# PHILOSOPHICAL FOUNDATION OF EDUCATION

*By*


**MAHAVEER SINGH**
*M.Sc., M.Ed., M.Phil., (Ph.D)*
*Lecturer*
*Translam College of Education*
*Meerut, Uttar Pradesh*

**UDAIVEER SINGH**
*M.Ed., (Ph.D)*





UNIVERSITY SCIENCE PRESS

(An Imprint of Laxmi Publications Pvt. Ltd.)

An ISO 9001:2008 Company

BENGALURU • CHENNAI • COCHIN • GUWAHATI • HYDERABAD
JALANDHAR • KOLKATA • LUCKNOW • MUMBAI • RANCHI • NEW DELHI
BOSTON (USA) • ACCRA (GHANA) • NAIROBI (KENYA)

# PHILOSOPHICAL FOUNDATION OF EDUCATION



Printed and bound in India
*Typeset at* : Kalyani Computer Services, New Delhi.
*First Edition* : 2010, *Second Edition* : 2017
*ISBN* : 978-93-80386-99-7



PUBLISHED IN INDIA BY
UNIVERSITY SCIENCE PRESS
(An Imprint of Laxmi Publications Pvt. Ltd.)
An ISO 9001:2008 Company
113, GOLDEN HOUSE, DARYAGANJ, NEW DELHI-110002, INDIA
Telephone : 91-11-4353 2500, 4353 2501
Fax : 91-11-2325 2572, 4353 2528
www.laxmipublications.com info@laxmipublications.com

Branches

| | |
|---|---|
| ✆ **Bengaluru** | 080-26 75 69 30 |
| ✆ **Chennai** | 044-24 34 47 26 |
| ✆ **Cochin** | 0484-237 70 04, 405 13 03 |
| ✆ **Guwahati** | 0361-254 36 69, 251 38 81 |
| ✆ **Hyderabad** | 040-27 55 53 83, 27 55 53 93 |
| ✆ **Jalandhar** | 0181-222 12 72 |
| ✆ **Kolkata** | 033-22 27 43 84 |
| ✆ **Lucknow** | 0522-220 99 16 |
| ✆ **Mumbai** | 022-24 91 54 15, 24 92 78 69 |
| ✆ **Ranchi** | 0651-220 44 64 |

C— 11969/016/05
*Printed at* : N.K. Book Binder, Delhi.

# CONTENT

# SYLLABUS

## EDM-101

## Course-1: PHILOSOPHICAL FOUNDATION OF EDUCATION

**Maximum Marks:100**
**Time Allowed : 3 Hrs.**

**Note:** There will be nine questions in the question paper. Students are required to attempt five questions in all. All questions shall carry equal marks.

Question no.1 shall be compulsory which will comprise of eight short answer type questions/parts and students are expected to answer any five parts.

There will be eight other questions comprising of two questions from each of the four units. Students are expected to attempt one question from each unit.

**Course Contents:**

**UNIT-1**

Relationship between Education and philosophy.

Schools of Philosophy:-

Samkhya, Vedanta, Nyaya,

Buddhism and Jainism with special reference to there educational implications

**UNIT-2**

Western Philosophies: Major Schools:-

Naturalism
Idealism
Pragmatism
Realism
Logical
Positivism
Existentialism
Marxism

Their educational Implications with special reference to epistemology, axiology and the process of education.

**UNIT-3**

Contributions of following Indians Philosophers to Education Thought:-

Vivekananda
Tagore
Gandhi
Aurobindo, and
J.Krishanamurthy

**UNIT-4**

Education, national values and the constitution of India

Nature of knowledge and the knowledge getting process

Social Philosophy of Education- Freedom, equality, Democracy and Responsibility.

# UNIT-1

## LEARNING OBJECTIVE

**Relationship between Education and philosophy.**
**Indian Schools of Philosophy:-**
**Samkhya, Vedanta, Nyaya,**
**Buddhism and Jainism with special reference to there educational implications**

# Relation Between Philosophy And Education

"Philosophy and education are like the two sides of the same coin; the one is implied by the other; the former is the contemplative side of life, while the latter is the active side."-J. S. Ross

**Meaning and Definition of Philosophy**

Etymological Meaning of Philosophy-The word philosophy is derived from two Greek words-`**Philos**' and '**Sophia**' `**Philos**' means love and 'Sophia' means wisdom. Thus, philosophy means love of wisdom. In this way, search of wisdom or truth is called philosophy, and the man who engages himself in this search is called a philosopher. In his famous book `Republic' Plato says-"He who has a taste for every sort of knowledge and who is curious to learn and is never satisfied may be justly termed a philosopher."

**Specific Meaning of Philosophy**-To be precise and definite, one may call philosophy as that deep thinking and meditation which concerns itself to the God, the soul and the Nature. This concentration and deep thinking is for revealing the bidder and immortal realities of existence namely-What is the nature of life, whence human being has come and what will be his final destination, how does external nature affect human life, how does this cosmos operate, how does the heavenly bodies affect human life, is there any life after this, what is heaven and hell. All these are the subjects and topics of philosophical thinking and ultimate realization. As these mental activities are abstract and difficult in nature, only capable and great persons can indulge in them. Common people cannot do this type of deep and concentrated thinking. Henderson and his colleagues have well said-"Philosophy **is a rigorous, disciplined and guarded analysis of some most difficult problems which man has ever faced."**

**Wider Meaning of Philosophy**-Philosophers do not form a specific and special group themselves. All those persons are philosophers who in one-way or the other search for truth and realities. A deep study reveals the fact that a man undergoes various kinds of experiences throughout his long life from birth to death. These experiences provide him with new knowledge. As a result, he develops a capacity to discriminate between right and wrong, proper and improper, relevant and irrelevant through these experiences, In a sense, each of us does this search work in some way or the other to some lesser greater extent. This search is essential for life to go on smoothly in this world full of diversities. In this sense, each of us becomes a philosopher at some time or the other. As this search for truth is philosophy, the great German philosopher Schopenhour rightly remaks-"Every man is a born metaphysician."

The above discussion shows clearly that every man is engaged in the search of truth to understand well the realities of things and occurrences. Through this thinking, he gets knowledge out of which he deduces a set of principles for his own use. He forms a set of ideas and values and begins to believe in them often implicitly. Thus, according to Huxley-"**Men live in accordance with their philosophy of life; their conception of the world. This is true even of the most thoughtless. It is impossible to live without metaphysics.**"

**Definition of Philosophy**

To make the meaning of philosophy more clear, the following definitions are being given: -

(1) " **Philosophy is a persistent attempt to give insight into the nature of the world and of ourselves by means of systematic refelection.**" R. W Sellars

(2) "**Philosophy like other studies aims primarily at knowledge** " .

- Bertrand Russell

**Features of Philosophy**

Philosophy is born out of experiences and circumstances with: which it is closely related. But it has an intimate relation with science as well. We discuss below these two special features of philosophy: -

**(1). Philosophy According to Experience and Situation-** the first special feature of philosophy is that it comes out of specific experiences, special circumstances and situations. This is the reason why different persons adopted different philosophies of life *in accordance with the* specific circumstances and conditions wherein they spent their lives. They not only accepted their philosophies as mental beliefs only. But they tried to translate their principles and philosophical beliefs into practice also. As for example, Gautam Buddha pondered over the ways to alleviate human sufferings, which he saw with his own eyes. Prophet Mohammad and Christ both prescribed ways of life to alleviate human misery. These ways' later came to take the form of Religions, which they expected to be followed by their followers, and it did happen. Hitler believed in a militant philosophy of courage and dash and so he propounded authoritarianism and despotism. Omar Khayyan believed in the philosophy of pleasure and indulgence and hence he preaches pleasure seeking. In our country the cult of Charvakism propagated a philosophy of: materialism and advocated individuals to cat drink and be merry by all means and at all times. On the other hand, Mahatma *Gandhi -was a* believer in spiritual *and* moral values of life and his *philosophy of non-violence* preaches abstinence, pity, kindness, fellow feeling and piety in all spheres of life. Hence, we can conclude that a certain philosophy is the product of times and circumstances and is born out of human experiences related to those times and conditions of life and society.

(2) **Philosophy and Science**-Philosophy is also closely related to Science. Science deals with realities of nature and life, animal or human. Those realities are integral part of the life of a child. These serve as raw material for the structuring of experiences for human beings. This interaction and experiences go to form philosophy. In short, realities of life are as essential as thoughts. Both co-operate to give rise to philosophy. A child must study both. science and philosophy to know and understand truth and reality of natural and human phenomena. Aims propounded by philosophy and sciences are the goal of education to pursue and realize in actual human life. Truth is related to circumstances and situations-political, social, economic and spiritual. These circumstances and situations condition our thinking and our view of truth and reality. We shall be propagating these truths and realities of life by various means of education.

**What is Education**

Education is not a dead process. It is a lively dynamic bipolar process of transformation. According to this view, there must be two poles for its operation-the one is the teacher and the other is the child as student. The teacher possesses some beliefs, ideals and values and these influence the child. In other words, we can say that the teacher, is a philosopher, who tries to mould and develop the child according to his philosophy to attain a desirable type of individual. Adams has rightly remarked-

"Education **is the dynamic side of philosophy. It is the active aspect of philosophical belief."**

## Relation Between Philosophy and Education

Interpreting philosophy and education separately, it is clear that both aim to impart knowledge of the truths and realities of life and develop the child accordingly. Both philosophy and education are integrally and interdependently related to each other. We are discussing below this interdependency in some greater details.

Education is dependent on Philosophy due to following reasons: -

**(1). Philosophy determines the real Destination Towards Which Education Has to** Go-Education is a conscious dynamic process which needs proper guidance and supervision. Without proper guidance and supervision, it cannot achieve its goal. Philosophy determines the goal of' life and also provides suitable and effective guidance and supervision for education to achieve that goal. Without the help of philosophy, education cannot be a successful process of development and achievement. Spencer has rightly remarked-"**True education is practicable only icy a true philosophy."**

(2) **Philosophy Determines** the Various Aspects of Education-Some scholars believe that philosophy is concerned with abstract items and conceptions only, while education deals with practical, concrete things and processes. Hence, the two are different and there exists no relation between them. But this is a wrong belief. Both philosophy and education are intimately and integrally connected with each other. Separation between the two is not possible on any account. It is the philosophy, we must know, that has been influencing all aspects of education since the very beginning and will go on influencing education for all times to come. Once again it will be better to recollect the saying of Ross that-"Philosophy and education are like the sides of **the same** coin, present different views of the same thing and that one **is implied by the other."**

(3) **Great Philosophers Have Been Great Educationists** Also-History bears eloquent testimony to the fact that great philosophers have been great educationists also of their times. Plato, Socrates, Locke, Commenius, Rousseau, Froebel, Dewey, Gandhi, Tagore, Aurobindo Ghosh and others who were great philosophers of their times have also talked about education. Their philosophical treatises have been important

guidebooks for educational planning and determination of educational aims for children of the world. In other words, all great philosophers have employed education as a means to translate their philosophical ideas into practice for the people to follow and develop themselves.

Philosophy is dependent of education due to following reasons: -

**(1) Education is the Dynamic Side of** Philosophy-Two things are essential for completing any task-(1) Thought or plan and (2) Application or practicability. Philosophy is the thought or plan side and education is the application or practical side. Philosophy determines the aim of life and by analysis lays down the principles to, be followed for achieving the set aims. Education translates these principles and ideas into practice, because the purpose of education is to mould human behaviour. Thus, Adams has rightly said -**"Education is the dynamic side of philosophy."**

**(2) Education is a Means to Achieve the Goal-**As said above it is philosophy which determines the aims of life. Through analysis and classification these are divided into goals to be achieved by the process of education. Herbart holds the same opinion - **"Education has no time to make holiday till all the philosophical questions are once for all cleared up:'** At times educationists and educators put before philosophers such problems which face them and defy solutions. In this way, education contributes to new thinking and new philosophy may born out of this thinking and analysing. So close are these two, the philosophy and the education, that it will be better to discuss this relation in greater details as Philosophy and Aims of Education, Philosophy and Curriculum, Philosophy and Methods of teaching, Philosophy and Discipline, Philosophy and Text-books and so on.

**Philosophy of Aims and Education**

**(A) Determination of Aims of Education by Philosophy**-Education sets itself into operation to realize some aims. It is why education is a purposeful activity. It should be remembered that the aims of education are related to the aims of life and the aims of life are the creations of the philosophy of a certain time. Hence, the aims of education are determined according to the aims and philosophy of life. This cycle goes on and on as time passes on. Thus, we come to the conclusion that education tries to achieve aims of life as goals of education and these aims of life are determined by the philosophy of life prevalent at the time. Different philosophers, in view of their own thinking keeping into consideration the demands of society of their times, have formulated different aims of life and education has always tried to achieve those aims as different goals of education. Thus, as aims of life change, aims of education also change accordingly. As such, one can have a general estimation of the aims of education at some time by knowing the philosophy of life at that time.

**(B) Determination of Aims of Education in Europe and** India-From earliest times to modern age, the aims of education in Europe and India at different times, bear eloquent testimony to the fact that they were determined by the philosophy of life prevalent during those days. In the following lines more light is being thrown on this close relationship as borne by history-

**(1) Ancient Period**-First of all let us take the example of Sparta state in ancient Greece. It should be remembered that Sparta was under a, constant attack by the enemies. Hence, the state needed resolute commanders and brave soldiers to defend its freedom and integrity. Hence, the aim or philosophy of ancient Sparta came to be a constant struggle against the enemy. To achieve this aim, the system of education tried to inculcate in children virtues of patriotism, courage, fearlessness, bodily powers, strict discipline and a spirit of self-sacrifice at the call of the state. Weakness of body was condemned- as vice and death in the service of the state was considered as the highest virtue, After Sparta, let us come to Rome, Athens and. India. Romans were conscious of their rights and duties and as such Roman education catered to the needs of fullest development of children in all spheres of human activity. In Athens, the aim of life was to have beauty of physique, beauty, of character, and a sense of appreciation for the objects of beauty. Hence, the aim of education was the development of wholesome character and inculcation of qualities, which enable children to lead their lives comfortably. Thus, children were given full freedom and ample opportunities to develop themselves physically, mentally and emotionally. One can note here that with a change in the philosophy of life aims of education in Athens were quite different to those of Rome and Sparta. In ancient India, religion was regarded as most essential. The aim of life was to perform all worldly duties and then achieve salvation from worldly ties to rebirth.

Hence, education, during those days, wads organized to attain happiness, bliss and in the end salvation.

**(2) Medieval Period**-Philosophy of life during medieval times saw great ups and downs. Aims of life changed from time to time and so the aims of education also changed accordingly. In those days Islam and Christianity were busy with proselytisation programmes in a very aggressive manner. Hence, religion entered the precincts of education also. The chief aims of Muslim education in India were-(1) Propagation of Islam, (2) Spread of education among Muslims, (3) Extension of Islamic kingdoms, (4) Development of morality, (5) Achievement of material wellbeing, (6) Propagation of Shariyat and (7) Building of character. In Europe Reformation and Renaissance criticised the infalliability of Catholism. People asserted their right to know the truth themselves and did not believe blindly in the rituals and ceremonies. Thus, aims of education changed again. Education was to develop critical insight and reasonableness in all beliefs and activities. It was expected of education to demolish all blind beliefs and mechanical rituals.

**Modern Period**-Philosophy of life again changed in modern period. As a result, revolutionary changes began transforming education also. Philosophy of Locke fell from prominence and it came to be agrued that education should develop the inherent qualities, aptitudes and capacities of children. Psychological tendency began to influence education very powerfully. Education became child-centred and according to famous educationist Pestalozzi the aim of education was declared to develop the personality of the child to the fullest extent. Herbart advocated the aim of education to be the formation of character. As times went by, aims of life changed again. The industrial revolution had its impact on education. As a result, one of the aims of education, namely, development of vocational efficiency *came* to the forefront. At present, all nations of the world are organizing their educational systems according to their needs and ideologies. In countries where the sentiment of democracy is strong, the aims of education are the inculcation of democratic values and promotion of democratic principles. On the contrary, countries where communism, facism or other kinds of despotism prevails as political ideology, education is so organized as to promote absolute obedience, blind beliefs and rigid discipline in children.

In England and America where democratic values prevail, aims of education inculcate democratic ideals and values. The chief aim is to develop fully the individuality of the child. In America the philosophy of pragmatism is in vogue. This has influenced education to be really practical, useful and purposive. Utility is the motto of all activities and experience. On the contrary, Russia and China exploit education as an instrument of indoctrination of enforced obedience and rigid discipline. During the British rule in India the purpose of education was to prepare native clerks to run the administrative machinary efficiently. After the attainment of independence in 1947, we have declared our country as a Republic and Socialistic welfare State. As such, the prime aim of our education is to develop dynamic citizens devoted to the service of the nation. Thus, we see that changing philosophy of, nation always brings about corresponding changes in the aims of education.

**Philosophy and Curriculum**

By means of curriculum desired behavioural changes are sought to be achieved to attain the goal of life determined by a particular philosophy. Thus, as philosophy determines the aims of education, so also it determines the curriculum. In other words, the philosophy of a country at a particular time determines the curriculum in which such subjects, activities and experiences arc included which are supposed to meet the emerging demands of the society at that time.

**Philosophy and Methods of Teaching**

Philosophy is also closely related to the methods of teaching. It is why changing philosophies change the methods of teaching accordingly. In reality method of teaching is impreceptibly conditionod by the philosophy of the nation. In a sense, philosophy is a way of thinking and a way of working. As such, these two factors determine the nature, style and actual operation of methods of teaching.

Philosophy of naturalism emphasizes the child more than the curriculum. Thus, according to Naturalism, the child's individual tastes, interests, aptitudes and capacities are to be, developed to the fullest extent_ For-this, the naturalists advocate Dallon Plan, Learning by doing, Heuristic method. Montessori method and other self learning and self-developing methods so that children gain knowledge in their own way and apply it according to their choice. The Pragmatists also advocate full and free development of individuality and for this, they advocate Project method as more practical and experimental. The Idealists advocate question-answer method, discussion, lecture and any other method, which ensures the total development of child's personality. Since different philosophies advocate different methods of teaching, it proves clearly that philosophy and methods of teaching are closely related to each other.

## Philosophy and Discipline

Philosophy determines the, nature and form of discipline. Whether school discipline should be strict and rigid or flexible and free is also a philosophical problem. It may be noted that the social, economic and philosophical thinking of a particular country always determine the nature of discipline. Despotic and authoritarian governments enforce rigid discipline while democratic countries give more or less freedom of action to children in schools. Adams in his famous hook `Modern Development in Educational Practice' has discussed the following three forms of discipline: -

(1). Repressionistic.

(2) Impressionistic.

(3) Emancipatory.

**(l) Repressionistic Discipline-**This concept of discipline is based upon despotic and authoritarian ideologies. This refers to arbitrary and dictatorial tendencies of the rulers. There is no freedom for children at all. They are kept under rigid control and unquestioning obedience is enforced upon them_ Physical punishments and creation of fear in the minds of children are the tools of enforce this type of discipline.

**(2) Impressionistic Discipline** -Impressionistic discipline is based upon the philosophy of Idealism. Idealists believe that the role of teacher has a powerful influence upon the thinking and behaviour of children. Thus, the teacher should, by his moral character and conduct, infuse a sense of self-discipline in all the children of school. The impression of the teacher's behaviour and the conducive influence of the whole school environment develops this sense of self-discipline. There is no need of physical punishments and creation of fear in the minds of children. Instead, love, sympathy, and affection transform the feelings and actions of children into desirable channels. This self-discipline is the surest and most effective way to self-development.

**(3) Emancipatory Discipline**-This type of discipline is based upon the philosophy of naturalism. Naturalists believe in the inherent goodness of the nature of a child. Hence, they advocate full freedom for the child to think and behave as he likes.. This freedom will develop him like a flower of a plant. Nature will flower out his innate qualities of goodness and virtue. Thus, there should be no repression or rigid control nor a scheme of giving impressions to the child at all. He will himself learn by the discipline of natural consequences. He should be allowed full self-expression This concept of discipline if generally accepted by educationists all over the world today. Hence, Freedom and Discipline' is a common talk in the field of education these days.

## Philosophy and Text-Books

To achieve aims of life and of education, text-books are of great importance and value. As curriculum is powerfully influenced by the philosophy of times, so also the textbooks are effected by the prevailing philosophy of the day. Since text-books contain matter which reflects the ideology, ideals and values of society, the government should keep an eye on the production of desirable books for children. For this, really standard books of utility for children should be made available and undesirable books should be discouraged and banned from production and circulation.

## Philosophy and Teacher

Philosophy has a great influence on the teacher both in the area of thinking and behaving. Really speaking, a teacher is not a teacher alone. He is a philosopher also. In other words, a teacher himself has a philosophy of his own and he influences children accordingly. As such, his philosophy of life should be such which develops the individuality of children to the fullest extent. For this, the teacher should know fully well the needs of children and the demands of society and then plan his methods of teaching. He must keep in mind that his own beliefs, ideology and principles of behaviour have a powerful impact on the development of children. Hence, he must possess a good understanding of all the philosophies of life and choose good and wholesome elements from them to form his own philosophy. Further, he must be a man imbued with high ideals and possess moral and spiritual values which go to form his character and shape his conduct. He must also be well conscious of national needs in all spheres and plan his teaching activities of fulfil those needs. Only such teachers imbued with high ideals, moral and spiritual values together with a sense of national responsibility for national prospertity and honour can create patriotic, dynamic, resourceful and enterprizing citizens devoted to national service and international goodwill.

It is clear from the above discussion that philosophy is inseparably linked with education and influences it powerfully in all areas and in all aspects. In short, philosophy leads and education follows the path shown by philosophy. The following remark is to the point-.

**"The belief that men may continue to educate without concerning themselves with philosophy means a failure to understand the precise nature of education.... The process of education cannot go on right lines without the help of philosophy."** ***-Gentile***

# SANKHYA

## INTRODUCTION

**SANKHYA** undoubtedly one of the oldest systems of Indian Phislophy. We find references to the Sainkhya-Yoga doctrines in some of the Upanisads, e.g., in the Chhandogya, the Prashna, Katha and particularly in the Shvetashvatara; in the Mahabharata in the Gita; and in the Smrtis and the Puranas. Badarayana, the author of the Vedanta-sutra, repeatedly refers to the view whether the Sankhya' can be regarded as the teaching of the Upanisads and rejects it, besides undertaking refutation of the Sankhya in the Tarkapada on rational grounds. Shankaracharya regards it as the `main opponent' (pradhana malla) of Vedanta and says that though Sankhya and Yoga are generally accepted by the wise as conducive to the Highest Good, yet these system advocate dualism and cannot be supported by the Shruti. These words are used in the Shruti and the Smrti in the sense of knowledge and action respectively and words like Mahat, Avyakta etc. are used in the sense of names and forms . The fact that Badarayana and Shankara. are keen to reject the view that Sainkhya, though accepted by the wise, is not based on the Upanisads because it advocates dualism, suggests that there must have been some thinkers belonging to the Sankhya .claimed it to be the teaching of the Upanisads. Though nothing can be said with absolute certainty, it seems highly probable that t o Sankhya in the beginning was based on the Upanisads and had accepted the theistic Absolute, but later on, under the influence of the Jaina and the Buddhist thought, it rejected theistic monism and was content with spiritualistic pluralism and atheistic realism. And it is this Saiikhya to which Badarayana and Sharikara are opposed. This also explains why sortie of the later Sainkhyas, e.g. Vijnanabhiksu in the sixteenth cen' tried to revive the earlier theism in Safikhya.

Tradition regards Kapila as the founder of this system. But Sark pravachana-sutra which is attributed to him is generally regarded by scholars as a work of the fourteenth century A.D., because it has not been referred to by the earlier writers of the other schools, because it criticizes the rival systems and because it wants to revive theism. So far as theism is concerned, we maintain that the original Sankhya was theistic. But the fact that this work has been ignored and Ishvarakrsna's Karika has been referred to instead by the other earlier writers, as well as the fact that it criticizes other systems go against this work being regarded as that of Kapila himself. As Ishvarakrsna himself speaks of Kapila, Asuri, and Pafichashikha, it seems probable that these were historical personages whose works have been lost. Kapila certainly flourished before Buddha and he must. have composed Sankhya-sutra which work was unfortunately lost long ago. Ishvarakrsna's SankhyaKarika seems to be the earliest available and the most popular work of this system. Besides this we have Gaudapada's Sankhya-Karikaohasya, Vachaspati Mishra's Tattva-Kaumudi and Vijiiana-bhiksu's Sankhya-pravachana-bhasya.

The word `Sankhya' is derived from the word `Sankhya' which means right knowledge as well as number. The Gita uses this word in the sense of knowledge, so does the Mahabharata ' at other places also. Sankhya means the philosophy of right knowledge (samyak khyati or jMina). The system is predominantly intellectual and theoretical. Right knowledge is the knowledge of the separation of the Purusa from the Prakrti. Yoga, as the counterpart of Sankhya, means action or practice and tells us how the theoretical metaphysical teachings of Sankhya might be realized in actual practice. Thus Sankhya-Yoga forms one complete system, the former being the theoretical while the latter being the practical aspect of the same teaching. Sankhya is also the philosophy of numbers, because it deals with twenty-five categories. As a philosophy of numbers, it might have influenced the Pythagorean philosophy.

Ishvarakrsna (fifth century A.D.) is the representative of the classical Sankhya which had divorced itself from the Upanisads under the influence of Jainism and Buddhism, yet the Vedantic teaching of absolutism with which the original Sankhya was associated, asserts itself implicitly in Ishvarakrsna. We have seen that absolutism is implicit in Jainism and explicit in Mahayana Buddhism and we shall see how it is implicit in Ishvarakrsna also.

Sankhya maintains a clear-cut dualism between Purusa and Prakrti and further maintains the plurality of the Purusas, and is silent on God. It is a pluralistic spiritualism and an atheistic realism and an uncompromising dualism.

## THEORY OF CAUSATION

LET us first consider the Sankhya theory of causation on which its doctrine of Prakrti is based. The basic question involved in any theory of causation is: Does the effect pre-exist in its material cause? 'Those who answer this question in the negative are called Asatkaryavidins, while those who answer it in the affirmative are called Satkaryavadins. According to the former, the effect is a new creation, a real begining. The effect (karya) does not pre-exist (asat) in its material cause. otherwise, there would be no sense in saying that it is produced or caused. If the pot already exists in the clay and the cloth in the threads and curd in milk, then why should the potter exert himself in producing the pot out of the clay, and why should not the threads serve the purpose il the cloth and why should not milk taste like curd? Moreover, its production would be its repeated birth, which is nonsense. Nyaya, Vaishesika, Hinayana Buddhism, Materialism and some followers of Mimamsa believe in Asatkaryavada, which is also known as Arambhavada.; the view that production is a new beginning. Materialism believes in Svabhavavada; Hinayana Buddhism in Anityaa paramanuvada or Ksanabhangavada and Nyaya-Vaishesika and some followers of Mimamsa in Nitya-paramanu-karanavada. The Satkaryavadins, on the other hand, behave the effect is not a new creation, but only an explicit manifestation of that which was implicitly contained in its materialcause. Here, another important question arises: Is the effect a real transformation or an unreal appearance of its cause? Those who believe that the effect is a real transformation of its cause are called parinamavadins (parinama = real modification); while those who believe that it is an unreal appearance are called Vivartavadins (vivarta =unrealappearance). Sankhya, Yoga and Ramanuja believe in Parinamavada. The view of Sankhya-Yoga is called Prakrti-parinama-vada, while the view of Ramanuja is called Brahma-Parinamavada. Shunyavada, Vijnanavada and Shankara believe in Vivartavada. Their views be respectively called Shonyata-vivarta-vada, Vijnana-vivarta-vac and Brahma-vivarta-vada. The view of Jainism and of Kumarila becalled Sadasatkaryavada because according to them the effect real as.well as unreal before its production-real as identical w the cause and unreal as a modal change thereof, though ultimately incline towards Parinamavada.

Sankhya believes in Satkaryavada. All material effects modification (parinama) of Prakrti. They pre-exist in the eternal bosom of Prakrti and simply come out of it at the time of creation and return to it at the time of dissolution. There is neither new production nor utter destruction. Production means development or manifestation (avirbhava); destruction means envelopment or dissolution (tirobhava). Production is evolution; destruction is involution. Sainkhya gives five arguments in support of Satkaryavada:

**(1)** If the effect does not pre-exist in its cause, it becomes a mere nonentity like the hare's horn or the sky-flower and can never be produced (asadakaranat).

**(2)** The effect is only a manifestation of its material cause, because it is invariably connected with it (upadanagrahanat).

**(3)** Everything cannot be produced out of everything. This suggests that the effect, before its manifestation, is implicit in its material cause (sarvasambhavabhavat).

**(4)** Only an efficient cause can produce that for which it is potent. This again means that the effect, before its manifestation, is potentially contained in its material cause. Production is only an actualization of the potential (shaktasya shakyakaranat). Were it not so, then curd should be produced out of water, and cloth out of reeds, and oil. out of sandparticles.

**(5)** The effect is the essence of its material cause and as such identical with it. When the obstrucfions in the way of manifestation are removed, the effect naturally flows out of its cause. The cause and the effect are the implicit and the explicit stages of the same process. The cloth is contained in the threads, the oil in the oil-seeds, and the curd in the milk. The effect pre-exists in its material cause (karanabhavat).

## PRAKTI

**THE theory that** causation means a real transformation of the material cause leads to the concept of Prakrti as the root-cause of the world of objects. All worldly effects are latent in this uncaused cause, because infinite regress has to be avoided. It is the potentiality of nature `the receptacle and nurse of all generation'. As the uncaused root-cause, it is called Prakrti; as the first principle of this Universe, it is called

Pradhana; as the unmanifested state of all effects, it is known as Avyakta; as the extremely subtle and imperceptible thing which is only inferred from its products, it is called Anumana; as the unintelligent and unconscious principle, it is called Jada; andas the ever-active unlimited power, it is called Shakti. The products are caused, dependent, relative, many and temporary as they are subject to birth and death or to production and destruction; but Prakrti is uncaused, independent, absolute, one and eternal, being beyond production and destruction. The extra me subtleness of Prakrti makes it unmanifest and imperceptible; we i far its existence through its products. Motion is inherent in it in the from of Rajas. As the source of the inanimate world, it is unconscious. the entire world of objects is implicit in the bosom of Prakrti. Evolution is the explicit manifestation of this world of objects, while dissolution-: is the returning of this world to Prakrti. Sankhya believes that consciousness cannot be regarded as the source of the inanimate world, as Vedanta and Mahayana believe, because an intelligent principle cannot transform itself into the unintelligent world. On the other hand, the material atoms of the physical elements too cannot be regarded as the causes of this world, as Charvakas, Nyaya and Vaishesika, Jainism and Hinayana Buddhism, and Mimarnsa wrongly believe, because they cannot explain the subtle products of matter like intellect, mind and ego (these are different from pure consciousness which belongs to Purusa a r, a, and are regarded here as internal organs), and further because the unity of the universe points to a single cause while the atoms are scattered and many. Unintelligent, unmanifest, uncaused, ever-active, imperceptible, eternal and one Prakrti alone is the final source o world of objects which is implicitly and potentially contained in its bosom.

Sankhya gives five proofs for the existence of Prakfti which a follows

(i) All individual things in this world are limited, dependent conditional and finite. The finite cannot he the causes of the universe. Logically we have to proceed from the finite to the infinite, from the limited to the unlimited, from the *peros* the *aperos,* from the temporary to the permanent, frog, the many to the one. And it is this infinite, unlimited, exterenal and all-pervading Prakrti, which is the source of this universe (bhedanam parimanat).

(2) All worldly things possess certain common characteristics by which they are capable of producing pleasure, pain and indifference. Hence there must be a common source posed of three Gunas, from which all worldly things arise (samanvayat).

(3) All effects arise from the activity of the potent cause. Evolution means the manifestation of the hitherto implicit as the explicit. The activity which generates evolution must be inherent in the world-cause. And this cause is Prakrti (karyatah pravrttescha).

(4) The effect differs from the cause and hence the limited effect cannot be regarded as its own cause. The effect is the explicit and the cause is the implicit state of the same process. The effects, therefore, point to a world-cause where they are potentially contained (karanakaryavibhagat).

(5) The unity of the universe points to a single cause. And this cause is Prakrti. (avibhagat vaishvarupyasya).

Prakrti is said to be the unity of the three Gunas held in equilibrium (gunanam samyavastha). The three Gunas are Sattva, Rajas and Tamas. They are the constituents of Prakrti and through it of the worldly objects. Being subtle and imperceptible their existence is inferred from their effects-pleasure, pain and indifference respectively. Although they are called Gunas, yet they are not ordinary qualities or attributes like the Nyaya-Vaishesika Gunas. They themselves possess qualities like lightness, activity, heaviness etc. They are extremely fine and everchanging elements. They make up Prakrti, which is nothing apart from them. They are not the qualities which Prakrti, the substance, possesses; on the other hand they themselves constitute Prakrti.They are the factors or the constituents or the elements of Prakrti. They are called Gunas because they are the elements of Prakriti, which alone is called substantive; or because they are subservient to the end of. The Purusa, or because they are intertwined, like three strands, to make up the rope of Prakrti which binds the Purusas.

Sattva literally means real or existent and is responsible for the manifestation of objects in consciousness. It is called goodness and produces pleasure. It is light and bright, buoyant (laghu) and illuminating (prakashaka). Luminosity of light, power of reflection, upward movement, pleasure, happiness, contentment, bliss are all due to it. Its colour is white. Rajas, which literally means foulness, is the principle of motion. It produces pain. Restless activity,. feverish effort and wild stimulation are its results. It is mobile (chala) and stimulating (upastambhaka). Its colour is red. Tamas, which literally means darkness, is the principle of inertia. It produces apathy and indifference. Ignorance, sloth, confusion, bewilderment, passivity and negativity are its results. It is heavy (guru) and enveloping (varanaka) and as such is gpposed to Sattva. It is also opposed to Rajas as it arrests activity. Its colour is dark. These three gunas which constitute Prakrti are never separate. They bhedanam , parimagat, samanvayat karyatah pravrtteshcha. karanakaryavibhagad avibhagad vaishvarupyasya, 'Sankhya-Karika,Guna means 'quality', 'secondary' and 'strand of a rope' .conflict and yet co-operate with one another and are always found intermingled. They are compared to the oil, the wick and the flam of a lamp, which, though opposed, yet co-operate to produce the light of a lamp. They are imperceptible and are inferred from their effect: All things are composed of these three gunas and their differences are due to the different combinations of these gunas. The nature of a thing is determined by the preponderance of a particular guna. There are called a good, bad or indifferent; intelligent, active or slothful; pure, impure or neutral, on account of the predominance of sattva, rajas or tamas respectively. When these gunas are held in a state of equilibrium, that state is called Prakrti. Evolution of worldly objects does not take place at state. These gunas are said to be ever changing. They cannot remain static even for a moment. Change is said to be of two kinds-homegenerous or sarupa-parinama and heterogeneous or virupa-parinama. During the state of dissolution (pralaya) of the world, the gunas change homogeneously, i.e., sattva changes into sattva, rajas into rajas and tama into tamas.into tamasThis change does not disturb the equilibrium of the gunas and unless the equilibrium is disturbed and one predominates over the other two, evolution cannot take place. Evolution starts when there is heterogeneous change in, the gunas and one predominates over the other two and brings about terrific commotion in the bosom of Prakriti.Rasalina beautifully brings out the nature of these gunas in a Hindi couplet. The poet says that the eyes of the beloved, are white, red and dark, and are full of nectar, intoxication and poison, with the result that once they pierce the heart of the lover, he experinces the joy of life, the agony of restlessness and the inertia of death. The recollection of the beloved gives him joy and makes life worth living; separation causes acute pain and makes him restless; intensity of love makes him everything and become inactive, unconscious and almost dead.' Sattva is white and is like nectar and gives : rajas is red and is like intoxication and gives pain; tamas is dark and is like poison and produces unconsciousness. `We bow to Prakrti,' says ishvarakrsna, `the red-white-dark, the unborn mother and" nurse receptacle of all generation". Such is the conception of Prakrti in Sankhya.

## PURUSA

THE other of the two co-present co-eternal realities of Sankhya. is the Purusa, the principal of pure Consciousness. Purusa is the soul, the self, the spirit, the subject, the knower. It is neither body nor senses nor brain, nor mind (manas) nor ego (ahankara) nor intellect (buddhi). It is not a 'substance which possesses the quality of Consciousness. Consciousness is its essence. It. is itself pure and transcendental Consciousness.. It is the ultimate knower which is the foundation of all knowledge. It is the pure subject and as such can never become an object of knowledge. It is the silent witness, the emancipated alone, the neutral seer, the peaceful eternal. It is beyond time and space, beyond change and activity. It is self-luminous and self-proved. It is uncaused, eternal and all pervading. It is the indubitable real, the postulate of knowledge, and all doubts and denials pre-suppose its existence. It is called nistraigunya, udisina, akarta, kevala, madhyastha, saksi, drasta, sadaprakashasvarupa, and jnata .Sankhya gives the following five proofs for the existence of. The Purusa:

(I) All compound objects exist for the sake of the Purusa. The body, the senses, the mind and the intellect are all means to realize the end of the Purusa. The three gums, the Prakrti, the subtle body-all are said to serve the purpose of the self. Evolution is teleological or purposive. Prakrti evolves itself in order to serve the Purusa's end. This proof is teleological (sangh'ataparatrthatvat).

(2) All objects are composed of the three gunas and therefore logically presuppose the existence of the Purusa who is the witness of these gums and is himself beyond them. The three gunas imply the conception of a nistraigunya-that which is beyond them. This proof is logical (trigunadiviparyayat).

(3) There must be a transcendental synthetic unity of pure Consciousness to co-ordinate all experiences. All knowledge necessarily presupposes the existence of the self, The self is the foundation (adhisthana), the fundamental postulate of all empirical

knowledge. All affirmations and all negationln' equally presuppose it. Without it, experience would not become experience. This proof is ontological (adhisthanat).

**(4)** Non-intelligent Prakrti cannot experience its products. So there must be an intelligent principle to experience the worldly products of Prakrti. Prakrti is the enjoyed (bhogya) and so there must be an enjoyer (bhokta). All objects of the world have the characteristics of producing pleasure, pain and bewilderment. But pleasure, pain and bewilderment have meaning only when there is a conscious principle to experience them: Hence Purusa must exist This argument is ethical (bhoktrbhavat).

**(5)** There are persons who try to attain release from the suffering of the world. The desire for liberation and emancipation implies the existence of a person who can try for and obtain liberation. Aspiration presupposes the aspirant. This proof is' mystical or religious (kaivalyartham pravrtteh).

Unlike Advaita Vedanta and like Jainism and Mimamsa, Sankhya believes in the plurality of the Purusas. Like the Jivas of the Jainas the souls of Ramanuja and the monads of Leibnitz, the Sankhya Purusas are subJect to qualitative monism and quantitative pluralism. The, selves are all essentially alike; only numerically are they different. Their essence is consciousness. Bliss is regarded as different from consciousness and is the product of the sattvaguna. Sankhya gives the following three arguments for proving the plurality of the Purusas:

**(1)** The souls have different sensory and motor organs and undergo separate births and deaths. Had there been only one Purusa, the birth of death of one should have meant the birth or death of all and-any particular experience of pleasure, pain or indifference by -one should have been equally shared by all. Hence; the souls must be many.

**(2)** If. the self were one, bondange of one should have meant: bondage of all and liberation of one should have meant liberation of all. The activity of one should have made all persons active and the sleep of one should have lulled into sleep all other persons.

**(3)** Though the emancipated souls are all alike and differ only in number as they are all beyond the three gunas, Yet the bound souls relatively differ in qualities also, since in some sattva tpredominates, while in others rajas, and in still others tamas, Hence their difference.

## EVOLUTION

We have seen that Prakrti is regarded as essentially dynamic. If motion were not inherent in Prakrti, it could not be given to it by any outside agency; and if motion once ceased in Prakrti, it could not yet reappear. Hence Prakrti is always. changing. Even in dissolution There is homogeneous change (sarupa or sajatiya parinama) in Prakrti when all the three gunas are in the state of equilibrium. It is only when heterogeneous change takes place and rajas vibrates and makes sattva and tamas vibrate that the equilibrium is disturbed and evolution takes place. Sattva, the principle of manifestation and rajas, the principle of activity were formerly held in check by tamas, the principle of no manifestation and non-activity. But when rajas, the principle of activity vibrates and makes the other two vibrate, the process of creation begins. And creation is not the new creation of the worldly objects, but only their manifestation. It is only making explicit of that which was formerly implicit. Evolution is regarded as cyclic and not linear. There is no continuous progress in one direction, but alternating periods of evolution (sarga) and dissolution (pralaya) in a cyclic order. Evolution is again said to be teleological and not mechanical or blind. Evolution takes place for serving the purpose of the Purusa. Prakrti, the gunas, the senses, the mind, the ego, the intellect, and the subtle body-all are constantly serving the end of the Purusa. This end is either worldly experience (bhoga) or liberation (apavarga). Purusa needs Prakrti for enjoyment as well as for liberation, for sarnsara as well as for Kaivalya. Evolution supplies objects to be enjoyed to the Purusa and also works for his liberation by enabling him to discriminate between himself and Prakrti

Now the question is: How does evolution take place? Evidently when heterogeneous motion arises and rajas disturbs the equilibrium of the gunas. But how is the equilibrium disturbed? Sankhya fails to answer this question satisfactorily. The fundamental blunder of Sankhya has been to separate Prakrti and Purusa as absolute and independent entities. As a matter of fact, the subject and the object are two aspects of the same reality, which holds them together and yet transcends them. All realistic pluralism, of whatever brand it may be, has failed to answer this question satisfactorily. If Prakrti and Purusa are absolutely separate and independent entities, then they can never unite together,. nor can there be any *tertium quid* to unite them. And if they cannot unite evolution cannot take place. Sankhya says that the disturbance of the equilibrium of the gunas, which starts evolution, is made possible by the contact of Purusa and Prakrti. Purusa without Prakrti is lame and Prakrti without Puma is blind. `Theory without practice is empty and practice without theory is blind.' Concepts without percepts are empty and percepts without concepts are blind.' Prakrti needs Purina in order to be known, to be seen, to be enjoyed (darshanartham); and Purusa needs Prakrti in order to enjoy (bhoga) and also in order to obtain liberation (apavarga), in order to discriminate between himself and Prakrti and thereby obtain emancipation (kaivalyartham). If Prakrti and Purusa remain separate, there is dissolution. For creation they must unite. Just as a lame manned a blind man can co-operate and the lame may sit on the shoulders of the blind and point to him the way, while the blind may walk and thus both can reach the destination, though neither of them could have done that separately, similarly the inactive Purusa and the non intelligent Prakrti co-operate to serve the end, and this union disturbs the equilibrium of the gums and leads to evolution.' But how can the two opposed and independent entities really come into contact? Sankhya realizes this difficulty and in order to avoid it says that there is no real contact between Purusa and Prakrti and that only the proximity of the Purusa, only the fact that Purusa is near to Prakrti (purusa-sannidhi-matra), is sufficient to disturb the equilibrium of the gunas and thus lead to evolution. But here Sankhya falls into another difficulty. The Purusa being always never to Prakrti (for the inactive Purusa cannot move), evolution should nee. e stop and dissolution would become impossible. Evolution, then, would be beginning less and the very conception of Prakrti as the state of equilibrium of the three gunas would be impossible. Sankhya find itself between these two horns of a dilemma-either no contact and hence no evolution or else no equilibrium and hence no Prakrti and no dissolution. In order to avoid these difficulties, Sankhya now posits the theory of the semblance of a contact (samyogabhasa). Of course, there is no real contact (samyoga) between Purusa and Prakrti; there is the semblance of a contact and it is this semblance that leads to evolution. Purusa is reflected in the intellect (buddhi) and wrongly identifies himself with his own reflection in tale buddhi. It is this reflection of the Purusa, which comes into contact with Prakrti, and not the Purusa himself. But buddhi or mahat is regarded as the first evolution of Prakrti and how can it arise before evolution to receive the reflection of the Purusa? To avoid this difficulty it is said that the Purusa is reflected in the Prakrti itself. If so, then liberation and dissolution would become impossible because Prakrti being always there and it being the essential nature of the Purusa to identify himself with his reflection in the Prakrti .he would never get liberation and the very purpose for which evolution' starts would get defeated. Moreover, the reflection being always there would be no dissolution and so no equilibrium of the gunas and hence no Prakrti. Again, if semblance of a contact is sufficient to disturb the equilibrium, then evolution itself becomes a semblance of evolution an appearance only (vivarta) and no real transformation (parinam) of Prakrti. Thus we see that in order to defend the initial blunder of regarding Purusa and Prakrti as absolute and independent entities, Sankhya commits blunders after blunders.

## THE EVOLUTERS

THE first product of the evolution is called Mahat, the Great. It is the germ of this vast world of objects including intellect, ego and mind. It is cosmic in its nature. But it has a psychological aspect also in which it is called buddhi or intellect. Buddhi is distinguished from consciousness. Purusa alone is pure consciousness. Buddhi or intellect, being the evolute of Prakrti, is material. It is made of finest matter and is thus capable of reflecting clearly the consciousness of the Purusa, like a wireless set capable of receiving the aerial waves. On account of the reflection of the Purusa-in it, it becomes apparently conscious and intelligent. The senses, the mind and the ego function for buddhi or intellect which functions directly for the Purusa. Its functions are said to be ascertainment and decision. It arises when sattva predominates. Its original attributes are virtue (dharma),: knowledge (jnana), detachment (vairagya) and power (aishvarya). When it gets vitiated by tamas, these attributes are replaced by their opposites. Memories and recollections are stored in buddhi.

Mahat produces Ahankara. It is the principle of individuation. Its function is to generate self-sense (abhimana). It produces the notion of the `I' and the `mine'. If is the individual ego-sense. Purusa wrongly identifies himself with this ego and knows himself as the agent of actions, desirerf of desires and striver for ends, and possessor and enjoyer of ideas, emotions and volition and also of material objects. Ahalikara is said to be of three kinds:

(1). Vaikarika or, sattvika,- when sattva predominates. Viewed as cosmic, it produces manas and five sensory organs and five motor organs. Viewed as psychological, it produces good deeds.

(2). Bhutadi or tamasa, when tamas predominates. Viewer' as cosmic, it produces the five subtle elements (tan-matras). Viewed as psychological, it leads to indifferent acts or to idleness and sloth.

(3). Taijasa or rajasa, when rajas predominates. Viewed as cosmic, it supplies the energy by which the Sattvika and the Tamasa produce their respective evolutes. Viewed as psychological, it produces evil deeds.

Manas or mind, which arises from the Sattvika Ahankara, is the subtle and central sense organ. It can come into contact with the-several sense organs at the same time. According to the Nyaya-Vaishesika School, manas is eternal and atomic and cannot come . id creation will several senses simultaneously. According to Safikhya, it is .on of Prakrtl, nor atomic. It is made up of parts and so can come into cont., evolutes, and different senses simultaneously. Saiikhya assigns to manas the function of synthesizing the sense data into determinate perce passing them on to the ego, and carrying out the orders of the through the motor organs.

The Sattvika Ahankara produces, besides manaa; the five sensory and the five motor organs. The five sensory organs (jnanendriva) are the functions of sight, smell, taste, touch and sound. According to the Nyaya-Vaishesika, the five sensory organs are derived from the five gross physical elements. But according to the Safikhya, the five senses are the functions of the mind and are derived from Ahankara. The five motor organs (karmendriya) are the functions of speech, prehensior movement, excretion and reproduction.

Buddhi, ahankara and manas represent the three psychological aspect of knowing, willing and feeling or cognition, conation and affection respectively. Safikhya calls them material and derives them from Prakrti. They shine through the light of the Purusa and are apparently conscious. All the three are called the internal organs or antahkarana and vital breaths (pranas) are said to be their modifications. The five sensory and the five motor organs together are called the ten external organ or bahyakarana. These are the thirteen karanas or organs of the Sankhya.

From the Tamasa Ahankara arise the five subtle essences, which are called Tanmatras or 'things-in-themselves'. These are the essences of sight, smell, taste, touch and sound. Unlike the Nyaya-Vaishesika ones, they are not derived from the gross elements. Rather the gross element themselves arise out of these. They are neither the qualities nor the differentia of the gross elements nor the functions that are the senseory organs, but the subtle essences, which produce the gross elements as well as their qualities. From the essence of sound (shabdatanmatra) arises the element of ether (akasha) together with the quality of sound. From the essence of touch combined with the essence of sound, arises the element of air together with the qualities of sound and touch. From the subtle essence of colour or sight combined with those of sound and touch, arises the element of fire or light together with the qualities of sound, touch and colour. From the essence of taste combined with the of sound, touch and colour, arises the element of water together with qualities of sound, touch, colour and taste. And lastly, from essence of smell combined with those of sound, touch, colour and taste arises the element of earth together with the qualities of sound, together colour, taste and smell with the Purusa who is a mere spectator and outside the play of evolution, are the twenty-five categories of Sankhya. Out of these twenty-five principles, the Purusa is neither a cause nor an effect; Prakrti is only the cause and not the effect; Mahat, Ahankara and the five subtle essences are both causes and effects; while the five sensory and the five motor organs and the five gross elements and manas are effects only.' *This* may be depicted by the following table:

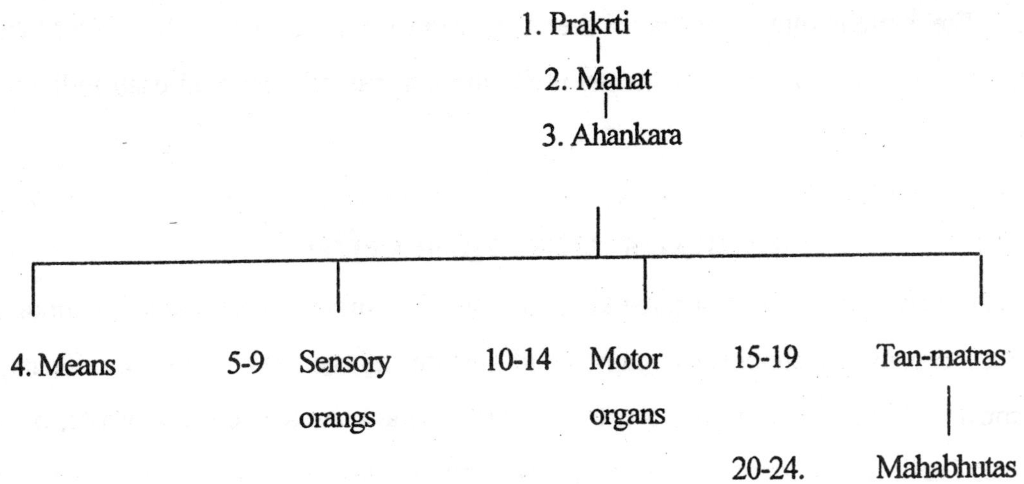


The evolution is teleological. Everything works to serve the purpose of the Purusa though unconciously. Just as non-intelligent trees grow fruits, or water flows on account of the declivity of the soil, or ironfilings are attracted towards a magnet, or milk flows through the udders of the cow in order to nourish the calf, similarly everything unconsciously tends to serve the purpose of the Purusa, whether it is enjoyment or liberation.' Prakrti is the benefactress of Purusa. Though Purusa is inactive and indifferent and devoid of qualities, yet the virtuous and the generous Prakrti which is full of qualities and goodness ceaselessly works through various means in a spirit of detachment for the realization of the Purusa, without any benefit to herself. Prakrti works to liberate the Purusa. There is immanent teleology in Prakrti. Though Purusa is neither a cause nor an effect, yet relatively it is he who should be regarded as the efficient cause as well as the final cause of evolution though Saiikhya regards Prakrti as both the material and the efficient cause.` He is like Aristotle's God, the unmoved mover who is beyond evolution. God, the pure intelligence, like the Purusa, does not actively participate in evolution. He is the end towards which the creation moves. And the creation moves by His mere presence. The gunas, which mutually differ and yet always co-operate, work like the oil, wick and flame of a lamp and illuminate the entire purpose of the Purusa and present it to the buddhi or the intellect.' All the organs work for the realization of the Purusa's end and for no other end. The subtle body too works for the sake of the Purusa's end.' Thus the whole creation unconsciously tends towards the realization of the purpose of the Purusa. And creation will continue till all the Purusas are liberated. The entire evolution of Prakrti therefore, right from the first evolute, the Mahat, up to the last evolutes the gross elements, is for the purpose of liberating each individual Purusa.

## BONDAGE AND LIBERATION

THE earthly life is full of three kinds of pain. The first kind, called adhyatmika, is due to intra-organic psychnphysical causes and includes all mental and bodily sufferings. The second, adhibhautika, is due to extra-organic natural causes like men, beasts, birds, thorns etc. The third, adhidaivika, is due to supernatural causes like the planeis, elemental agencies, ghosts, demons etc. Wherever there are gunas there are pains. Even the so-called pleasures lead to' pain. Even the life in heaven is subject to the gunas. The end of man is to get rid of these kinds of pain and sufferings. Liberation means complete cessation of all sufferings which is the *'summum bonum,'* the highest end of life (Apavarga or Purusartha).

Purusa is free and pure *consciousness.* It is inactive, indifferent and possesses no attributes. Really speaking, it is above time and space merit and demerit, bondage and liberation. It is only when it mistake reflection in the buddhi for itself and identifies itself wrongly with to the *internal* organ-the intellect, the ego and the mind, that it is said to be bound. It is the ego, and not the Purusa, which is bound. When the Purusa realizes its own pure nature, it gets liberated which in fact it always was. Hence bondage is due to ignorance or non-discrimination between the self and the not self and liberation is due to right knowledge or discrimination between the self and the not self. Liberation cannot be obtained by means of actions. Karma, good or had or indifferent, is the function of the gunas and leads to bondage and not to liberation. good actions may lead to heaven and bad actions to hell but heaven and hell alike, like this wordly life, are subject to pain. It is only knowledge that leads to liberation because bondage is due to ignorance and *ignorance* can be removed only by knowledge. The Jiva has to realize itself as title pure Purusa through discrimination between Purusa and Prakrit Actions and fruits, merits and demerits, pleasure and pain all belong; to the not self. The knowledge that 'I am not (the not-self)', that 'nothing is mine', that 'ego is unreal', when constantly meditated upon, becomes pure, incontrovertible and absolute and leads to liberation. Sankhya admits both Jivanmukti and Videhamukti. The moment right knowledge dawns, the person becomes liberated here and now, even though he may be embodied due to prarabdha karma. On account of the momentum of past deeds, the body continues to exist for some time, just as the wheel of a potter goes on revolving for some time due to previous momentum even though the potter has withdrawn his hand from it. As the liberated saint, though embodied, feels no association with the body; no new karma gets accumulated as all karma loses' energy.' The final and the absolute emancipation, the complete embodied isolation automatically results after death. Sankhya liberation is a state of complete isolation, freedom from all pain, a return of the Purusa to its pure nature as consciousness. There is no pleasure or happiness or bliss here, for pleasure presupposes pain and is relative to it. Pleasure is the result of sattva guna and liberation transcends all gunas.

Sankhya believes that bondage and liberation alike are only phenomenal. The bondage of the Purusa is a fiction. It' is only the ego, the product of Prakrti, which is bound. And consequently it is only the ego, which is liberated. Purusa, in its complete isolation, is untouched by bondage and liberation. If Purusa were really bound, it could not have obtained liberation even after hundred births, for real bondage can never be destroyed. It is Prakrti, which is bound, and Prakrti, which is liberated. Ishvarakrsna frankly says: Purusa, therefore, is really neither bound nor is it liberated nor does it transmigrate; bondage, liberation and transmigration belong to Prakrti in its manifold forms.[3] Prakrti binds itself with its seven forms. There is nothing finer and subtler than Prakrti; she is so shy that she never reappears before that Purusa who has once `seen' her in her true colours.' Just as a dancing girl retires from the stage after entertaining the audience, similarly Prakrti also retires after exhibiting herself to the Purusa.

## GOD

The original Sankyha was monistic and theistic. But the classical Sankhya, perhaps under the influence of Materialism, Jainism and Early Buddhism, became atheistic. It is orthodox because it believes in the authority of the Veda. It does not establish the non-existence of God. It only shows that Prakrti and Purusas are sufficient to explain this universe and therefore there is no reason for postulating a hypothesis of God, But some commentators have tried to repudiate the existence of God, while the later Sankhya writers like Vijnanabhiksu have trig revive the necessity for admitting God. Those who repudiate the existence of God give the following arguments: if God is affected by selfish motives, He is not free; if He is free, He will not create this we: pain and misery. Either God is unjust and cruel or He is not free and all-powerful. If the law of Karma determines him, He is not free if not, He is a tyrant. Again, God being pure knowledge, this material world cannot spring from Him. The effects are implicitly contained in, there cause and the material world, which is subject to change, requires an unintelligent and ever-changing cause and not a spiritual and immutable God. Again, the eternal existence of the Purusas is inconsistent with God. If they are the parts of God, they must have some divine power. If God creates them, they are subject to destruction. Hence there is no God.

## GENERAL ESTIMATE

Let us now proceed to give a critical estimate of the Sankhya system. The logic of the Sankhya system, like that of Jainism, impels it to embrace idealistic monism or absolutism but it clings, like Jainisr to spiritualistic pluraiism and dualistic realism. The fundamental blunder of Sankhya is to treat Prakrti and Purusa as absolutely separate and independent realities. The Prakrti and Purusa of Sankhya thus become mere abstractions torn away from the context of concrete experience. The object and the subject are relative and not independent and absolute. Experience always unfolds them together. Like the two sides c: she same coin, they are the two aspects of the same reality. To dig a chasm between them is to undermine them both. And that is what Sankhya has done. The logic of Sankhya requires it to maintain the ultimate reality ofthe transcendental Purusa alone and to regard Prakrti as its inseparable power. When this Purusa is reflected in its own power Prakrti, it becmes the empirical ego, the Jiva, the phenomenal. Plurality belongs to this Jiva, not to the transcendental Purusa. The subject and the object, the Jiva and the Prakrti, are the two aspects of the Purusa, which is their transcendental background. It is the Purusa which sustains the empirical dualism between Prakrti and Jiva and which finally transcends it. Every jiva is the potential Purusa and liberation consists in the actualiation of this potentiality. This is the philosophy to which the Sankhya logic points and which is throughout implicit in Sankhya, but whit: is explicitly rejected by Sankhya with the inevitable and unfortunate result that Sankhya has reduced itself to a bundle of contradictions.

If Prakrti and Purusa are absolute and independent, they can never come into contact and hence there can be no evolution at all. As Sharikara has pointed out,Prakrti being unintelligent and Purusa being indifferent and there being no third principle, no *tertium quid,* there can be no connection of the two. Neither real contact (sarhyoga) nor semblance of contact (samyogabhasa) nor mere presence of Purusa (sannidhya-matra), as we have noticed above, can explain evolution. Sankhya realizes the mistake, but in order to defend the initial blunder it commits blunders after blunders."

The Sankhya account of Prakrti makes it a mere abstraction, an emptiness of pure object. The original state of Product not a harmony, but only a tension of the three gunas. The gunas *to* a state beyond them. It is this state which gives harmony to the gunas and transcends them. Prakrti does not do that. Hence it is not real. Reality is the Purusa alone. Again, Prakrti is unconscious and unintelligent. How can it then explain the teleology, which is immanent in creation? If Prakrti is unconscious and blind, evolution must be mechanical and blind and there can be no freedom of the will. And if Prakrti and all its evolutes from Mahat to the Mahabhutas tend to serve the purpose of the Purusa, it can be neither unconscious nor independent. Again, if Prakrti is blind and non-intelligent, it cannot evolve this world that is full of harmony, order, design and purpose. Stones, bricks and mortar cannot account for the design of a building. Mere clay cannot fashion itself into a pot. How can Prakrti explain the original impetus, the first push, and the *elanvital, which* disturbs the equilibrium of the gunas? The argument that Prakrti works unconsciously for the emancipation of the

Purusa just as unintelligent milk flows for the nourishment of the calf is untenable because milk flows as there is a living cow and there is the motherly love in the cow for the calf. Nor can the modification of Prakrti be compared to that of grass that turns into milk. Grass becomes milk only when a milk cow eats it, and not when it lies uneaten or is eaten by a bull. The simile of the blind and the lame is also misleading since the blind and the lame are both intelligent and active beings that can devise plans to realize a common purpose, while Prakrti is unconscious and Purusa is indifferent and there is no common purpose. The simile via magnet and iron is also misleading because the proximity of the Purusa being permanent, there would be no dissolution and hence no liberation and the very state of Prakrti as the equilibrium of the gunas would be impossible since the presence of the Purusa would never permit the state of equilibrium. Moreover, activity is said to belong to Prakrti and enjoyment to Purusa. This overthrows the moral law of Karma and brings in the charge of vicarious liability; Poor Purusa suffers for no fault of its own. Prakrti performs actions and Purusa has to reap their fruits, good or bad. And Prakrti knows how to make delicious dishes, but not to enjoy them.

Though Prakrti is called absolute and independent yet there is a note of relativism in the conception of Prakrti. As a triad of the gunas it. Points towards the nistraigunya Purusa as the transcendental reality. At every step, it shows its dependence on Purusa. It cannot evolve this world by itself without being influenced by the Purusa-whether that influence is due to real contact or semblance of contact or mere presenco. How can Prakrti be absolute then? An absolute Prakrti is contradiction in-terms. If it is absolute why should it care to serve the purpose of the Purusa? Does it not make it subservient to the Purusa? And if it is unconscious and blind, how can it serve this purpose? Though Sankhya calls Prakrti as impersonal, yet its descriptions of Prakrti are. full of personal notes. Prakrti is called a dancing girl; she is feminine, she is virtuous and generous; she is the benefactress of the Purusa; she serves Purusa's purpose in a spirit of perfect detachment for no gain to herself; and yet she is blind; she is extremely delicate and shy and cannot stand the eye of the Purusa; she is seven-rainbow-coloured and wants to attract the Purusa. How can such Prakrti be absolute and impersonal? Purusa is untouched by bondage, liberation and transmigration. It is Prakrti who binds herself and liberates herself and transmigrates. Prakrti is said to vanish for that Purusa who has `seen' her, though she continues to exist for others. Does this not make Prakrti relative? If she `vanishes', how can she be absolute and eternal? Why not frankly equate Prakrti with Avidya? Either maintain a plurality of Prakrtis or equate it with Avidya. These descriptions of Prakrti clearly show that Vedanta is *implicit* in Sankhya.

Sankhya throughout makes a 'confusion between the Purusa, the transcendental subject and the Jiva, the empirical ego, the product of the reflection of Purusa in Buddhi or Mahat. Sankhya rightly emphasizes that the Purusa is pure consciousness and that it is the foundation of all knowledge and that it is beyond bondage, liberation and trans-migration. Purusa has really nothing to do with the play of Prakrti. It is a mere spectator and is not among the *dramatis personae.* It is net contaminated by action. It is self-proved and self-shining. It is the transcendental subject that appears as the phenomenal ego. We cannot derive consciousness from Prakrti or matter, nor can we regard consciousness as a quality. The self is not a substance but a subject It is the Alone, the unseen seer, the transcendental Absolute. But Sankhya soon forgets its own position and reduces the ultimate Purusa the level of the phenomenal ego. Some of the proofs advanced in support of the existence of Purusa, are proofs only for the phenomenal ego. Purusa is called enjoyer and Prakrti enjoyed. But if Purusa the transcendental subject, how can it be an enjoyer? If it is passive, indifferent and inactive, how can it enjoy? Again, how can the tray cendental reality be split into the many reals? How can there be a plurality of the transcendental subjects, the Purusas? Of course, no one denies the plurality of the empirical egos, the Jivas. But the many-ness of the egos, the empirical souls, does not lead us to the manyness of the transcendental selves, the Purusas. In fact, all the arguments advanced by Sankhya to prove the plurality of the Purusas turn out to be arguments to prove the plurality of the Jivas which none has ever denied. Sankhya to proves the plurality of purusas by such flimsy arguments that if there were only one Purus the birth or death or bondage or liberation or experience of pleas or pain or indifference of one should lead to the same result in the case of all, forgetting its own doctrine that the Purusa is not subject to birth or death or bondage or liberation or any action. Realizing this grave defect, the commentators like Vachaspati, Gaudapada and Vijnanabhiksu have maintained the reality of one Purusa only. If

Sankhya can reduce all objects to one Prakrti, why can it not reduce all the empirical souls to one Purusa by the same logic? And why can Prakrti and the empirical Purusa be not reduced to the Absolute Purusa by the same logic? Again, if all the Purusas are essentially similar, if the essence of all is pure consciousness, how can they be really many? Differences and distinctions constitute individuality. If all the Purusas are essentially the same, there is no meaning in proclaiming their quantitative plurality. Numerical pluralism is sheer nonsense.

Another grave defect in Sankhya is in its conception of liberation. Liberation is regarded as a negative cessation of the three kinds of pain and not as a state of positive.bliss. Sankhya feels that bliss is a product of Sattva guna and cannot remain in liberation, which is the state beyond the gunas. But Sankhya forgets that the bliss in liberation is not empirical happiness produced by sattva. This bliss is also transcendental in character. It is beyond both pain and pleasure. What is related to pain is empirical pleasure and not transcendental bliss. The negative Kaivalya suggests an influence of the Hinayana Nirvana. Will the liberated Purusas; the eternally isolated units not represent 'a vast array of sad personalities'? If liberation is an annihilation (nasmi, naham) of human personality and not its perfection, the ideal of liberation is most untmspiring. It must be substituted by an ideal of positively blissful eternal existence in the bosom of the Absolute.

Sankhya, therefore, should let its Prakrti glide into Avidya, the inseparable power of the Purusa; its Prakrti-parinama-vada into Purusavivarta-vada; its so-called empirical Purusa into phenomenal Jiva; its negative Kaivalya into positively blissful Moksa, and should, instead of maintaining the plurality of Purusas and creating arrunbridgable chasm between the subject and the object, recognize the Absolute Purusa, the transcendental subject which gives life and meaning to the empirical subject and object and holds them together and ultimately transcends them both.

## METAPHYSICAL VIEWS

To quote Dr. S. Radhakrishnan: `It is impossible to read Shan kara's writings, packed as they are with serious and subtle thinking, without being conscious that one is in contact with a. mind of a very fine penetration and profound spirituality . . . . His philosophy stands forth complete, needing neither a before nor an after ... whether we agree or differ, the penetrating light of his mind never leaves us where we were'.

Ultimate Reality, according to Shankar is Atman or Brahman which is Pure Consciousness (jfiana-svarupa) or Consciousness of the Pure Self (svarpa-jnana) which is devoid of all attributes (nirgiuna) and all categories of the intellect (nirvishesa). Brahman associatecd with its potency (shaktri) may or mulayidya appears as the qualified

Brahman (saguna or savishesa or apara Brahma) or the Lord (Ishvara) who is the creator, preserver of this word that is His appearance.

Jiva or the individual self is a subject-object Complex-Its subject element is Pure. Consciousness and is called the-Saksiu. Its objectelement is the internal organ called. the antahkarana which is bhautika as it is composed of all the five elements, with the predominance-of tejas which makes it always active except in- deep sleep-or states like swoon or trance. The source of the internal organ is Avidya that causes individuality. In perception, the internal -organ,. When a sense organ comes m contact with an object assumes the.'form'.of that object. It is the written or the mode of the internal organ... This written inspired by the Saksin takes the form of empirical knowledge. In waking state, the internal organ is aided by the senses; in dream state, it functions by itself; and in deep sleep it is lost in its cause Avidya. In This state too individuality persists because the Saksin is associated with Avidya. In liberation, Jfiana destroys Avidya and the Saksin is realized as the Brahman, which it always is.

Maya or Avidya.is not pure illusion. It is not only absence of knowledge. It is also positive wrong. Knowledgedge. It is a cross of the real the unreal (satyanrte mithuni krtya). In fact it is indescribable.it is neither existent nor non-existent nor both. It is not existent for 'IC existent is only the Brahman. It is not non-existent for it is responsible for the appearance of the Brahman as the world. It cannot be both existent and non-existent for this conception is self-contradictory. It is called neither real nor unreal (sadasadvilaksana). It is false or mithya. But it is not a non-entity like a hare's horn (tuchchha). It is positive (bhavarupa). It is potency (shakti). It is also called superposition. When (adhyasa). A shell is mistaken as silver. The shell is the ground on which the silver is superimposed. When right knowledge (prama) arises, this error (bhranti or bhrama) vanishes. The relation between the shell and the silver is neither that of identity nor of difference nor of both. It is unique and is known as non-difference (tadatmya). Similarly, Brahman is the ground on which the world appears through Maya. When right knowledge dawns and the essential unity of the jiva with the Paramatman is realized, Maya or Avidya vanishes.

Shaidkara emphasizes that from the phenomenal point of view the world is quite real. It is not an illusion. It is a practical reality. He distinguishes the dream state from the waking state. Things seen in a dream are quite true as long as the dream lasts; they are sublimed only when we are awake. Similarly, the world is quite real so long as true knowledge does not dawn. But dreams are private. They are creations of the jiva (jivasrsta). The world is public. It is the creation of Ishvara (Ishvara-srsta). Jiva is ignorant of the essential unity and takes only diversity as true and wrongly regards himself as agent and enjoyer. Avidva conceals the unity (avarana) and projects names and forms (viksepa). Ishvara never misses the unity. Maya has only its viksepa aspect over him. The Highest Brahman (para-Brahma) is both the locus (ashraya) and the objective saya) of Maya. When the jiva through knowledge and knowledge alone, karma being subsidiary, this essential unity, liberation is attained here and now (jivan-mukti) and final release. (videha-mukti) is obtained after the death of the body.

This is a short summary of Shankaracharya's philosophy He too is considerably influenced by Buddhism) He preserves the best that was in Mahayana in his own philosophy.He uses many words, especiaiiy in his Upanisad-Bhasyas, which were commonly used in Mahayana literature. But outwardly he is an enemy of Buddhism. Gaudapada had love and respect for Mahayana. Shankara has nothing but strong and even bitter words for it. It is very important and interesting too to: note that Shankara does not at all criticize the two most important schools` of Mahayaana, the Shunyavada and the Vijnanavada. What he criticizes under the name of Vijnanavada is in fact

Svatantra-Vijnanavada; -And he summarily dismisses Shunyavada as a self-condemned nihilism that is below criticism. Shankara observes that there are three important. Schools of Buddhism – the Sarvastovada, the Vijanawavada and the Shunyavada school of Hinayana, which, according to sankara, includes both the Vaibhsdiks and the Sautrantika school\,was bitterly cities by the Mahayanists themselves. Shankaras criticism against it is not new. It must be admitted that Shaker's exposition of fied. He avoided Shunyavada by taking the word Shunya in its popular sense and easily dismissing Shunyavada as nihilism.and he did not at all touch real Vijananavada.by Vijmamavadins he means Svatantra-Vijnanavadins who were his immediate predecessors.it was easy for him to criticeze their momentary consciousness. no reference do we find to asanaga or Vasubandhu or to their doctrines with the solitary exception however of the Alaya-Vijanana.on the other hand we find verses quoted from Dinnaga and Dharmakirti and their views correctly exposed and criticized. And we also find references to and criticisms of the views of shanitaraksita as well as rplirs to the objection raised by Shantarakshares in common with Vijananavada also .but here it loses much of its force because vijanavada regards consciousness as absulet and permanent. Shankara, however, represent a definite advance on Vasubandu as well as on Gaudapada who agrees with Vasubhandu .

## CRITICSM OF THE PRAKARTI-PARINAMA-VADA OF SANKHYA

We have given the arguments advanced by Sankhya in faviour of its prakrti. Shankara agrees with sankaya in maintaining that the design, harmony or order in the universe must presuppose a single cause which is enternal and unlimited. But he criticizes Sankhya when it says that such a casuse is the unintelligent Prakrui. According to Shankara the intelligent nature be explained by unintelligent Prakrti? We do proceed from the finite to the infinite, from the limited to the unlimited, from the peros to the *aperos, from* the effect to the cause, from pluralitu to unity but only the conscious Brahman asscociated with its Maya Shakti can be the creator, Preserver and destroyer of his world. Unintelligent Prakrti is too poor and too powerless to be its causes. We see that stones, bricks and mortar cannot fashion themselves in a well designed building without the help of intelligent workmen. How can, then the unintelligent. Pradhana account for the beauty, symmetry, order and harmony of this grist universe-internal and external? Again, how can Pradhana explain the original impetus, the first push, and the *elan, which* is supposed to disturb the equilibrium of the three gunas? Mere clay, without a potter, cannot fashion itself into a pot. Chariots cannot move without horses etc. Why should Sainkhya hesitatingly admit that the initial activity comes from the mere presence of the Purusa (purusa-sane matra)? Why should it not frankly admit that it comes from the conscious Brahman?' Again, the argument of Sankhya that just as unintelligent milk flows for the nourishment of the calf, similarly unintelligent Prakrti works for the emancipation of the Purusa is untenable because milk flows as there is a living cow and a living calf and there is also the motherly love in the cow for the calf. Again, because Prakrti is regarded as an absolutely independent entity in itself. It cannot be related in any way to the indifferent Purusa who can neither energize nor restrain it. Then, Prakrti should sometimes evolve and sometimes should not evolve. Nor can the modification of Prakrti be compaired to that of grass which turns into milk. Grass becomes milk my when it is eaten by a milch cow, not when it lies uneaten or is eaten by a bull.

Again, even if we grant activity to Pradhana, it cannot explain the teleology, which Sankhya takes to be immanent in nature. Unconscious, Pradhana can have no purpose; indifferent neutral Purusa too can have no purpose. If Safikhya tries to solve the difficulty by pointing out that Prakrti and Purusa combine like the blind and the lame and then Purusa , like the magnet moving the iron, may move Prakrti to accomplish his goal, it is mistaken, for the blind and the lame persons arc both intelligent and active beings, while Prakrti is unconscious and Purusa is indifferent. The simile of the magnet and the iron also wrong. If the mere presence of the Purusa is sufficient to move the Pradhana, then Purusa being always co-presented, there should be perpetual movement. Thus creation should have no beginning and no end. The liberation of Purusa will also become impossible. Again, Prakrti and Purusa can never be related. Prakrti is unconscious; Purusa is indifferent; and there is no third principle, no *tertium quid,* to relate them. The chasm which Sankhya has created by postulating two independent and eternal' entities, one the subject and other the object, can never be bridged by it. It must therefore recognize a higher conscious principle that transcends and yet gives meaning to and preserves at a lower level, the subject object duality.

Moreover, by regarding Pradhana as a mere agent and Purusa as a mere enjoyer, Sankhya opens itself to the charge of vicious suffering which throws all moral responsibility overboard. Why should Purusa suffer for the actions of pradhana? And how can it be possible that Prakrti knows only to do and not to enjoy?

Brahman alone, therefore, is the cause and it is universally declared to be so by all the Vedanta texts. The words like mahat, avyakta etc. used in certain Upanisads, e.g. in the Katha, do not denote the mahat and avyakta of Sankhya. They simply mean the potentiality of names and forms in their cause Brahman. They are not independent of it. Sankhya and Yoga are generally accepted by the wise as conducive to the highest well. But these systems advocate dualism and cannot be supported by the Shruti. The Shruti uses these words only in the sense of knowledge_ and meditation respectively. We accept those doctrines of these systems, which do not clash with Advaita, also. Shankara calls Sankhya as the `principal opponent' (pradhana-malla) of the Vedanta and says that its refutation implies the refutation of paramanukarana-vada etc.

Sankhya, therefore, should let its Prakrti glide into Maya, its Prakrti-parinamavada into Brahma-vivarta-vada, its satkaryavada into satk'arana-vada, its Purusa into jiva, its negative kaivalya into positively blissful moksa, and should, instead of maintaining the plurality of Purusas representing `a vast array of sad personalities' and creating an unbridgable chasm between the subject and the object, recognize the non-dual Purusa, the Brahman transcending the subject-objcet duality.

## CRITICISM OF ASAT-KARYAVADA

SHANKARA believes in sat-karyavada but his interpretation of it is different from that of Sainkhya. By it he really means satkaranav'ada. His view is known as vivartav'ada. The effect, no doubt, must pre-exist in the cause. But ultimately the effect is not something different from the cause. The cause alone is real; the effect is only its appearance.

Shankara agrees with the Shunyavadins and the Svatantra-Vijnanavadins in maintaining, against Sainkhya, that if the effect were real and if it really pre-existed in the cause, then it is already an accomplished fact and its production will be a vain repetition. He also agrees with them, against Nyaya-Vaishesika, that if the effect were a non-entity,. it would be like a hare's hom and its production would be impossible. We have seen that for the Svatantra-Vijnanavadin asatkaryavada is a misnomer for he does not advocate the production of a non-entity. Reality' itself, to him, is efficient causation .Shankara, however, agrees with the Shunyavadin, against Svatantra-Vijiianavadin, in maintaining that causation in a real sense is an impossibility. Production cannot called be the own essence' of a thing for ultimately there can be neither production nor destruction nor any momentary entity.

The effect, says Sharikara, can never exist independently outside of the cause either before or after its manifestation. There f, it cannot be said that the effect does not pre-exist in the cause effect is only an appearance of the cause. Though the effect and cause are non-different, yet it is the effect that exists in and deper on the cause and not *vice versa.*

We see that milk produces curd, clay produces pots and gold produces ornaments. Curd cannot be produced from clay nor can pots be produced from milk. But according to asatkaryavada this should be possible-If it is rejoined that the cause has a certain peculiarity (atishaya) according to which only certain effects can be produced from certain causes, we reply that if this peculiarity means `the antecedent condition of the effect', asatkaryavada is abandoned; and if it means `the power of the cause to produce a particular determined effect', then it must be admitted that this power is neither different from the cause nor r existent because if it were either, production would be impossible.

Again, the relation between the cause and the effect, like that between, substance and qualities, must be that of identity (tadatmya). It cannot be of the nature of inherence (samavaya) because inherence will require another relation to relate it to cause and effect and this relation' another relation and so on *ad infinitum;* or inherence itself will impossible for without being related to the two terms it cannot hang in the air.

Again, according to asatkaryavada, the effect and the cause can have no connexion because connexion is possible only between two exist entities and not between an existent and a non-existent entity or between, two non-existent entities. Nobody says that the son of a barren woman was a king. He is a non-entity and never was or is or will a king.

Again, the theory that when the effect is produced the cause is destroyed is absolutely wrong. The cause can never be destroyed. When milk changes into curd, it is not destroyed. Nor is the seed destroyed when it becomes the sprout. If the cause in the process of change is destroyed, recognition will become impossible.

Hence it is impossible to produce an effect which is different from its cause and which does not pre-exist in it even within a hundred years.

## CRITICISM OF THE PARAMANU-KARANA-VADA OF NYAYA-VAISHESIKA

This school maintains that the four substances (earth, water, fire and air) in their subtle (amurta) form as causes are eternal and atomic. Akasha, though itself not atomic, binds the atoms together. The atoms of Democritus are only quantitatively different, are in motion and make up souls also. But the Vaishesika, atoms are both quantitatively and qualitatively different, are by nature at rest and are distinct from souls. God assisted by the Unseen Power (adrsta) of the jivas generates motion in. the atoms. This motion (parispanda) joins two atoms together which make a dyad (dvyaquka). Three such dyads make a triad (tryanuka), Four dyads fona a quartrad (chaturanuka) and so on till the gross objects of the world are produced. An atom is infinitesimal and spherical (parimandala); a dyad is minute (apu) and short (hrasva); and a triad and others are great (mahat) and long (dirgha). The things produced are not mere aggregates, but wholes composed of parts, the parts and the whole being relatrd by inherence (samdviiya). The Vaishesika says that the cause must transmit its qualities to the effect, e.g., white threads make white cloth, and black threads make black cloth. Therefore conscious. Brahman cannot be the cause of theunconscious world. Atoms are its cause.

Sharikara in refuting this theory points out that it is not necessary for the cause to transmit all its qualities to the effect. Even on the Vaishqika hypothesis an atom which is spherical produces a dyad which is not spherical, but minute and short; and a dyad produces a triad which is neither minute nor short, but great and long. If this is so; why should not the conscious Brahman produce an unconscious world?

Are the atoms essentially active or inactive or both or neither? If active, then creation would become permanent; if inactive, then there would be no creation : if both, the conception would he self-contrialictory; and if neither, then their activity must come from outside and this outside agency must be either seen or unseen; if seen, then it should not exist before creation; and if unseen, then it being always present near the atoms, creation would become permanent and if the proximity of the unseen to the atoms is denied, then creation would be impossible. In all cases therefore there can be no creation from atoms.'

## CRITICISM OF THE CATEGORIES OF NAYA-VAISHESIKA

This school assumes six categories (padartha) which unlike the Aristitelian categories which are mere logical predicates are metaphysical objects these categories says Shankara are regarded as absolutely different from one another and still it is maintained that qualities action etc, depend upon the substance if so then substance alone should exist if in order to avoid this difficulty it is maintained that substance and qualities are

Inseparably connected (ayutasiddha), then this inseparable connection must be either in space or in time or in herself.and none of these alternatives can support the Vaishesika theory If it is inseparable in space, then the Vaishesika. Doctrine that substance produce other substance and qualities other qualities will be upset. If it is inseparable in time, then the two horns of a cow would be inseparably connected. If it is inseparable in itself, then no distinctions could be made between substance and qualities.

Shankara like Nagarjuna Dharmakirti and Shantaraksita challenges the distiniction of parts and whole. The whole can be not neighter a more aggregate of parts nor can it be something apart from parts. The whole cannot abide in all the parts taken together, for then it would not be perceived, as it is impossible to perceive all the parts. If it is said that the whole abides in allthe parts taken together through the help of other parts, then it would lead to infinite regress as we would airways be forced to assume further parts. Again, the whole cannot abide in each separate part because if it abides in one part, it cannot abide in another part, just as Devadatta cannot be present at the same time in two different places. Moreever, if the whole were present in separate parts, then they would sita, the whole is unreal and the parts alone are real, for Nagarjuna and Shanakara, both the whole and the parts are relative and therefore ultimately unreal.

The Vaishesika maintains that Atman is a substance, which is unintelligent in it and becomes intelligent on account of its contact with mind (mans). This, says Shankara, is highly absurd. To say that the unqualified and indeterminate Atman really comes into contact with something different from itself is to violate the established canon of logic again either the qualities of pleasure pain etc.will be reduced to the Atman, and they too will become permanent or the Atman will be reduced to the qualities and will become impermanent. By no stretch of reasoning can it be proved that the Atman can feel pleasure or pain or that it is made up of parts or that it is changing.

Action or motion (karma) is impossible and with it creation too is impossible because the adrsta can produce no motion in the atoms. It can inhere neither in the souls nor in the atoms. Hence there can be neither creation nor dissolution.

The universal- is also ultimately unreal. We perceive no universal cow' in the individual cows. It is only the generic qualities that are present in individual cows. If the `universal cow, as a `whole', is present in each cow, then even the horns or the tail of a cow should yield milk.

Inherence too is impossible..Tnherence (samavaya) is a. category while samyoga or conjunction is a quality, according to Nyaya-Vaishesika Inherence is regarded as an eternal, imperceptible, inseparable and reat relation subsisting between parts and whole, qualities and substance, action and agent, universal and particular etc. A dyad is supposed to be related to its two constituent atoms by this samavaya. Sharikara, like Chandrakirti, Dharmakirti and Shantaraksita and like Zeno and Bradley, points out that inherence must lead to infinite regress. Inherence, being different from the two things which it relates;

stands in need of another inherence to relate it with them. This second inherence again requires another inherence and so on *ad infinitum. If* it is maintained that samavaya does not inhere in the samavay in by another samavaya; but is identical with it, then even samyoga should be regarded as, identical with the things it conjoins; and as both equally require another relation to relate them to the two terms; no talk of calling samavaya a category and sarnyoga a quality can remove the.difculty. Shankara's point is that a relation, whatever may be its nature and howsoever intimate it may be regarded, can never be identical- with the terms, which it relates. If $t_1$ and $t_2$ are two terms that are to be related by $r_2$ the relation, then the following difficulties -are bound, to occur:

(1) . If r inheres in $t_i$, it cannot relate it with $t_2$;

(2). If r inheres in $t_2$, it cannot relate it with t1;

(3). The same r cannot inhere in both t1 and $t_2$;

(4). If r is absolutely different from ti and $t_2$ and falls outside both, then r itself becomes another term and requires a further relation which can relate it with -$t_1$ and $t_2$., Thus infinite regress is sure to creep in:

Thus we see that the distinction between samyoga-and samavaya is untenable. One and the same thing, may be called by different names

According to different considerations the same Devadatta may be called a Brahaman, a learned man, a boy, a youth, an old man, a father, a son, a grandson, a brother, as on in law etc. etc.

The six categories of the Vaishesika therefore, are nothing but mere assumption and if we priceed with mere assumptions there is nothing to check us if we assume hundres and thousands of caregories instead of six.

## CRITICISM OF THE DICRTINE THAT GOD IS THE EFFICIENT CAUSE ONLY

Some Yogins and some Vaishesikas and other hold that God is the eddicient cause only for. He is the ruler of primordial Matter and Souls this makes according to his sweet will some persons great, some ordinary and other loe loe then, he will be rightally charged of being actuated by partilitu, attachment and harted and hence he will be one like us and no real god. Nor can the harted and hence. He will be rightly charged of being actulated by partiality, attachment and harted and hence He will be one like us and no real god. Nor can the blind remove the difficulty.

Moreever, God cannot be the ruler of Matter and souls without being connected with them and there can be no such connection. It cannot be conjunction because God, Souls and Matter are regarded as infinite and without parts. It cannot be inherence because it is impossible to decide as to which is the abode and which the abiding thing. For us the difficulty does not arise at all because we maintain the identify (tadatmya) of the cause and the effect. Again, if Prakrti ceases for the liberated soul, it must be finite and there would be nothing to rule. Moreover, these three infinite principles will limit one another and will collapse into a void. The infinite can be only one. Further, if Matter and souls are infinite, God cannot rule over them and then hen will be neighter neither omniscient nor omnipotent.

## CRITICISM OR BRAHAMA-PARINAMA-VADA

SANKARA maintained Brahma-karana-vada as he recognizes that Brahama is the causes of the world. But his theory is called Brahma-vivarta-vada because it takes the world to play only a phenomenal appearance of Brahaman. Neither Brahaman nor vada opposes Shankara to real creation for him, the world is neighter a real creation by Brahaman nor a real modification of Brahman. Brahman associated with its power Maya is the ground on which the phenomenal world is super-imposed. When true knowledge dawns and the essential unity of the jivat man with the Paramatman is realized, the world is sublated. Modification or change in a realistic manner (satattvato'nyatha pratha), like the change of gold into ornaments or of clay into pots or of milk into curd, is called parinama or vikara. Unreal change or seeming modification (atattvato'nyatha pratha), like the appearance of water into waves, bubbles, foam etc., is called vivarta. They are not, as Sarvajnatma Muni rightly points out, absolutely opposed; parinamavada logically leads to vivartavada, which is only a step ahead of it. The world, which cannot be called real either in the beginning or in the end, must be unreal in the middle also.

This entire diverse universe of names and forms, of agents and enjoyers, of space, time and causality, says Shankara, proceeds from that omniscient, omnipotent and omnipresent cause, the Brahman which alone is the creator, preserver and destroyer of it. Brahman is the material cause as well as the efficient cause. All the sacred texts which declare Brahman as undergoing modification or change (parinama) do not at all mean a real modification or change, as it is illogical. Their real aim is to teach that the world is only a phenomenal appearance of Brahman which is in fact beyond all plurality and phenomena and which is the same as the Real Self. Thus Ishvara or Saguna Brahman associated with Maya is the cause of this world.

Shankara gives some of the objections raised by Shantaraksita and others and refutes them. He says that some people object to the simile given in some Upanisads that just as a spider produces, maintains and devours a cobweb, similarly Brahman creates, maintains and destroys this world. They say that a spider, on account of its desire to eat small insects, emits saliva, which produces the web. What such desire and what external means can Brahman have?' To this we reply that creation is not something ultimately real. It is only an appearance, Moreover, Brahman being Consciousness can need no other external means except its own potency, Maya. Again, it is objected that Ishvara cannot be the creator of this world for then the charges of inequality and cruelty will be leveled to Him. Why should He make some people happy and others miserable? Is He not partial to some and prejudiced against others? We reply that He cannot be so charged. The Shruti and the Smrti declare that the inequality in the creation is due to the merits and demerits of the creatures. Just as a cloud rains the same water, though different seeds fructify according to their different potentialities, similarly Ishvara is the common cause of creation, though different creatures reap different fruits on account of the difference in their actions. The objection that before creation merits and demerits do not exist is invalid, for creation has no beginning. Actions and inequality, therefore, like seeds and sprouts, are both cause and effect.' But it should he remembered that ultimately creation is an impossibility. Shankara agrees with the Shunyavadins and with Gaudapada here. Brahman is the only Reality. It cannot he produced from itself because there can be neither any peculiarity (atishaya) nor any change (vikara) in the eternal. It cannot he produced from anything other than itself for every other thing except Brahman is non-existent and unreal. Again, why should Brahman really create? It has no desire or ambition to fulfil. If it has, it is not perfect. Shruti can prove either by independent reasoning or no desire or ambition of Brahman. (Aptakamasya ka spriha?). Therefore it must be remembered, says Shankara, that whenever we talk of creation, we do not mean real creation; we mean only a phenomenal appearance of Brahman due to Avidya and this creation-appearance is real only as long as Avidya lasts. When Avidya is removed by right knowledge, God, the Ruler, Soul, the Enjoyed, and all are merged in the Highest Brahman.

## CRITICISM OF JAINISM

The Jainas believe in the theory of Relativity called the Sapta-bhangi-naya or the Syadvada: (r) Relatively, it is; (2) Relatively, it is ; (2,}Relatively, it is not (3)Relatively, it both is and is not; (4) Relatively, it is indescribable (5) Relatively, it is and is indescribable; (6) Relatively, it is not and is indescribable; (7) Relatively, it both is and is not and is also indes-cribable. They also say that a thing may he one as 'well as many, eternal as 'well as momentary.

Shankara, like Dharmakirti and Shantaraksita, bitterly criticize this theory. He points out that contradictory attributes like existenc non-existence, unity and plurality, eternity and momcntarinee etc cannot belong to the sane thing, just as light and darkness cannot remainingat the same place or just as the same thing cannot be hot and cold at the same time. According to this view, the theory of Syadvada itself may not he correct. Relativity cannot be sustained without the Absolute, which is rejected by the Jainas. The theory looks like the word of a lunatic. Again, the judgments cannot be indescrihshle, for they are clearly set forth. To describe them and to say that they are indescribable is a contradiction in terms.

## CRITICISM OF BUDDHISM

*(a) Criticism of the Sarvastivada School:-This is* the most important School of Hinayana. It is divided, according to Sharikara, into two major schools-the Vaibhasika

and the Sautrantika. The former attaches itself to Vibhasa, a Commentary on an Abhidharma work and may be called presentationism or naive realism as it maintains the independent existence of mind and matter. The latter attaches itself to the Sutra and may be called representationism or critical realism as it maintains that the existence of external objects is inferred through mental presentations, even as eating of good food is inferred through corpulence or a country is inferred through language. But both these schools are equally realistic and reduce mind to fleeting ideas and matter to fleeting sensations.

Shankara takes both these schools under the name of `Sarvastivada' and says that its followers hold that external reality is either element (bhuta) or elemental (bhautika) and that internal reality is either mind (chitta) or mental (chaitta). Earth, water, fire and air are elements. Colour etc. and the sense organs like eye etc. are elemental. The internal world consists of the five skandhas-of sensation, idea, feeling, conception and forces.

Shah kara objects that these two types of aggregates-external as well as internal-can never be formed at all The unintelligent momentary atoms and the momentary skandhas cannot form any systematic whole. No intelligent principle-enjoyer or ruler-which may unite these aggregates is admitted by the opponents. If it is urged that the momentary vijfiana unites the aggregates, it is untenable, for the vijfiana must come into existence in the first moment and must unite the aggregates in the second moment which would mean that the vijnana exists at least for two moments and is therefore not momentary. Nor can the aggregates be formed on account of Dependent Causation, for in the Wheel of Causation each preceding link is the immediate efficient cause of the succeeding link only, not of the whole series. The momentary atoms too cannot combine by themselves. When it is impossible even for the permanent atoms of the Vaishesika to combine, it is more so with the atoms in Buddhism which are momentary.'

Again, the Buddhists maintain that existence arises from nonexistence, that a seed must be destroyed before a sprout can spring up or milk must be destroyed before curd can come into being. Shaflkara replies that an entity can never arise from a nonentity. Had it been so anything would arise from anything? Nothing can originate from the horns of a hare. And even when Buddhists themselves admit that aggregates arise from atoms and mental states from the skandha why should they confuse the world with worse than useless contradictions.

*(b) Criticism of the Theory of Momentariness (,ksanadha.vada):*The antecedent link in the causal series, says Shankara, cannot even be regarded as the efficient cause of the subsequent link because, accordinge to the theory of momentariness, the preceding link ceases to exist when the subsequent link arises. If it is urged that the antecedent moment-when -fully developed (parihispannavasthah) becomes the cause of the subsequent moment, it is untenable;, because the assertion that a fully developed moment has a causal efficiency necessarily: presupposes its connection with the second moment and this repudiates the theory of universal momentariness. Again, if it is urged (as is done by the Svatan-tra Vijfianavadins) that the mere existence of the preceding moment means its causal efficiency (bhava evasva vvaparah), this too is impossible, because no effect can arise without imbibing the nature of the causes and to admit this is to admit that the cause is permanent as it continues, exist in the effect and thus to throw overboard the doctrine of momen- tariness.

Again, are production and destruction the nature of a thing (vastunah svarupameva) or another state of it (avasthantaram va) or a different thing (vastvantarameva va): All these alternatives are impossible. In the first case, production and destruction would become synonymous with the thing itself. Again, if it is said that production is the beginnings thing is the middle, and destruction is the end, then a thing, being connected with three moments, would not be momentary. And if it be mainted that production and destruction are two absolutely different things like a horse and a buffalo, then the thing, being different from production and destruction would become permanent. Again, if production and destruction are regarded as perception and non-perception, then too, erception and non-perception, being the attributes of the perceiving mind and not of the thing, the thing would become permanent. In all cases therefore the theory of momentariness is entirely untenable.

Again, if the opponent says that things arise without a cause, he violates dates his own statement that things arise depending on causes and conditions"'. Then anything may arise out of anything. And if the opponen says that the preceding cause lasts only up to the arising of the succeeding effect, this would imply that the cause and the effect are simultaneous.

Again, there can be neither conscious destruction (pratisankhyanirodha, e.g., of a jar by a stick), nor unconscious destruction (apm.' isankhyanirodha, e.g., the decay of things), because these can related themselves neither to the series (santana-gochara) as in all the series the members are causally related in an uninterrupted manner, nor to the members of the series (bhava-gochara) as a momentary thing cannot be completely annihilated because it is recognized in different states as having a connected existence.

Again, if Right Knowledge destroys Ignorance, then the Bud-dhistic doctrine that universal destruction is going on without any cause is given up; and if it is destroyed by itself, then the Buddhistic teaching pertaining to the 'Path' to help the destruction of Ignorance becomes futile. Moreover, bondage and liberation are also impossible. If the soul is momentary, whose is the bondage and whose is the liberation? Again, there will be vicarious liability in moral life. He who performs an act will lose its fruit and another will have to reap it.

The fact of memory and recognition gives a deathblow to the theory of momentariness. The past is recognized and remembered in the present and this implies the existence of a permanent synthesizing subject without whom knowledge shall always remain impossibility. Identity cannot mean similarity. Even similarity requires a permanent subject I who knows two things to be similar. When the Buddhist himself recognizes all his successive cognitions, till he breathes his last, as belonging to the same Self, should he not tremble in maintaining shamelessly the doctrine of momentarincss?' Everything may be doubted but the self can never be doubted for the very idea of doubt presupposes the self. Indeed, when philosophers fail to admit a self-evident fact, they may try to uphold their view and refute the view of their opponents, but in doing this, they entangle themselves in mere words and, honestly speaking, they convince neither their opponents nor even themselves.

***(c) Criticism of 'Vijndnavada'*** **(really of Svatantra-Vijnanavada):-**By the term 'Vijnanavada', Shankara really means `Svatantra-Vijnanavada'. These

Buddhists, says Shankara, maintain the existence of momentary ideas only. They say that Buddha taught the reality of the external world to his inferior disciples who cling to this world, while to his superior disciples he gave his real teaching that ultimate reality is the momentary vijnana only. Shankara, taking his stand mainly on the Alambanapariksa of Dinnaga, exposes the Buddhist view as follows:

If external things exist they should be either atoms or aggregates of atoms like posts etc. And both are impossible. Atoms cannot be perceived and their aggregates can be regarded neither as identical with nor as different from the atoms. It is the ideas themselves, which appear as different external objects, as a post, a wall, a pot, a cloth etc. The fact that the idea is identical with the external object is proved also by the rule that the internal idea and the external object are always experienced simultaneously-esse *est prescipi* (sahopalambhaniyama). There is also difference between waking and dreaming states. Just as in states likes, dreams, magical illusions, mirage, sky-castles, etc. etc., it is the ideas themelves which appear as objects though there are no external objects Similarly in waking state too the ideas themselves appear as external objects. The plurality of the ideas is due the beginningless impression (madi vasana), and not due to the plurality of the so-called external objects. In the beginning less samsara ideas and impressions succeed each other, like seeds and sprouts, as causes and effects.

Shankara vehemently criticizes this view. According to him it is objective idealism. And the tragedy is heightened by the fact that ideas are regarded" as `momentary. Shainkara's standpoint here is that of *psychological realism* which is compatible with Absolute Idealism. The external world must exist because we perceive it. If things and ideas are presented together it does not mean they are identical. If objects depend on the mind it does not mean that they are a part of the mind. To be perceived by the mind is not to be a portion of the mind. The arguments of the Buddhist in denying thc external world though he is hims'' riencing it, are like the words of a person who while he is eating and feeling satisfied, says he is not eating or feeling satisfied. We perceive a black cow and a white cow. Now, the attributes of blackness and whiteness may differ but cowness remains the same. Similarly in cognition of ajar' and `cognition of a cloth', jar and cloth being objects differ while consciousness remains the same. This proves that ideas and objects are distinct.

If the Buddhist replies that he is not denying the *consciousness of objects* but he is only asserting that he perceives no object apart from consciousness, he is only making a purely arbitrary statement which he cannot prove by any sound argument. Nobody is conscious of his perception only, but everybody perceives external objects like post, wall etc. Even the Buddhist while explicitly denying the external object implicitly accepts it. Dinnaga says that `internal consciousness itself appears *as if* it is something external'. Now, if there is no external world how can he say that consciousness appears as if it is something external? Indeed, no sane person says that Visnumitra appears like the son *of* a barren woman. There can be no hypothetical without a categorical basis. Possibility always involves actuality. The possibility or impossibility of things can be determined only through means of right knowledge. Means of right knowledge themselves do not depend on pre-conceived possibility or impossibility. That is possible which can be proved by any valid means of cognition like perception etc. And that is impossible which cannot be so proved. Now, the external objects are apprehended. by all valid means of cognition. How can their existence be legitimately denied?' Shankara also quotes a verse from Dharmakirti to the effect non-dual consciousness itself is wrongly viewed *as if* it appears as subject-object duality'. Shankara criticizes this view also from the standpoint from which he criticizes that of Dinnaga Lie objects to phrase *`as if external'*. He points out that the Buddhists should say Consciousness appears as the external world, and not that it appears *as if* it is something external. Thus Shankara himself admits that is entire subject-object universe is only an appearance of the Atman which is Pure Consciousness. His point is simply to reject subjective idealism and to emphasize the phenomenal reality of the external world.

Shankara also emphasizes that the dream state and the waking states, cannot be placed on a par. These states are entirely different. Thing seen in a dream are sublated in the waking state. Their falsity and illusory character are realized when the dreamer awakes. But the thing like posts, walls etc. seen in the waking state are not so contradicted sublated. Dreams are private; waking life is public.

Dreams are remenm bered; things in waking life are directly perceived. They cannot be treated on the same level on the pretext that both are equally experience through consciousness. Even the Buddhist himself realizes the act difference between the two and what is directly experienced cannot be refuted by their intellectual jugglery.

Again, the Buddhistic assertion that the plurality of ideas is due tot plurality of impressions and not due to the plurality of external object is also wrong, because if the external objects do not exist then impression themselves cannot arise. And even if these impressions are held be beginning less, this position is like a series of the blind, leading to the fallacy of infinite regress and at once negating all practices of this work. Moreover, impressions being mental modifications require a substratatum: to inhere and in the Buddhistic view there is no such substratum' Alayavijnana too which is held to be momentary cannot be, like ind'vidual cognitions (pravrttivijnanas), the substratum of to inhere and in the Buddhistic view there is no such substratum Alayavijana too which is held to be memory cannot be, like individual conditions (pravrttivijnanas), the substratum of impressions.

Shankara says that his criticism of the theory of momentariness equally applies to this school also.? Momentary ideas cannot ideas themselves. There must be a permanent self to synthesize the fleeting ideas and give them a unity and a meaning. The preceding and the succeeding ideas become extinct as soon as they become objects e consciousness. They can neither apprehend nor be apprehended. Hence the various Buddhistic theories like the theory that fleeting ideas succeed one another, the theory of momentariness, the theory of the Unique particular and the General, the theory that the preceding idea leaves an impression which causes the succeeding idea to arise, the theory of ignorance, the theory of Existence and Non-Existence of things, the theory of Bondage and Liberation etc'all crumble down.'

If the Buddhist replies that the idea is self-conscious and is apprehended by itself like a luminous lamp, he is wrong, for to say that the momentary idea illuminates itself is as absurd as to say that, fire burns itself. If he again urges that to say that an idea is apprehended by something else is to involve oneself in infinite regress as this something else would require another thing to apprehend it, and therefore the only way to avoid this infinite regress is to maintain that an idea is self-luminous like a lamp, both these arguments put forth by him are fallacious. In fact it is only the permanent self, which apprehends the manifold ideas and synthesizes them into a unity and which may be regarded self-luminous like a lamp needing nothing else for its illumination. But an idea cannot be so regarded. The self therefore apprehends an idea. An idea, therefore, is just like an object in relation to the knowing self that is the subject. As the self who apprehends the ideas requires nothing else for its own apprehension, the charge of infinite regress does not arise at all. And so the second objection also becomes ineffective. The self-alone is the knowing subject; an idea is only a known object. The witnessing self is a self-evident fact. Its existence is self-proved and can never be denied. Moreover, the view that a momentary idea, like a lamp, manifests itself without being illuminated by the self means that knowledge is possible without a knowing subject. It is as absurd as to maintain that a thousand lamps manifest themselves inside a deep impenetrable rock.' If the Buddhist says that by idea he means consciousness and that we vedantins too who accept the ultimate reality of consciousness, accept his view, he is utterly mistaken, because for us an *idea* is only like an object requiring for its manifestation the self-luminous Self which is the knower. Again, if the Buddhist rejoins that our witnessing self which is self-luminous and self-proved is only his idea in disguise, he is wrong because, whereas his ideas are momentary and manifold and are no better than a scattered chaos, originating and dying away, our Self, on of the other hand, is non-dual and permanent and is the ultimate knowing subject which synthesizes these scattered ideas into a unity and gives them a meaning." Therefore we see that the difficulty in Buddhism is not removed even if we grant self-consciousness to the viinanas, for the vijnanas being momentary and manifold will only add to confusion It is only the Self, the permanent knower and the eternal seer whose sight is never destroyed.' Even hundreds of Buddhists cannot depress the self-proved self nor can they replace it by their momentary idea just as a dead person cannot be brought back to life again.

These Buddhists believe, says Shankara, that knowledge itself (dhireva), being self-luminous consciousness (chitsvarupavabhasaka) (vena), appears in its own form as subject (svakara) as well as in the form of external objects (visayakara cha), that it is the idea (vijnana) its which manifests itself as subject and as object (grahyagrahakakara) and that this transparent (svachchhibhutam) and momentary (ksanikar.) idea (vijnanam) ultimately transcends the subject-object duality (grahyagrahaka-vinirmuktam).

All these assumptions, says Shankara, are obstacles to the Vedic passleading to the Highest Good. The illumination of a lamp is not its own comes from the self. In this respect there is no difference between a pot and a lamp for both are equally objects. Thus the momentary vijnana which is only an object to the self which knows it, cannot manifest.: itself as the subject-object duality. The momentary vijnanas must be known by the self (vijnanasyapi chaitanyagrahyatvat). This self, which knows the manifold vijnanas and gives them unity and meaning, is different from them and is the only light or the self-luminous knower. If the ideas alone were real, then they would be synonymous with pots, cloths etc. for they are all objects to the knowing-self. This would lea to the abolition of the distinction between subject and object, meant and end, actions and results and would further lead to the annihilation of all phenomenal practices (sarva-samvyavaharalopaprasanngah). Bordage and Liberation would be impossible. The sacred texts of the Buddhists would be useless · (upadesha-shastranarthakyaprasangah) and their authors would have to be regarded as ignorant (tatkarturajnana. prasangah). There would be also vicarious liability (akrtabhyagama) and destruction of deeds (krtavipranasha). If the self-conscious vijnana is the only reality and them is no self, then the qualities of momentarincs soullessness etc. would not be imposed on it. Nor can these qualities v regarded as a part of the vijnana for it is impossible that qualities lit suffering etc. which are enjoyed should he a part of the vijnana, which is the enjoyer. Nor can these qualities be natural to vijnana for if th were so, it would be impossible to remove suffering etc. and then liberation would be impossible. Nor can the annihilation of the vijnana be regarded as the cessation of suffering etc. for surely if a person who is pierced by a deadly thorn dies, he cannot be said to have been cured of the pain produced by that thorn. Death, certainly, is not the remedy of a disease.' Now, it will be easy to see that the view, which Shankara exposes, and cnticizes under the name of `Vijnanavada' is in fact Svatanntra - Vijnanavada. We do not find any reference to the doctrines of Lankavatara Asanga and Vasubandhu. But we find that Shankara has quoted half' verse from Dinnaga, one verse from Dharmakirti and has often referrend to the views of Shantaraksita without however mentioning_ the names of any. We also see that his exposition of `Vijnjanavada is infact correct and a clear exposition of Svatantra Vijnanavada. We should remember that Svatantra-Vijnanavadins were his immediate predecessors All these facts support our view that the so-called criticise of 'Vijnanavada' by Shankara is really the criticism of the Svatantra-Vijnanavada School; the real Vijnana-vada of Asanga and Vasubandhu' is not refuted by it.

***(d) Advance on L gndnavida and on Gaudapada:-It may*** he pointed out however that in regard to those views which Vijnanavada share in common with Svatantra-vijnanavada, Shafikara's criticism applies to Vijfianavada also. But it is *very* important to note that here; Shafikar's criticism loses much of its force. The Alambana-Pariksa of Dinnaga is not a very original work. Almost all its ideas are based on Vasubandhu's works. We know that Vasubandhu in his Vimshatika and in his Bhasya on it criticized the atoms of the Vaishesikas and of the Vaibhasil We also know that he declared external objects to be inside consciousness. We also know that he placed dream state and waking state almost on equal footing.' We also know that Gaudapada too agreed complete with Vasubandhu in many respects. Shafikara's criticism, therefore applies in some respects to Vasubandhu and Gaudapada. But we say that this criticism loses much of its force because, firstly, Vasubandhu and Gaudapada do not deny the *objectivity* of the external world as the objects appear as *objects* to the knowing subject, and secondly, because they hold pure Consciousness which is the same as the self-luminous: Self to be the *permanent* background of all phenomena. Their view is not subjective idealism. It is absolutism. When it is maintained that pure and permanent Consciousness, which is self-luminous and which transcends the subject-object duality, is the only reality and that the I world is only its appearance, the criticism of Shankara falls off the mark because he himself believes in this view.

The difference between Vasubandhu and Gaudapada on the one band, and Shankara on the other is not the difference of kind but only of degree. The difference is only of emphasis. We know that Vasubandhu and Gaudapada distinguish between the illusory (parkalpita) and the relative (paratantra) aspects. They place these two states on a par only in order to emphasize *the ultimate unreality of* the world. Shafkar the other hand is keen--and herein his greatness lies-to emphasize *the phenomenal reality* of the world. Secondly, he wants to prove the unreality of the external world not by saying that it does not fall outside consciousness but by saying that it is essentially false (mithya) because it can be described neither as existent nor as non-existent (sadasadanirva chaniya). We have seen that Gaudapada and Shunyavada accepted this doctrine. Thirdly, in Shankara Vasubandhu's Vijnaptimatra gives place to Brahman or Atman, Alavavijnana to Ishvara, Klista Manovijiiana to Jiva, Visayavijiiapti to Jagat, and Parinama to Vivarta. Shankara in fact develops the ideas found-in Shunyavada, Vijiianavada and Gaudapada almost to perfection and spotless purity.

Shankara's criticism therefore, applies and is intended by him to apply, with full force tc Svatantra-Vijnanavada only, which degrades Consciousness merely to momentary and manifold ideas.

***(e) Criticis;, of Shunyavada:-***Shankara takes the word `Shunya' in the sense of mere negation and says that Shunyavada which is pure nihilism is contradicted by all valid means of cognition. It stands selfcotidemned. The Shunyavadin says Shankara, cannot legitimately negate all phenomenal practices unless he finds some higher truth (anyattattva). Shankara therefore summarily dismisses. Shunyavada taking it to be below criticism.' But really Shunyavada does admit such higher truth (Tattva) and is absolutism.

***(f) General Criticism of Buddhism:-The*** more we examine the Buddhistic system, says Shankara, the more it gives way like a well dug in sand. It has no solid foundation. There is no truth in it. It can serve no useful purpose. Buddha by teaching three mutually contradictory systems of Bahyarthavada, Vijnanavada and Shunyavada, has proved it beyond doubt that either he was fond of making contradictory statements or his hatred of people made him teach three contradictory doctrines so that people may be utterly confused and deluded by accepting them. Therefore all persons who desire the Good should at once reject Buddhism.

We thus see that Shankara's attitude towards Buddhism is that of hatred and animosity lie uses harsh words for Buddha and for Buddhists. The spirit of Gaudapada is gone. As for his criticism of Buddhism we may make the following remarks: Shankara finds it easy to dismiss Shunyavada taking the word Shunva in its popular sense of pure negation or void. When he remarks that Shunyavada cannot dismiss the world as pure negation nor even as relative existence unless it finds some higher truth (tattva), he takes it for granted that it has no such hither truth. But our entire treatment of Shunyavada bears ample witness to the fact that Shunyavada declares the world to he relative and therefore ultimately unreal only because it emphatically believe in the reality of the higher truth or Tattva which it calls Paramatah. Shaiikara, therefore, only avoids Shunyavada. We have also noticed that Shankara does not refute real Vijnanavada. So far as Bahyarthavada or Sarvastivada is concerned we know that this school of Hinayana was bitterly criticized by the Mahayanists themselves and Shafkara's criticism against it cannot be regarded as altogether new or original, although it is perfectly valid. The full force of Shankara's criticism is therefore directed against the Svatantra-Vijnanavada school, especially against its theory of momentariness. The criticism is fully justified.

We have noticed Shafikara's dialectical criticism of the various schools of philosophy where we have also explained Shafkara's own standpoint. We now turn to his exposition of his own philosophy.

## MAYA AND BRAHMAN

There is a famous saying that the entire system of Advaita Vedanta may be summarized in half a verse which runs as follows: Brahman is the only Reality; the world is ultimately false; and the individual soul is non-different from Brahman.' Brahman and Atman or the Supreme Self are synonymous terms. The world is a creation of Maya. The individual selves on account of their inherent Avidya imagine themselves as different from Brahman and mistake Brahman as this world of plurality, even as we mistake a rope as a snake. Avidya vanishes at the dawn of knowledge-the supra-relational direct and intuitive knowledge of the non-dual self, which means liberation.

The words Maya, Avidya, Ajnana, Adhyasa, Adhyaropa, Anirvachaniya, Vivarta, Bhranti, Bhrama, Mama-rupa, Avyakta, Aksara, Bijashakti, Mula-prakrti etc. are recklessly used in Vedanta as very nearly synonymous. Of these May˜a, Avidya, Adhyasa and Vivarta are very often used as interchangeable terms. There are two schools among later Advaitins divided on the question whether playa and Avidya are identical or different. The general trend of the Advaitins including Shafkara himself has been to treat these two terms as synonymous and to distinguish between the two aspects of Maya or Avidya which are called avarána and viksepa, the former being the negative aspect of concealment and the latter the positive aspect of projection. The advocates of the other school who treat Maya and Avidya as different say that Maya is something *positive,* though absolutely dependent on and inseparable from Brahman, which provides a medium for the reflection of Brahman and for the projection of this world, being an essentially indistinguishable power (shakti) of Brahman, while Avidya is entirely *negative* in character, being pure ignorance or absence of knowledge of Reality. Secondly, Maya, the cosmic power of projection, conditions Ishvara who is not affected by Avidya; while Avidya, the individual ignorance, conditions the Jiva. Brahman reflected in Maya is the Ishvara and Brahman reflected in Avidya is the Jiva. Hence, though the individual ignorance is dispelled by knowledge-, Maya, being the inherent nature of Brahman, cannot be so dispelled, Thirdly, Maya is made mostly of sattva, while Avidya is made of all the three-sattva, rajas and tamas. But really speaking the two schools are not opposed. Whether Maya is called the cosmic and positive power of projection and Avidya the individual and negative ignorance, or Maya and Avidya are treated as synonymous and as having two aspects of concealment and projection, the fundamental position remains the same. Further, both the schools agree that Ishvara is ever free from the negative aspect of Ignorance and that in Him sattva preponderates. Hence, whether concealment is called Avidya or Tulavidya and projection Maya or Mulavidya, the difference is only in words.

Shankaracharya brings out the following characteristics of Maya or Avidya:

**(1)** Like the Prakrti of Sankhya, it is something ***material and unconscious*** (jada) as opposed to Brahman (Purusa in the case of Sankhya) which is Pure Consciousness, though unlike Prakrti, it is neither real nor independent.

**(2)** It is the inherent *Power or Potency* (shakti) of Brahman. It is coeval with Him. It is absolutely dependent on and inseparable from Brahman. It is non-different (ananya) from Him. The relation of Maya and Brahman is unique and is called tadatmya; it is neither identity nor difference nor both. Maya is energized and acts as a medium of the projection of this world of plurality on the non-dual ground of Brahman.

**(3)** It *is beginning less* (anadi).

**(4)** It is something *positive* (bhavarupaa), though not real. It is called positive in order to emphasize the fact that it is not merely negative. It has two aspects. In its negative aspect it conceals (avarana) Reality and acts as a screen to hide it. In its positive aspect it projects (viksepa) the world of plurality on the Brahman-Ground. It is non-apprehension as well as misapprehension.

**(5)** It is *indescribable and indefinable* for it *is neither real nor unreal nor both* (sadasadanirvachaniya). It is not real, for it has no existence apart from Brahman; it is not unreal, for I karyopadhir ayam jivab karanopadhir Ishvarah. it projects the world of appearance. It is not real, f vanishes at the dawn of knowledge; it is not unreal, f(..- it is true as long as it lasts. It is not real to constitute a limit to Brahman and yet it is real enough to give rise to the world of appearance. And it is not both real and unreal, for this conception is self-contradictory.

**(6)** It has *a phenomenal and relative* character (vyavaharikasa) It is an *appearance* only (vivarta).

**(7)** It is of the nature of *superimposition* (adhyasa). It is an error (bhranti) like that of a 'rope-snake' or a 'shell-silver'. It is the superimposition upon one thing of the character of another thing. It is wrong cognition or misapprehension.

**(8)** It is *removable by Right Knowledge* (vijfiananirasya). When Vidya dawns Avidya vanishes. When the rope is known, the 'rope-snake' vanishes.

**(9)** Its locus (ashrava) as well as object (visaya) is Brahman and yet Brahman is really untouched by it, even as a magician is uneffected by his magic or the colourless akasha is untouchby the dark colour attributed to it.

It is self-evident, says Shankara, that the subject and the object are absolutely opposed to each other like light and darkness. The subject is Pure

Consciousness; the object is Unconsciousness. The one is he ultimate 'I'; the other is the 'non-F. Neither these two nor their attributes can, therefore, be identified. Yet it is the natural and common practice of people that they wrongly superimpose the object and is attributes upon the subject and *vice versa* the subject and its attributes . upon the object. This co-mingling of the subject and the object, `his mixing up of truth and error, this coupling of the real and the unreal (satyanite mithunikrtya) is called superimposition (adhyasa) or error (bhrama) or illusion (maya) or ignorance (avidva). All definition error agrees in maintaining that error is the superimposition of one thing on another, e.g., the superimposition of silver on shell or the illusion of the moons on a single moon. This superimposition that carried all 'ignorance', and the realization of the true nature of reality by discarding error, they call 'knowledge'. This transcendental Ignorance is the pre-supposition of all practices of this phenomenal world. Superimpose therefore, is the notion of a thing in something else (atasmin tadbuddhih). This unreal beginning less cycle of superimposition goes on leading to the false notions of the agent and the enjoyer and to alt phenomental. Practices. The study of tithe Vedanta texts is undertaken in order to free oneself from this false notion of superimposition and thereby realize the essential or unity of the Self'. This superimposition is not secondary or figurative (gauna); it is false (mithya). It is really pitiable that even learned people who distinguish between the subject and the object confuse these terms, like ordinary goatherds and shepherds.

We do not admit any antecedent state of this world as its independent cause. We only admit an antecedent state of this world dependent on Ishvara. This state is called Nescience or Ignorance (avidya). It is the germinal power or causal potentiality (bija-shakti). It is unmanifest (avyakta). It depends on Ishvara (Parameshvarashraya). It is illusion (mayamayi). It is the universal sleep (mahasupti) wherein are slumbering the worldly souls forgetting their own real nature. All difference is due to Ignorance. It is not ultimate. Names and forms (namarupe) are only figments of Ignorance. They are neither real nor unreal. Ishvara is limited by His own power of Nescience• and appears as many phenomenal selves even as space appears as different `spaces' limited by the adjuncts of jars etc. The omniscience, omnipresence and omnipotence of Ishvara are all due to the adjuncts of

Ignorance; they are not ultimate. Where the essential unity of the Atman is realized, they all vanish. Creation, therefore, is due to Ignorance. It is not ultimately real?

Maya is not only absence of knowledge; it is also positive wrong knowledge (mithyachararupa).It is not only non-apprehension, but also misapprehension.[3] It makes the infinite appear as finite. It produces the manifold phenomena when in fact there is only the non-dual Atman. It makes the unlimited Atman appear as limited jivas. It produces the false notions of plurality and difference. But it is not the real characteristic of Atman or Brahman because it is destroyed by true knowledge, just as rope-snake is sublated by the knowledge of the rope. Brahman, through Avidya, appears as the manifold world of names and forms, just as pure water appears as dirty foam.' The questions like: What is Avidya? Whose is Avidya? Where does it appear? etc. are useless (nirarthaka), for if Avidya is not known they cannot be solved, and if the true nature of Avidya is realized, the locus and object of Avidya is also realized. Brahman itself is the locus and object of Avidya.[5] Avidya is the darkening power (tamasa-pratyaya).Its essential nature is to cover or hide the real (avaranatmakatvadavidy3). It operates in three ways: (i) as positive wrong knowledge (viparitagrahika), (ii) as doubt (sámshayop asthapika), and (iii) as absence of knowledge (agrahanatmika).

Really it can do no harm to Reality, just as mirage-water cannot make the sandy desert muddy.?

The phenomenal world is often condemned by Shankara as unreal exactly in the inspirit of Mahayana Buddhism and of Gaudapadapada. It is said to be mirage-water (maricyambhah) rope-snake (rajju-sarpa), Shell silver (shukti-rajata), dusty surface of the sky, (akasha-tala-malinata), city of Gandharvas (Gandharvanagara), illusion (naya) plantain-trunk (kadali-garbha), dream (svapna), bubble (jala-budb da) foam (phena), moving fire-brand (alata-chakra), magical elephant (mayanirmita-hasti), hair etc. seen floating in the atmosphere on account of defective vision (keshondraka; timiradrsti), illusion of double-n`r)on (dvichandradarshana), pure magic (Indra-jala) etc.' Like Gaudapada, Shankara also uses many words which were commonly used in Mahayana. We have already remarked that such words were the heritage o` the common language and not the monopoly of Mahayana. But they definitely go to prove the influence of that age on Shainkara. Much passage is found in Shankara that can be exactly compared with some Buddhistic writings. For example, Shafikara observes: Knowing the true nature of all phenomena which represent the cycle of birth-and-death, which are manifest and unmanifest, which are the cause of mutual production like the seed and the sprout, which are beset with innumerable evils, which are unreal like plantain-trunk, illusion, mirage, sky-castle, dream, bubble, foam, which are being destroyed every moment 'and which are the result of ignorance, attachment and other defiled action and which consist of subject and object, merit and demerit, knowing such phenomena in their reality, a Brahmana should practice renunciation. The beginningless sariisara which is of the nature of suffering and which is rooted in Ignorance is like a continually flowing stream of water. Just as a person of defective vision sees double-moon or mos-quitoes and flies floating in the atmosphere, or just as a dreamer sees many things in a dream, similarly this world of plurality of names and forms is imagined through Ignorance. From the Absolute is this world illusion expanded, like the magical illusion from a magician.[5] Ultimately the Absolute is not at all touched by it.

It is very important to remember that the world is not condemned to be utterly unreal even by Mahayana and Gaudapada., much less by Shankara. Sharikara uses such words only to emphasize the ultimate' unreality of the world. The metaphors are metaphors and should not be stressed beyond the breaking point. The world is only an appearance It is not ultimately real. It becomes sublated when knowledge dawns But so long as we are in this world, we cannot take it to he unreal. It is a practical reality. It is a workable hypothesis 'absolutely necessary though in the end most indefensible'. Far from condemning this world Shafikara claims some sort of reality even for error and illusion. No appearance is so low that the Absolute does not embrace it is the Real, which appears, and hence every appearance is low that the absolute does not embrace it. It is the real, which appears, and hence every appearance must have come degree of truth in it, though none can be absolutely true. Objects, seen in a dream are quite real as long as the dream lasts. The water in a dream can quench the thirst in a dream. It is only when we are awake that we can realize the falsity of the dream state. So long as a rope is mistaken for a: snake, it is sufficient to frighten the person who mistakes it. It is only when the rope is known that the person may laugh at his folly. Similarly, so long as we are engrossed in Ignorance, the world is quite real for us. It is only when true Knowledge dawns that the world becomes sublated. Just as foam, bubbles, ripples, waves etc. exist separately, though in fact they are not different from water, similarly the subject and the object, the enjoyer and the enjoyed do exist separately, though in fact they are not different from Brahman.- The manifold world of experience is the effect; the highest Brahman is the cause. And the effect has no independent existence apart from the cause. Plurality of effects is only a creation of Ignorance.

To the objection that how can unreal Maya cause the real Brahman to appear as the phenomenal world and how, again, can false personalities through false means reach true end? Shankara's reply is that a person entangled in mud can get out of it through the help of mud alone, that a thorn pricked in-the body can be taken out with the help of another thorn, and that there are many instances in this life which show that even unreal things appear to cause real things, e.g., a reflection in a mirror is unreal but it can correctly represent the reflected object; the roaring of a tiger in a dream is unreal but it may make the dreamer, =tremble with-ear and may awaken him.[2] The objection loses its force when it is remembered that the manifold world is taken to be real as long as the essential unity of the Jiva with the Brahman is -not realized. As long as this knowledge does not dawn, all secular and religious practices are taken to be real.

The opponent again says that he fails to understand as to how unreal Maya can cause-the real Brahman to appear. If the world is unreal, unreal means like the Vedanta texts cannot lead to real liberation; if the world is real, it cannot be Maa. The dilemma which the opponent puts -forth is: either frankly admit' that the world is real or remember 'that a philosophy which has nothing better to say than that unreal personalities are unreally striving in an unreal world through unreal mean's to attain an unreal end is itself unreal. Verily, one bitten by a rope-snake does not die nor can one use mirage-water for drinking or bathing.

Shankara replies that the objection is wrong. If a person imagines himself to have been bitten by a poisonous snake, end if the imagination is very strong, it may result in heart failure or in some psychological disaster. Again, the water in a dream can quench the thirst in a dream and a person bitten by a snake in dream may feel himself to he dead in the dream. We have seen that even unreal things can cause real things. The opponent hopelessly confuses the two different standpoints- the empirical and the absolute, even as he is confusing the imaginary with the empirical. The unreality of the effects of the imaginary standpoint (pratibhasika) can be realized only -when the empirical standpoint of (vyvaharika) is attained. Similarly, the unreality of the empirical- at standpoint can he realized only from the absolute standpoint (paramarthika). The falsity of the dream-objects is realized when the dreamer gets awake. And even then, though these dream-object, are sublated, the *consciousness* that the dreamer had experienced these objects in the dream is not sublated even in the waking state. Consciousness' is, therefore, eternal and real. Right knowledge is not useless because, firstly, it removes ignorance, and secondly, it cannot be sublated. It is only from the absolute standpoint when right knowledge is attained that the Vedanta declares the world to be unreal.

Many critics have failed to understand the real significance of Maya or Avidya and have therefore charged Shapkara with explaining the world away. But this charge is based on a shifting of the standpoint Shankara, as we have shown above, has granted, nine degree of reality even to dreams, illusions and errors. How can he, then, take away the reality of this world? Shankara takes the words 'real' and 'unreal' in their absolute sense. Real means *real for all time* and Brahman alone can be real in this sense. Similarly, unreal means absolutely unreal like the hare's horn, which this phenomenal world is not. Hence this world is neither real nor unreal. This shows its self-contradictory and therefore incomprehensible nature. It is relative, phenomenal, finite. But it is not illusory. It is *true for all practical purposes.* What does it matter to us, worldly people, if it is not *absolutely true* in the philosophical sense? When the *'reality'* which is denied to this world means *'reality for all time'*, the *unreality'* which is attributed to it means *'non-eternality.'* Who can stand up and say that the world is not 'unreal' if 'unreal' means 'non-eternal'? Again, the world will be sublated only when knowledge dawns and not before. This should make us humbly strive after true knowledge rather than engage ourselves in futile quarrels. Shankara's intention is perfectly *clear-none can condemn this world as unreal he* who does it, *is not qualified* to do so and he who is qualified to d, so, *will not do so,* for he would have risen above language and finite thought.

## ISHVARA AND BRAHMAN

BRAHMAN is the only Reality. It is absolutely indeterminate and non-dual. It is beyond speech and mind. It is indescribable because no description of it can be complete. The best description of it is through the negative formula of *'neti neti'* or `not this, not this'. Yet Brahman is not an abyss of non-entity, because it is the Supreme Self and stands self-revealed as the background of all affirmations and denials. The moment we try to bring this Brahman within the categories of intellect or try to make this ultimate subject an object of our thought, we miss its essential nature. Then it no more remains Unconditioned Consciousness, but becomes conditioned as *it were*.. This Brahman, reflected in or conditioned by Maya, is called Ishvara or God. Ishvara is the personal aspect of the impersonal Brahman. This is the celebrated distinction between God and the Absolute, which Shankara, following the Upanisads, makes. Ishvara is also known as Apara Brahma or lower Brahman as contrasted with the unconditioned Brahman, which is called Para Brahma, or Higher Brahman.

The phenomenal character of Ishvara is quite evident. He is the highest appearance, which we have. Some critics have missed the *significance* of Ishvara. They believe that Ishvara *in* Advaita is unreal and useless. But they are sadly mistaken. Missing the true significance of Maya is at the root of this mistaken belief. Ishvara becomes `unreal' only for *him* who has realized his oneness with Brahman by rising above speech and mind. For us Ishvara is all in all. Finite thought can never grasp Brahman. And therefore all talks about Brahman are really talks about Ishvara. Even the words `unconditioned Brahman' refer really to `conditioned Ishvara', for the moment we speak of Brahinan, He ceases to be Brahman and becomes Ishvara.

Ishvara or God is the Sat-Chit-Ananda, the Existence-Consciousness Bliss. He is the Perfect Personality. He is the Lord of Maya. He is immanent in the whole universe, which He controls from within. He is the Soul of souls as well as the Soul of Nature. As the immanent inner ruler, He is called Antaryamin. He is also transcendental, for in His own nature He transcends the universe. He is the Creator, Sustainer and

Destroyer of this universe. He is the Source of everything. He is fie final haven of everything. He is the Concrete Universal, the Supreme. Individual, the Whole, the Identity-in-difference. He is the object of devotion. He is the inspirer of moral life. He is all in all from the practical stand - point. Thus the description of Brahman, which Ramanuja gave at a much later date, is essentially an elaboration of Shankara's Ishvara.

Shankara, like Kant, believes that God cannot he *proved* by our finite thought. All attempts to do so end in failure. They lead to, what Kant has called, the antinomies. The cosmological proof can give only a finite creator of this finite creation and all finite creators is no creator at The teleological proof can only point to the fact that a conscious principle is working at the root of creation. The ontological proof can give only idea of God and not God as *a real object.* The Nyaya arguments to prove the existence of God are futile. God is an article of faith Shruti is the only *proof* for the existence of God. As Kant falls back on faith, so Shankara falls back on Shruti. Shankara agrees with Gauda-real pada's view of Ajati. There is no a *real* creation. God, therefore, is no *'real'* Creator. God alone is *real;* the creation is only an *appearance of* God.

Ishvara has been a taxing problem for the followers of Shankara.. According to some, Ishvara is the reflection of Brahman in Maya, while jiva is the reflection of Brahman in Avidya. According to others, Brahman, limited or conditioned by Maya is Ishvara, while Brahman limited by Avidya or the internal organ (which is a product of Avidya is jiva. The former view is called Reflection Theory (pratibimbavada) and the latter Limitation Theory (avachchhedavada). Some regard jiva as the reflection of Ishvara. The defect in the Reflection Theory is title Brahman and Maya both being formless, how can a formless original be reflected in a formless receptacle? To avoid this some have suggested the Identity of the Original and the Reflected Image (bimbapratibimbabhedavada). But this too cannot be accepted. The defect in the Limitation Theory is as to how can Maya or Avidva constitute limitation to Brahman? Those who do not agree with either of these theories have suggested a third, the Appearance Theory, according to which Ishvara and jiva are inexplicable appearances of Brahman (abhasavada). The post-Shankarites have indulged in needless hair-splitting. The problem was not at all taxing to Shankara. He uses the similes of the reflection of the Sun or the Noon in the waves or in the different vessels of water, the simile of the reflection of the red colour of the flower in the crystal as well as the simile of the limitation of the universal space as the different `spaces in the jars'. He uses them only as metaphors for their suggestive value. They should not be taken literally and stressed beyond the breaking point. Shankara himself seems to favour Appearance Theory (abhasavada) because for him Ishvara and jiva are the *inexplzrcirhle appearances* of Brahman. They are due to Maya or Avidya or Adhzsa. They are only appearances (vivarta). The `why' and the `how' reacting Avidya are illegitimate questions and therefore an isolable mystery. God is God only to the jiva who is labouring under Avidya. God himself never feels Himself as God; He feels Himself essentially one ' the Brahman, for Avidya in its negative aspect of concealment never operates on Him. God is the Lord of Maya, while Maya constantly troubles jiva. God always enjoys the Bliss of Brahman while jiva is tortured by the pangs of Avidya. When Brahman is viewed 'as samsara, God 'soul and Nature arise simultaneously and when Brahmin's own essence is realized, God, Soul and Nature vanish simultaneously.

## JIVA AND BRAHMAN

QUALIFIED Brahman is Ishvara. Phenomenally there is a difference between jiva and Ishvara. The former is the agent and the enjoyer, . acquires merit and demerit, experiences pleasure and pain, while the latter is not at all touched by all this. The Mandaka (III, I, I) declares that `one bird (jiva), eats the sweet fruit, while the other (Ishvara) merely looks on'. Jiva enjoys (pibati), while Ishvara makes him enjoy (payayati). One is the enjoyer, the other is the ruler. The Katha (I, 3, r ; III, 3, 34) only figuratively says that both of these enjoy (chhatrinvayena). But ultimately there is no difference at all between jiva and Brahman. Only so long as the jiva does not discard Nescience leading to duality and does not realize its own true nature, he remains the individual self. Slumbering in ignorance, when he is awakened by the Shruti, he realizes that he is not the body, senses, or mind, but is the non-dual universal Self-tat tvam asi (that thou art). Realizing his own true nature, he ever dwells in himself shining forth in his own true nature. Jiva through ignorance is regarded as tinged with the false notions of the `I' and the `Mine' which arise when mind through senses comes into contact with the fleeting sensations or ideas. It is viewer as something different from the eternal and self-luminous Consciousness, which is its immanent inner controller, as the reflection of that Consciousness, as identical with mind and its states, as associated with the seed of ignorance, as the possessor of momentary ideas etc. As long as these false notions about the self persist, the result is the empirical self and the objective world; and when these notions are destroyed by right knowledge, the result is liberation, though ultimately both bondage and liberation are phenomenal, because jiva is really non-different from Brahman.2 Even the view that he becomes Brahman is only a verbal statement (upacharamatra), for he is always Brahman.[3] Just as a pure transparent white crystal is wrongly imagined to be red on account of a red flower placed near it, or just as the colourless sky is wrongly imagined to be sullied with dirt by the ignorant, or just as a rope is wrongly taken to be a snake in the twilight, or just as a shell is mistaken for silver, similarly the non-dual Atman or Brahman is wrongly imagined to be the empirical self. Just as the Sun or the Moon appears many on account of the reflection in the different waves or vessels of water or just as the same space appears on account of the adjuncts of jars etc.as different `spaces', similarly the same Self appears as so many phenomenal selves on account of Nescience. Shan-kara says that he who wants to explain the Scripture as teaching that jiva is not really Brahman, and who thus wants to preserve the ultimate reality of bondage and liberation, is indeed lowest among the learned (panditapasada).'- To refute, etch and other vain speculations which hinder the realization of tire essential unity of the self and to show that there is only one real Self, eternal and unchanging, which is the Luminous Body of Pure Consciousness (Vijnana-dhatu), and which, through its own power, manifest. Itself as many, and that accept this there is no other Reality, no other Pure Consciousness, is the aim of the Shariraka-Bhasya.

## ATMAN- AND BRAHMAN

'ATMAN is the same as Brahman. It is Pure Consciousness. It is the Self which is Self-luminous and which transcends the subject-object duality and the trinity of knower, known and knowledge, and all the categories of the intellect. It is the Unqualified Absolute. It is the only Reality. Brahman is everything and everything is Brahman There is no duality, no diversity at all. This Self can never be denied. for the very idea of denial presupposes it. It cannot be doubts for all doubts rest on it. All assertions, all doubts, all denials pre-suppose it. It is not adventitious or derived (gantuka)'. It is self-proved or original (svayarnsddha). All means of cognition pramanas are founded on it. To refute this Self is impossible, for he who tries to refute it is the Self.[5] The knower knows no change, for eternal existance is his very nature. `Never is the sight of the seer destroyed' says the Brhadaranyaka. *'He who* knmvs Brahman becomes Brahman.' He who is the knower is the Self, for he is omnipresent. Everything else is relative and therefore ultimately unreal. The Self-alone is not relativity is, therefore, self-proved. The tragedy of human intellect is that it tries to know everything as ,an object. But whatever can be presented as an object is necessarily relative and for that very reason unreal. The knower can never be known as an object. Ultimately there is no distinction between the true knower and pure knowledge. 'How, O' dear, can the knower be known?' says the Brhadaranyaka. Hence all these who rely on the intellect are deluded because they can never truly describe the Self either as existent or as non-existent. It is essentially indescribable, for all descriptions and all categories fail to grasp it fully.' *As* a matter of fact Brahman ultimately transcends all categories. The best method of describing it, therefore, is by negative terms. But if we want to describe it positively, the best that we can say is that it is Pure !) Consciousness, which is at oncc Pure Existence and Pure Bliss. True, we cannot say that Brahman *is self-conscious* of its consciousness or that it *enjoys* its own bliss. These determinations of the intellect fail here. The fact is that Brahman itself is Pure Existence, Pure Consciousness and Pure Bliss-all in one. It is its very nature to be such. It cannot be regarded as a substance having these qualities or even as a subject knowing or feeling these qualities. All distinctions of substance and qualities, of subject and object, all determinations of' the intellect cease here.' Dvaita does not deserve to be, taught, for everybody normally assumes it in all phenomenal practices. Therefore taking the normal dualism which people naturally take for granted on account of transcendental ignorance, the Shastra teaches that though dualism is a practical necessity, yet it is not ultimately real. Brahman is the only reality. It is the End (upeya); and Brahmavidya, or the knowledge of the no difference of the jivatman and the Paramatman, is the means (upaya) to realize this end. When the end is realized the Shastra itself is transcended.

Existence and consciousness are one. 'The Real is the Rational and the Rational is the Real'. But ultimately Brahman-is-devoid of all charm˙ cteristics. -It cannot be defined as mere Existence and not as Consciousness, for the Shastra says that it is All-Consciousness (vijnanaghana); nor can it be defined as mere Consciousness and not as Existence, for the Shastra says: 'it is'; nor can it be defined as both Existence and Consciousness, for to admit that Brahman is characterized by Existence different from Consciousness or by Consciousness different from Existence, is to admit duality in Brahman; nor can it be defined as characterized by Existence non-different from Consciousness for if Existence is Consciousness and Consciousness is Existence why should there be any controversy at all whether Brahman is Existence or Consciousness or both?[5] Again, to say, that Reality exists but is not known is a contradiction in terms, for at least Reality is known as unknowable by intellect. It is like saying that 'colored objects exist but there is no eye to see them'. Reality, therefore, must exist for us and it is only Pure Consciousness that can ultimately exist. We cannot know it by finite intellect but we can realize it directly through pure intuition. It is non-dual Consciousness where all distinctions, all plurality, all determinations, all qualities, all characteristics, all categories and all concepts are transcended. All determinations of language and intellect are merged in this indeterminate and unqualified Reality. Being and not-being, one and many, qualified and unqualified, knowledge and ignorance, action and inaction, active and inactive, fruitful and fruitless, seedful and seedless, pleasure and pain, middle and not-middle, shunya and ashunya, soul and God, unity and plurality etc. etc.-all these determinations do not apply to the Absolute. He who wants to grasp the Absolute by any of these determinations, indeed tries to roll up the sky like a skin or tries to ascend space like a stair-case or wishes to see the footprints of fish in water of birds in the sky.

The Shastra, therefore, becomes silent after saying-'not this, this.' If a man does not understand that he is a man when lie is told that he is not a non-man, how can he be able to understand, then, if he is told that he is a man?[3] The two 'no'-is in the formula 'neti neti' are meant for emphasizing the fact that whatever can be presented as an object is ultimately unreal. They cover the entire field of objective existence and point out that it is not real. There is no better way of describing the Absolute than this negative method. But it should be never missed that all these negations pre-suppose and point towards the positive Brahman. The Absolute can he unknowable only for those who are ignorant of the Vedanta tradition, who do not know the means of right knowledge and who desperately cling to the world. True, the Absolute cannot known as an object by the intellect. But being the only Reality and being always present and so not at all foreign, it is directly realized through spiritual experience (samyagjndna).the phrase 'neti net" negates all characteristics of Brahman, but it does not negate Brahman itself. It implies that there is something about it. which something is denied. Appearances can be negated only with reference to Reality. Effects alone can be negated, for they are unreal But the cause, the Brahman, cannot be negated, for it the ultimate ground on which all effects or phenomena are superposed.

## KNOWLEDGE AND ACTION

SHANKARA repeatedly asserts that the Absolute can be realized through knowledge and knowledge alone; karma and upasana are subsidiary. They may. help us in urging us to know Reality and they may prepare us for that knowledge by purifying our mind (sattvashuddhi), but ultimately it is knowledge alone which, by destroying ignorance, the root-cause of this world, can enable us to be one with the Absolute. The opposition of knowledge and action stands firm like a mountain.' They are contradictory (viparite) and are poles apart (duramete). Those who talk of combining knowledge-with action, says Shafikara, have perhaps not read the Brhaddranyska nor are they aware of the glaring contradiction repeatedly pointed out by the Shruti and the Smrti. Knowledge and action are opposed like light and darkness. Actions are prescribed for those who are still in ignorance and not for those who are enlightened. Knowledge only removes ignorance and_ then Reality shines forth by itself.[3] A liberated sage, however, performs actions without any attachment and works for the uplift of humanity. Shankara's own life bears ample witness to this fact.

## KNOWLEDGE AND LIBERATION

ULTIMATE Reality (paramarthikainvastu) can neither be asserted nor denied by knowledge. Knowledge does nothing else except removing - ignorance. Shastra only generates right knowledge (jfiapakam). It does nothing else (nakarakam).

Knowledge of Brahman, which leads to eternal bliss, does not depend' on the performance of any act, for Brahman is already an accomplished fact. Religious acts, which lead to prosperity, depend on human performance. Religious texts enjoin injunctions or prohibitions. Knowledge merely instructs. Knowledge of Brahman culminates in immediate experience and is already an accomplished fact. Action, whether secular or Vedic, can be done, rnisdone or left undone. Injunctions, prohibitions, options, rules and-exceptions depend on our thinking. But knowledge leaves no option to us for its being this or that or for its existence or: non-existence. It is not in our hands to make, unmake, or chang. Knowledge. Our thinking cannot make a pillar a man. Knowledge of Brahman, therefore, depends on Brahman itself. It is always of the same nature because it depends on the existent thing.' True knowledge is produced by Pramanas and conforms to its objects. It can neither be produced by hundreds of injunctions nor can it be destroyed by hundreds of prohibitions. Knowledge is not mental activity, because it depends not on mind but on the existent fact.`' There is also no succession in knowledge. Once it dawns, it dawns forever and at once removes all ignorance and consequently all bondage. Liberation, therefore, means removal of ignorance by knowledge. That blessed person who has realized Reality is liberated here and now.[4] The Shruti says `just as a slough cast off by a snake lies on an anthill, similarly does this body lie. This is Jivanmukti. Final release (Videhamukti) is obtained after the death of the body. The Shruti says `the only delay for him is the death of the body'. Just as a potter's wheel goes on revolving for sonic time even after the push is withdrawn, similarly the body may continue to exist even after knowledge has dawned, though all attachment with the body is cut off. Like an arrow shot from the bow, the body continues to reap the fruits until it expires; but no new actions are accumulated.'

## ULTIMATE CRITERION OF TRUTH

WE have to discuss here the claims of Revelation, Reason and Intuition' each of which wants to be crowned as the ultimate criterion of truth in Shankara. Shankara attaches supreme importance to the revealed truths of the Vedas which are regarded as the `breath of God' (yasya nishavsitam Vedah). But it is only jnanakanda that is stressed, not the karmakanda. He who condemns Shankara as a mere theologian `whose faith is pinned to the Vedas', must be either hopelessly ignorant of Shankara-Vedanta or be himself nothing less than a prejudiced dogmatist. Shankara never accepts the Shruti blindly. It is only because he fully knows that the Shruti is the result of the highest realization of the ancient sages, that it is the most valuable pearl that the ocean of human experience can ever boast to yield after having been churned by the rod of the intellect, in short, it is only because Shankara is fully conscious of the fact that the Shruti is the shining pure gold tested at the touch-stone of reason and experience, that he builds his many destroyed magnificent palace of the Advaita on the firm foundation of the Shruti.

Many passages may be quoted from Shankara where he says that Brahman, being supersensuous, can be realized only through Revelation or Shruti? Here too, intellect is not driven out of the palace of philosophy, but kept there as an ancillary to the Revelation-Queen.

Shankara repeatedly asserts that discursive intellect cannot grasp Reality. Brahman cannot become the object of perception as it has no form, and it does not lend itself to inference and other means, as it has no characteristic mark. Partly accepting the position of Bhartrhari, which is criticized by Shantaraksita, Shankara remarks that reasoning, because it depends on individuals, has no solid foundation. Others more ingenious may prove arguments held valid by some, fallacious. Like Asanga, Shafikara declares intellect to be insecure and emphasizes the Agama.[5] But his criticism is directed towards *kutarka.* Mere logical quibbling, says Shankara, cannot set Shruti, aside. A false logician is a quibbler saying whatever he likes.? They, whose minds are fouled by logical, quibbling, are to be pitied because they do not know the tradition of the Vedanta. What grand feats of reasoning do such logicians who are bulls without horns and tails display! They are princes among liars and among those who violate the tradition of the wise. They cannot enter the Fort of Brahman, which is open only to those who are of excellent wisdom, who have the knowledge of the Shastra and blessings of the teacher. Debators like carnivorous animals for the sake of bait, fight against one another and fall from Reality. Themselves deluded they also delude innocent people. It is only for the sake that people, who desire liberation, which can be obtained by knowledge alone, should reject false views, says Shankara, that he criticizes other doctrines, not for any interest in discussion for its own sake.

It is, therefore, only logical quibbling or kutarka that is condemned by Shankara. Sutarka or refined intellect is admitted as supreme in the phenomenal world where its authority is said to be unquestionable. Only an intellectual, a rational being can understand the meaning of the Shruti. It cannot reveal itself to a beast. As Yaska said that he who only reau., or remembers the Veda but does not understand its meaning is only *a coolie* carrying a load of the Veda on his head and is no better than a pillar." Shankara never asks us to accept the Shruti blindly. He is never satisfied with a mere quotation from the scripture on a vital metaphysical issue but always defends it with reason. If we find apparent contradictions in the Shruti, we should interpret other passages of the Shruti in the light of that one central doctrine of the Shruti which appeals to reason. If the Shruti contradicts reason, reason must be our guide for it is nearer our experience.' Even if hundred Shrutis declare with one voice that fire is cool and without light or that the Sun does not shine, we cannot accept them. Reason is the sole means of knowing, truth and falsity. We cannot question the validity of intellect in the phenomenal world. Here, `You obey while you rebel'. Even the statement that `intellect stands condemned' must be made by intellect itself Infra-relational intuition is the animal instinct and supra-relation true intuition is the same as Pure Reason. Svanub have or Svanubhuti immediate experience or direct self-realization is the same as Pure Consciousness. Here finite intellect, casts off its garb of relationally *which* was put upon it by ignorance and becomes one with-the Absolute which is Pure Consciousness. Discursive intellect confesses its impotence only to be rejuvenated with new. life and eternal vigour, and what appears to be its suicide is, in fact, its consecration. Shall we not say then, with deeper meaning, that the ultimate criterion of truth in , Shanxara is immediate spiritual realization in this truer sense?

# NYAYA

## INTRODUCTION

The sage Gotama is the founder of Nyaya School. He also knew as Gautama and as Aksapada. Nyaya means argumenetation and suggests that the system is predominantly intellectual, analytic, logical and epistemological. It is also called Tarkashastra or the science of reasoning: Pramanashastra or the science of logic and epistemology; Hetuvidya or the science of causes; Vadavidvd or the science of debate; and Anviksiki or the science of critical study.

Gotama's Nyaya-sutra \vas commented upon by Vatsyayana in his Nyaya-bhasya. On this Uddyotakara wrote his Vartika, which was commented upon by Vachaspati in his Tatparya-tika. Udayana's Nvdya-kusumanjali and Javanta's Nyaya-manjari are the other important works of this school. The Nyvya-nyaya or the modern school of Indian logic begins with the epoch-making Tattva-chintamani of Gangesha. Vasudeva, Raghunatha, Mathuranatha, Jagadisha and Gadadhar, arc the eminent logicians of this school.

## NYAYA AND VAISHESIKA

NYAYA is a system of atomistic pluralism and logical realism. It is allied to the Vaishesika system, which is regarded as `Samanatantra' or similar philosophy. Vaishesika develops metaphysics and or logical Nyaya develops logic and epistemology. Both agree in viewing the earthly life as full of suffering, as bondage of the soul and in regarding liberation, which is absolute cessation of suffering as the supreme end of life. Both agree that bondage is due to ignorance of reality and that liberation is due to right knowledge of reality. Vaishesika takes up the exposition of reality and Nyaya takes up the exposition of right knowledge of reality. Nyaya mostly accepts the Vaisheşika metaphysics. But there are some important points of difference between them, which maybe noted. Firstly, while the Vaishesika recognizes seven categories and classifies all reals under them, the Nyaya recognizes sixteen categories and includes all the seven categories of the Vaishesika in one of them called Prameya or the table, the second in the sixteen. The first category is Pramana or means of knowledge. This clearly brings out the predominant logical and epistemological character of the Nyaya system. Secondly, while the Vaishesika recognizes only two Pramanas-perception and inference and reduces comparison and verbal authority to inference, the Nyaya recognizes all the four as separate-perception, inference, comparison and verbal authority.

## KNOWLEDGE AND PERCEPTION

KNOWLEDGE (jnana) or cognition (buddhi) is defined as apprehension (upalabdhi) or consciousness (anubhava). Nyaya, being realistic, believes that knowledge reveals both the subject and the object, which are quite distinct from it. All knowledge is a revelation or manifestation of objects (arthaprakasho buddhih). Just as a lamp manifests physical things placed before it, so knowledge reveals all objects, which come before it. Knowledge may be valid or invalid. Valid knowledge (prama) is defined as the right apprehension of an object (yatharthanubhavah). It is the manifestation of an object as it is. Nyaya maintains the theory of correspondence (paratah pramanya). Knowledge, in order to be valid, must correspond to reality. Valid knowledge is produced by the four valid means of knowledge-perception, inference, comparison and testimony. Invalid knowledge includes memory (smrti), doubt (sarhshaya), error (viparvava) and hypothetical reasoning (tarka). Memory is not valid because it is not presentative cognition but a representative one. The object remembered is not directly presented to the soul, but only indirectly recalled. Doubt is uncertainty in cognition. Error is misapprehension, as it does not correspond to the real object. Hypothetical reasoning is no real knowledge. It is arguine like this-' if there were no fire, there cannot be smoke'. When you see a rope as a rope you have right knowledge. If you are uncertain whether it is a rope or a snake, you have doubt. If you recall the rope you have seen, you have memory. if you mistake the rope for a snake, you have error.

Knowledge is produced in the soul when it comes into contact with the not-soul. It is an adventitious property of the soul, which is generated in it by the object. If the generating conditions are sound, knowledge is valid; if they are defective, knowledge is invalid. A man of sound vision sees a conch white, while a man suffering from jaundice sees it yellow. Correspondence with the object is the nature of truth. If knowledge corresponds to its object, it is valid; if it does not, it is invalid. Valid knowledge corresponds to its object (yathartha and avisamvadi). And leads to successful activity (pravrttisamarthya). Invalid knowledge does not correspond to its object (avathartha and visamvadi) and leads to failure and disappointment (pravrttivisamvada). Fire must burn and cook and shed light. If it does not, it is Knowledge intrinsically is only a manifestation of objects. The question of its validity or invalidity is a subsequent question and depends upon its correspondence with its object. Truth and falsity are extrinsic characteristics of knowledge. They are apprehended by a subsequent knowledge. They arise and are apprehended only when knowledge has already arisen. They are neither intrinsic nor self-evident. Validity and invalidity of knowledge arise (utpattau paratah pramanyam` after knowledge has arisen, and they are known (jfiaptau paratah pramatma after knowledge has arisen and they have also arisen. Correspondence is the content and successful activity is the test of truth. The Naya theory of knowledge, therefore, is realistic and pragmatic; realistic as regards the nature and pragmatic as regards the test of truth.

Perception, inference, comparison or analogy and verbal tesimony are the four kinds of valid knowledge. Let us consider them, one by one.

Gotama defines perception as 'non-erroneous cognition which is produced by the intercourse of the sense-organs with the objects, which is not associated with a name and which is well-defined'.' This definition of perception excludes divine and yogic perception, which is not generated by the intercourse of the sense organs with the objects. Hence Vishvanatha has defined perception as `direct or immediate cognition which is not derived through the instrumentality of any other cognition This definition includes ordinary as well as extra-ordinary perception and excludes inference, comparison and testimony. Perception a kind of knowledge and is the attribute of the self. Ordinary perception presupposes the sense organs, the objects, the manas and the self and their mutual contacts. The self comes into contact with the mans the manas with the sense organs and the sense-organs with the object The contact of the sense-organs with the objects is not possible unless the manas first comes into contact with the sense-organs, and the of the manas with the sense-organs is not possible unless the self comes into contact with the manas. Hence sense-object contact sarily presupposes the manas-sense contact and the self-manas necessarily. The sense organs are derived from the elements whose specific qualities of smell, taste, they manifest colour, touch and sound. The *manas* are the mediator between the self and the sense organs. The external object, through the senses and the manas, makes an impression on the self. The theory, therefore, is realistic.

The Naiyayika maintains two stages in perception. That is called indeterminate or nirvikalpa and the second, determination, savikalpa. They are not two different *kinds* of perception, but only earlier and the later stages in the same complex process of perception. Gotama recognizes these two stages in his definition of perception quoted above. Perception is 'unassociated with a name' (avyapadeshya) which means 'indeterminate', and it is 'well-defined' (vyavasayatmaka) which means 'determinate'. All perception is determinate, but it is necessarily preceded by an earlier stage when it is indeterminate. Nyaya recognizes the fundamental fact about knowledge which is said to be the distinct contribution of Kant to western philosophy that knowledge involves both sensation and conception. 'Percepts without concepts are blind and concepts without percepts are empty.' Perception is a complex process of experience involving both sensation and conception. All perception we have is determinate because it is perceptual knowledge or perceptual judgment. Sensation is the material and conception is the form of knowledge. Bare sensation or simple apprehension is nirvikalpa perception; perceptual judgment or relational apprehension is savikalpa perception. Nyaya avoids the fallacy of the psychical staircase theory that we have first sense-experience, then conception and then judgment. Perception is a complex presentative-representative process in which we cannot really separate direct awareness from relational judgment. Indeterminate perception forms the material out of which determinate perception is shaped, but they can be distinguished only in thought and not divided in reality. Nirvikalpa perception is the immediate apprehension, the bare awareness, the direct sense-experience, which is undifferentiated and non-relational and is free from assimilation, discrimination, analysis and synthesis. The consciousness of the 'that' is not yet determined by the consciousness of the 'what'. But as the 'that' cannot be really known as separated from the 'what', the 'substance' cannot be known apart from its `qualities', we immediately come to savikalpa perception where the mere awareness of the 'that' and the 'what' and their 'inherence' as something undifferentiated, unrelated, dumb and inarticulate, is transformed into differentiated; relational, conceptual and articulate knowledge involving assimilation, discrimination, analysis and synthesis. For example, when we go, from broad daylight, into a dark cinema hall to see a matinee show, we first do not see the seats or the audience clearly, but have only a dim sensation of the objects present there which gradually reveal themselves to us; the dim sense-experience of the objects in the hall is indeterminate perception while the clear perception of them is determinate perception. The mere apprehension of some object as something, as the 'that', is indeterminate perception, while the clear perception of it together with its attributes is determinate perception. We see in dusk a straight something lying on the road and find out by going near it that it is a rope. We see a white moving object at a distance and when it comes near we see it is a white cow. The earlier stage is indeterminate and the later one determinate perception. We are in a hurry to go somewhere and want to finish our bath before starting. We do not know whether the water was cold and the bath refreshing, though we did feel the coolness of water and the refreshing character of bath. We feel water and we feel its coolness but we do not relate the two. Indeterminate perception presents the bare object without any characterization. In determinate perception we relate the substance with its attributes. The feeling of indeterminate perception is psychological, but its knowledge is logical. As bare awareness, as mere apprehension, we *sense* indeterminate perception, we *feel* it, but the moment we try to *know* it even as 'bare awareness' it has passed into conception and has become determinate. Hence all our perception being cognition is determinate and is a perceptual judgment. We can setnarate indeterminate from determinate perception only in thought end not in reality. Hence, though we feel indeterminate perception also a psychological state of sense-experience, its knowledge even as indeterminate perception is a result of logical deduction. We do feel it directly but only as an awareness, not as a cognition. Mere apprehension, being infra relational, cannot be cognized. As cognition it is inferred afterwards when conception has transformed mere sensation into a perceptual judgment.

Vatsyayana says that if an object is perceived with its name we have determinate perception; if it is perceived without its name, we have indeterminate perception. Jayanta Bhatta says that indeterminate perception apprehends substance, qualities and actions and universets as separate and indistinct something and is devoid of any association with a name, while determinate perception apprehends all these together with a name. Gangesha Upadhaya defines indeterminate perception as the non-relational apprehended of an object devoid of all association of name, genus, differentia Annam Bhatta defines it as the immediate apprehension of an object as well as of its qualities, but without `he knowledge of the relation between them. The substance and the qualities the 'that' and the 'what' are felt separately and it is not apprehended that those qualities inhere in that substance or that the 'what characterizes the 'that'. Indeterminate perception is 'mere acquaintance which William James calls 'raw unverbalized experience', while determinate perception is relational apprehension.

Perception, again, may be ordinary (laukika) or extraordinary (alau - kika). When the sense organs come into contact with the objects present to them in the usual way, we have Laukika perception. And if the contact of the sense organs with the objects is unusual way, i.e., if the objects are not ordinarily present to they are conveyed to them through an extraordinary medium, we Alaukika perception. Ordinary perception is of two kinds-internal (manasa) and external (bahya). In internal perception, the mind (manas), which is the internal organ, comes into contact with the psychical states and processes like cognition, affection, conation, desire, pain, pleasure, aversion etc. External perception takes place when the five external organs of sense come into contact with the external objects. It is of five kinds-visual, auditory, tactual, gustatory and olfactory, brought about by the sense organs of sight, sound, touch, taste and smell respectively when they come into contact with the external objects. The external sense organs are composed of material elements of earth, water, fire, air, and ether and therefore each senses the particular quality of its element. Thus the sense organ of smell is composed of the atoms of earth and perceives smell, which is the specific quality of earth and so on.

Extra-ordinary perception is of three kinds-samanyalaksana, jnanalaksana and yogaja. Samanyalaksana perception is the perception of the universals. According to

Nyaya, the universals are a distinct class of reals. They inhere in the particulars, which belong to different classes on account of the different universals inhering in them. An individual belongs to a particular class because the universal of that class inheres in it. Thus a cow becomes a cow because it has the universal cowness inhering in it. Ordinarily we perceive only the particulars and not the universals. We perceive particular cows but we do not perceive a 'universal cow'. Hence the Nyaya maintains that the universals are perceived extraordinarily. Whenever we perceive a particular cow we first perceive the 'universal cowness' inhering in it. The second kind of extraordinary perception is called jnanalaksana perception. It is the 'complicated' perception through association. Sometimes different sensations become associated and form one integrated perception. Here an object is not directly presented to a sense organ, but is revived in memory through the past cognition of it and is perceived through representation. For example look at a blooming rose from a distance and say *'I see* a fragrant rose'. But how can fragrance be *seen?* It can only be *smelt.* Fragrance can be perceived by the sense organ of smell and not by the sense organ of vision that can perceive only colour. Here the visual perception of the rose revives in memory the idea of fragrance by association, which was perceived in the past through the nose. The perception of the fragrant rose through the eye, therefore, is called jnanalaksana perception or perception revived in memory through the cognition (jhana) of the object in the past. Other examples of it are: 'the piece of sandalwood *looks* fragrant', 'ice *looks* cold', 'stone *looks* hard', 'tea *looks* hot', etc. etc. Thc theory of illusion accepted by Nyaya called 'Anyathakhyati' is based on this kind of perception. When we mistake a rope for a snake, the idea of snake perceived in the past is imported in memory through this extraordinary jnanalaksana perception and is confused with the object (i.e., rope) which is directly presented to the sense-organ. When shell is mistaken for silver, the idea of silver perceived in the past in a shop (apanastha) (or anywhere else) is revived in memory through jnanalaksana percoration and is confused with the object (i.e., shell) which is directory presented to the sense-organ. The past impresses represents the object to our mind: Error is due to a wrong synthesis represented and –the represented objects. The represented object is (Majd with the pre sented one. The word 'anyatha' means 'else wise 'elsewhere' both these senses are brought out in an erroneous perception. The presented object is perceived else wise and the represented object exist elsewhere. The shell and the silver, the rope and the snake are both separately real; only their synthesis is unreal. The shell and the rope are directly presented as the 'this' (when we say: *'this is* silver' or *'this:* is a snake'), while the silver and the snake exist elsewhere and are revived in memory through jfianalaksana perception. The third kind of extra-ordinary perception is called yogaja perception. This is the intuitive and immediate perception of all objects, past, present and future possessed by the Yogins through the power of meditation. It is like the evalajnana of the Jainas, the Bodhi of the Buddhists, and the Kaivalya of the Sankhya-Yoga and the Aparoksanubhuti of the Vedantins. It is intuiture supra sensuous and supra relational.

## INFERENCE

THE second kind of knowledge is anuma or inferential or relation and its means is called anumana or inference. It is defined as that cognition which presupposes some other cognition. It is mediate and indirect and arises through a 'mark', the 'middle term' (linga or hetu) which is, invariably connected with the 'major term' (sadhya). It is knowledge: (myna) which arises *after* (anu) other knowledge. Invariable conmitance (vast or avinabhavanivama) is the nerve of inference. The presence of the middle term in the minor term is called paksadharmata. The invariable association of the middle term with the major term is called vyapti. The knowledge of paksadharmata as qualified by - vyapti is called paramarsha. And inference is defined as knowledge and using through paramarsha,' i.e., the knowledge of the presence of the major in the minor through the middle which resides in the minor (paksadharmata) and is invariably associated with the major (vyapti). Like the Aristotelian syllogism, the Indian inference has three terms. The major, the minor and the middle are here called sadhya, paksa and linga or hetu respectively. We know that smoke is invariably associated with fire (vyapti) and if we see smoke in a hill we conclude that there must be fire in that hill. Hill is the minor term; fire is the major term; smoke is the middle term. From the presence of smoke in the hill as qualified by the knowledge that wherever there is smoke there is fire, we proceed to infer the presser gust fire in the hill. This is inference. Indian logic does not separate sound on from induction. Inference is a complex process involving with. Indian logic also rejects the verbalist view of logic. It studies if. Ought as such and not the forms of thought alone. The formal and the material logic are blended here. Verbal form forms no integral part of the inference. This becomes clear from the division of inference into svartha (for oneself) and parartha (for others). In the former we do not require the formal statement of the different members of inference. It is a psychological process. The latter, the pararmatha, which is a syllogism has to be presented in language and this has to be done only to convince others. There are five members in the Nyaya syllogism. The first is called Pratijiia or proposition. It is the logical statement which is to be.<proved. The second is Hetu or `reason', which states the reason for the establishment of the proposition. The third is called Udaharana, which gives the universal concomitance together with an example. The fourth is Upanaya or the application of. the universal concomitance to the present case. And the fifth is Nigamana or conclusion drawn from the preceding propositions. These five propositions of the Indian syllogism are called `members' or avayavas. The following is atypical Nyaya syllogism:

**(1)** This hill has fire (pratijfia).

**(2)** Because it has smoke (hetu).

**(3)** Whatever has smoke has fire, e.g., an oven (udaharana).

**(4)** This hill has smoke which is invariably associated with fire (upanaya).

**(5)** Therefore this hill has fire (nigamana).

If we compare it with the Aristotelian syllogism, which has only three propositions, we will find that this Nyaya syllogism corresponds to the Barbara (AAA) mood of the First Figure which is the strongest mood of thee strongest figure. Though the Nyaya syllogism has five and tae Aristotelian has three propositions, the terms in both are only three--the sadhya or the major, the paksa or the minor and the beta or the middle. Out of the five propositions, two appear redundant and we may easily leave out either the first two or the last two, which are essentially the same. The first coincides with the fifth and the second with the fourth. If we omit the last two, the first three propositions correspond with the conclusion, of the minor premise and the major premise reactively. Or, if we omit the first two, the last three propositions corres to the major premise, the minor premise and the conclusion of Aristotelian syllogism. Hence if we leave out the first two member of the Nyaya syllogism which are contained in the last two, we find that it resembles the Aristotelian syllogism in the First Figure:

(1)All things, which have smoke, have fire (Major premise).

(2) This hill has smoke (Minor premise).

(3) Therefore this hill has fire (Conclusion).

And the typical Aristotelian syllogism may be stated in the . Form thus:

(1) Socrates is mortal (pratijfia).

(2) Because he is a man (hetu).

(3) Whoever is a man is a mortal, e.g., Pythagoras (udaharana)

(4) Socrates is a man who is invariably a mortal (upanaya).

(5) Therefore Socrates is mortal (nigamana).

But there are certain real differences between the Nyaya anti the Aristotelian syllogism apart from the nominal difference between the numbers of the propositions in each. The, Aristotelian syllogism is only deductive and formal, while the Nyaya syllogism is deductive-inductive and formal-material. The Nyaya rightly regards deduction and induction as inseparably related, as two aspects of the same process-the truth now realized in western logic. Inference, according to Nyaya, is neither from the universal to the particular nor from the particular to the universal, but from the particular to the particular through the universal The example is a special feature of the Nyaa syllogism and illustrates the truth that the universal major premise is' the result of a real induction based on the law of causation and that induction and deduction cannot be really separated. Again, while in the Aristotelian syllogism the major and the minor terms stand apart in the premises though they are connected by the middle term with each other, in the Nyaya syllogism all the three terms stand synthesized in the Upanaya. Again while the Aristotelian syllogism is verbalistic, the Nyaya recognizes the fact that verbal form is not the essence of inference and is required only to convince others. Some people like Dr. Vidyabhusana and Prof. Keith have suggested that Greek thought influences the Nyaya syllogism But it is absolutely false. We find the development of the Nyaya inference before Aristotle. There are also certain fundamental differences between the two views and the modern western logicians accept the view of Nyaya as better also. The view that vyapti the nerve of inference, was introduced by the Buddhist logician Dinnaga who was influenced by Greek thought is also wrong. Vyapti was recognized much before Diinnaga,I nor did he `borrow' his doctrine from Greece. It is more reasonable to explain the similarities between the two as due to a parallel development of thought. Indian logic has been a natural growth.

There are five characteristics of the middle term:

**(1)** It must be present in the minor term (paksadharmata); e.g., smoke must be present in the hill.

**(2)** It must be present in all positive instances in which the major term is present; e.g., smoke must be present in the kitchen where fire, exists (sapaksasattva).

**(3)**It must be absent in all negative instances in which the major term is absent; e.g., smoke must be absent in the lake in which fire does not exist (vipaksasattva).

**(4)** It must be non-incompatible with the minor term; e.g., it must not prove the coolness of fire (abadhita).

**(5)** It must be qualified by the absence of counteracting reasons which lead to a contradictory conclusion; e.g., `the fact of being caused' should not be used to prove the eternality' of sound (aviruddha).

Inference is generally regarded as of two kinds-Svartha and Parartha which we have already discussed. Gotama speaks of three kinds of inference-purvavat, shesavat and samanyatodrsta. The first two are based on causation and the last one on mere coexistence. A cause is the invariable and unconditional antecedent of an effect and an effect is the invariable and unconditional consequent of a cause. When we infer the unperceived effect from a perceived cause we have purvavat inference, e.g., when we infer future rain from dark clouds in the sky. When we infer the unperceived cause from a perceived effect we have shesavat inference, e.g., when we infer past rain from the swift muddy flooded water of a river. When inference is based not on causation but on uniformity of co-existence, it is called samanyatodrsta, e.g., when we infer cloven hoofs of an animal by its horns. According to another interpretation, a purvavat inference is based on previous experience of universal concomitance between two things, a shesavat inference is parishesa or inference by elimination, and a samanyatodrsta is inference by analogy. Another classification of inference gives us the kevalanvayi, kevalavy atireki and anvayavyatireki inferences. It is based on the nature of vyapti and on the different methods of establishing it. The method of induction by which universal casual relationship is established may be anvaya, vyatireka or both. The first corresponds to Mill's Mathod Agreement, the second to his Method of Difference, and the third to this Joint Method of Agreement and Difference or the Method of Double Agreement. We have kevalanvayi inference when the middle term is Always positively related to the major term. The terms agree in presence, there being no negative instance of their agreement in , absence, e.g.,

All knowable objects are nameable;
The pot is a knowable object;
The pot is nameable.

We have kevalavvatireki inference when the middle term is the differentium of the minor term and is always negatively related to the major term. The terms agree only in absence, they're being no positive instance of their agreement in presence, e.g..

What is not different-from-other-elements has no smell;
The earth has smell;
The earth is different-from-other-elements.

We have anvayavyatireki inference when the middle term is both positively and negatively related to the major term. The vyapti between the middle and the major is in respect of both presence and absence. There is Double Agreement between the terms-they agree in presence in the positive instances and they also agree in absence in the negative instances; e.g.,

All things which have smoke have fire;
This hill has smoke; This hill has fire; and No non-fiery things have smoke;
This hill has smoke;
This hill is not non-fiery;
i.e., This hill has fire.

In Indian logic a fallacy is called hetvabhasa. It means that the middle, term *appears* to be a reason but is not a valid reason. All fallacies are material fallacies. We have mentioned the five characteristic of valid middle term. When these are violated, we have fallacies. Five kinds of fallacies are recognized:

**(1) Asiddha or Sadhyasama:** This is the fallacy of the unproved middle. The middle term must be present in the minor term (paksadharmata). If it is not, it is unproved. It is of three kinds-

**(a) ashrayasiddha:** The minor term is the locus of the middle term. If the minor term is unreal, the middle term cannot be present in it; e.g., 'the sky-lotus is fragrant, because it is a lotus, like the lotus of a lake'.

**(b) svarupasiddha:** Here the minor term is not unreal. But the middle term cannot by its very nature be present in the minor term; e.g., 'sound is a quality, because it is visible'. Here visibility cannot belong to sound which is audible.

**(c) vyapyatvasiddha:** Here vyapti is conditional (sopadhika). We cannot say, e.g., wherever there is fire there is smoke'. Fire smokes only when it is associated with wet fuel. A red-hot iron ball or clear fire does not smoke. Hence 'association with wet fuel' is a condition necessary to the aforesaid vyapti. Being conditioned, the middle term becomes fallacious if we say: 'The hill has smoke because it has fire'.

**(2) Savyabhichara or Anaikantika:** This is the fallacy of the irregular middle. It is of three kinds:

**(a) Sadharana:** Here the middle term is too wide. It is present in both the sapaksa (positive) and the vipaksa (negative) instances and violates the rule that the middle should not be present in the negative instances (vipaksasattva); e.g., 'the hill has fire because it is knowable'. Here 'knowable'. is present in fiery as well as non-fiery objects.

**(b) Asadharana:** Here the middle term is too narrow. It is present only in the paksa and neither in the sapaksa nor in the vipaksa. It violates the rule that the, middle term should be present in the sapaksa (sapaksasattva); e.g., 'sound is eternal, because it' is audible'. Here audibility belongs to sound only and is present nowhere else.

**(c) Anupasarhhari**: Here the middle term is non-exclusive. The minor term is all-inclusive and leaves nothing by_ way of sapaksa or vipaksa; e.g., 'all things are non-eternal, because they are knowable'.

**(3) Satpratipaksa:** Here the middle term is contradicted by another middle term. The reason is counter-balanced by another reason. And both are of equal force; e.g., 'sound is eternal, because it is audible' and 'sound is non-eternal, because it is produced'. Here 'audible' is counter-balanced by 'produced' and both are of equal force.

**(4) Badhita:** It is the non-inferentially contradicted middle Here the middle term is contradicted by some other pramana and not by inference. It cannot prove the major term which is disproved by another stronger source of valid knowledge, 'fire is cold, because it is a substance'. Here the middle term `substance' becomes contradicted because its major term `coldness' is directly contradicted by perception.

**(5). Viruddha:** It is the contradictory middle. The middle term, instead of being pervaded by the presence of the major term, is pervaded by the absence of the major term. Instead of proving the existence of the major term in the minor term, it proves its non-existence therein; e.g., `sound is eternal, because it is produced'. Here 'produced', instead of proving the eternality of sound, proves its non-eternality. Here the middle term itself disproves the original proposition and proves its contradictory, while in the savyabhichara the middle term only fails to prove the conclusion, and in the satpratipaksa the middle term is inferentially contradicted by another middle term both of which are of equal force, and in the badhita the middle term is non-inferentially contradicted and the major is disproved by stronger pramana other than inference.

## COMPARISON

THE third kind of valid cognition is Upamiti and its means is called Upamana. It is knowledge derived from comparison and roughly corresponds to analogy. It has been defined as the knowledge of the relation between a word and its denotation.' It is produced by the knowledge of resemblance or similarity. For example, a man who has never seen a gavaya or a wild cow and does not know what it is; is told by a person that a wild cow is an animal like a cow, subsequently comes across a wild cow in a forest and recognizes it as the wild cow then his knowledge is due to upamana. He has heard the word `gavaya: and has been told that it is like a cow and now he himself sees the objected denoted by the word 'gavaya' and recognizes it to be so. Hence upama is just the knowledge of the relation between a name and the object denoted by that name. It is produced by the knowledge of similarly, because a man recognizes a wild cow as a`gavava' when he perceives its similarly to the cow and remembers the description that a gavaya is an animal like a cow'.

The Buddhists reduce Upamana to perception and testimony. The Sankhya and the Vaishesika reduce it to inference. The Jainas reduce it to recognition or pratyabhijfia. The Mimarnsakas recognize it as a separate source of knowledge, but their account **of it** is different from that of Nyaya, which will be considered in the chapter on Mimamsa.

## VERBAL TESTIMONY

THE fourth kind of valid knowledge is Shabda or Agama or authoritative verbal testimony. Its means is also called Shabda. It is defined as the statement of a trustworthy person (aptavakya) and consists in understanding its meaning. A sentence is defined as a collection of words and a word is defined as that which is potent to convey its meaning.' The power in a word to convey its meaning comes, according to ancient Nyaya, from God, and according to later Nyaya, from long established convention. Testimony is always personal. It is based on the words of a trustworthy person, human or divine. Testimony is of two kinds Vaidika and secular (laukika). The Vaidika testimony is perfect and infallible because God speaks the Vedas; secular testimony, being the words of human beings who are liable to error, is not infallible. Only the words of trustworthy persons who always speak the truth are valid; others are not. A word is a potent symbol, which signifies an object, and a sentence is a collection of words. But a sentence in order tote intelligible must conform to certain conditions. These conditions are four-akanksa, yogyata, sannidhi and tatparya. The first is mutual implication or expectancy. The words of a sentence are interrelated and stand in need of one another in order to express a complete sense. A mere aggregate of unrelated words will not make a logical sentence. It will be sheer nonsense, e.g., `cow horse man elephant'. The second condition is that the words should possess fitness to convey the sense and should not contradict the meaning. `Water the plants with fire' is a contradictory sentence. The third condition is the close proximity of the words to one another. The words must be spoken in quick succession without long intervals. If the words `bring', 'a', **and `cow' are** uttered at long intervals they would not make a logical sentence. The fourth condition is the intention of the speaker if the words are ambiguous. For example, the word 'saindhava' means `salt' as well as a `horse'. Now, if a man who is taking his food asks another to bring 'saindhava', the latter should not bring a horse.

The Nyaya admits only these four pramanas. Arthapatti or implication is reduced to inference. For example, when we say for Devadatta does not eat during day', the implication is that he must be eating during night otherwise how can he be fat:

Mimamsa grants the status of an independent pramana to implication. But Nyaya reduces it to inference thus:

> All fat persons who do not eat during day, eat during nig'
> Devadatta is a fat person who does not eat during day;
> Devadatta is a fat person who eats during night.

Abhava or non-existence, which also is regarded as a separate pramana by Bhatta Mimamsa, is reduced here either to perception or to inference. Abhava is non-existence of a thing and the same sense organ that perceives a thing, perceives its non-existence also. If the thing is imperceptible and can only be inferred, then, its non-existence too may be equally inferred.

## CAUSATION

LET us now consider the Nvaya theory of Causation. A cause is defined as an unconditional and invariable antecedent of an effect and an effect as an unconditional and invariable consequent of a cause. The same cause produces the same effect and the same effect is produced by the same cause. Plurality of causes is ruled out. The first essential characteristic of a cause is its antecedence; the fact that it should precede the effect (Ptirvavrtti). The second is its invariability; it must Invariably precede the effect (Nivatapurvavrtti). The third it its Unconditionally or necessity; it must unconditionally precede the effect (Ananyathasiddha). Unconditional antecedence is immediate and direct antecedence and excludes the fallacy of the remote causes Thus we see that the Nyaya definition of a cause is the same as that in Western inductive logic. Hume defines a cause as an in variable antecedent. J. S. Mill defines it as an unconditional and invariable antecedent. Carveth Read points out that unconditionally includes; idea immediacy. A **cause,** **therefore,** is an unconditional, immediate and invariable antecedent of an effect.' Nyaya recognizes five kinds of. ofaccidental (anyathasiddha) antecedents which are not real ruses. Firstly, the qualities of a cause are mere accidental antecedents. The colour of a potter's staff is not the cause of a pot. Secondly, the cause of a cause or a remote cause is not unconditional the potter's father is not the cause of a pot. Thirdly, the co-effect of a cause is they not causally related. The sound produces by the potter's staff is not the cause of a pot, though it may invariably precede the pot. Night and day are not causally related. Fourthly, eternal substances like space are not unconditional antecedents. Fifthly, unnecessary, things like the potter's ass are not unconditional antecedents; though the potter's ass may be invariably present when the potter is making. a pot, yet it is not the cause of the pot. A cause must be an unconditional and necessary antecedent. Nyaya emphasizes the sequence view, of causality. Cause and effect are never simultaneous. Plurality of causes is also wrong because causal relation is reciprocal. The same effect cannot be produced by any other cause. Each effect has its distinctive features and has only one specific cause. Further, like Western logic, the Nyaya regards a cause as `the sum-total of the conditions, positive and negative, taken together'. The cause is an aggregate of the unconditional or necessary and invariable antecedent conditions, which are called karanasamagri. The absence of negative counteracting conditions is called pratibandhakabh'ava.

An effect (karya) is defined as the 'counter-entity of its own prior non-existence' (pragabhavapratiyogi). It is the negation of its own priornegation. It comes into being and destroys its prior non-existence. It was non-existent before its production. It did not pre-exist in its cause. It is a fresh beginning, a new creation. This Nyaya-Vaishesika view of causation is directly opposed to the Sankhya-Yoga and Vedanta view of satkaryavaada. It is called asatkaryavada or arambhavada. The effect (karya) is non-existent (asat) before its creation and is a new beginning (arambha), a fresh creation, an epigenesis. It is distinct from its cause and can never be identical with it. It is neither an appearance nor a transformation of the cause. It is newly brought into existence by the operation of the cause.

There are three kinds of causes-samavayi, asamavayi and nimitta. The first is the samavayi or the inherent cause, also called as the upadana or the material cause. It is the substance out of which the effect is produced. For example, the threads are the inherent cause of the cloth and the clay is the inherent cause of a pot. The effect inheres in its material cause. The cloth inheres in the threads. -The effect cannot exist separately from its material cause, though the cause can exist independently of its effect. The material cause is always a substance (dravya). The second kind of cause is asamavayi or non-inherent. It inheres in the material cause and helps the production of the effect. The conjunction of the threads (tantusamyoga), which inheres in the threads, is the non-inherent cause of the cloth of which the threads are the material or the inherent cause. The colour of the threads (tanturupa) At the non-inherent cause of the colour of the cloth. The cloth itself is the inherent cause of its colour. The effect as well as its non-inherent cause both co-inheres in the material cause. The non-inherent cause is always a quality or an action (guna or karma). The third kind of cause is nimitta or efficient. It is the power, which helps the material causes to produce the effect. The weaver is the efficient cause of the cloth. The efficient cause includes the accessories (sahakari), e.g., the loom and shuttle of the weaver or the staff and wheel of the potter. The efficiency cause may be a substance, a quality or an action.

Sometimes a distinction is made between a general or an ordinary (sadharana) and a peculiar or an extraordinary (asadharana) causes Space, time, God's knowledge, God's will, merit, demerit, prior-non existence and absence of counteracting factors are the eight general causes. The extraordinary cause is called the karana or the instrument cause.and is included in the efficient cause. It is the motive power, which immediately produces the effect, e.g., the staff of the potter. The modern Nyaya regards the efficiency itself, which inheres in this cause as the real instrumental cause. The inherent cause, the non-inherent causes the efficient cause and the purpose correspond to Aristotle's material, formal, efficient and final causes.

## SOUL

THE law of Causation is subservient to the law of Karma. The Nyaya, like the Vaishesika, believes in teleological creation. The material causes of. This universe is the eternal atom of earth, water, fire and air and the efficient cause is God. The infinite individual souls are co-eternal **with atoms.** And God is co-eternal with atoms and souls and is external to both. Nyaya advocates atomism, spiritualism, theism, realism and pluralism. Creation means combinations of atoms and destruction means dissolution of these combinations through the motion supplied to or withdrawn from the atoms by the Unseen Power working under the guidance of God. The innumerable eternal atoms and the innumerable eternal souls are both beyond; creation and destruction. God can neither create them nor destroy them. God is not the real creator as He is not the material cause of this universe. And though He is called the. ruler of the Universe being regarded as the efficient cause, the real efficiency belongs to the Unseen Power. The view of causation is asatkaryavada because the different combinations of atoms are regarded as new creations, as real fresh beginnings. It is the doctrine of epigenesis as the new products arise as real creations having the distinctive features of their own and adding new properties to reality. The individual soul is regarded as the substratum of the quality of consciousness, which is **not its** essence but only an accidental property. The soul is a real knower, a real enjoyer and a real active agent and an eternal substance. **It is** not transcendental consciousness and it is different from God who is the Supreme Soul. Cognitions, affections and conations are the attributes of the soul, which is one, partless and all-pervading. Each soul has its manas during its empirical life and is separated from it in liberation. It is distinct from the body, the senses and the mind (mans). Bondage is due to ignorance and Karma. Liberation is due to Knowledge and destruction of Karma. The Vedas are the work of God and therefore claim absolute authority.

## GOD

NYAYA accepts the metaphysics of the Vaishesika School and the accounts of matter, soul and God are almost the same as those in the Vaishesika. We have discussed the metaphysics of the Vaishesika School and so we need not repeat it here. The categories, the doctrine of asatkaryavada, the account of creation and destruction, the nature of atoms and souls, the account of bondage and liberation, the authority of the Veda, the nature and function of God, the Unseen Power-all these are accepted by Nyaya. The criticisms, which we levelled against the Vaishesika, also apply against the Nyaya position in so far as both are identical. While Kanada himself has not specifically mentioned God, the later Vaishesikas and particularly the later Naiyayikas have given an elaborate account of God and the latter have made God's

Grace an essential thing for obtaining true knowledge of the realities which alone leads to liberation. They refer to God as the creator, maintainer and destroyer of this world and introduce the element of devotion. But in our opinion all this can be done only by courtesy. God, as an eternal external reality, is always limited by the co-eternal atoms and souls and has to be guided by the law of karma. Though the later Naiyayikas are forced to amend the absurd position that eternal consciousness is not the essence of God by raising consciousness from the position of a separable accident to the position of an inseparable attribute in the case of God, yet they have failed to rise to the correct position by not taking. : consciousness as the essence of God. An atomistic and spiritualistic pluralism can lead only to an external theism where God, souls and atoms all fall apart and the dualism of matter and spirit can never be overcome. God is said to possess all the six perfection in their fullness-majesty, power, glory, beauty, knowledge and freedom. But then why are the liberated souls not allowed to share these qualities? If liberation consists in getting rid of all qualities, then God will be regarded as eternally bound. Again, God is called the moral governor of all beings (prayojaka karta). But then, either the souls are not free or the law of karma is thrown overboard. If the law of karma represents the self-determination of God and therefore does not bind God, then Karma and God would become -aft identical and external theism would vanish. The Nyaya should reduced its so-called eternal and independent atoms to a single material principle and its so-called innumerable eternal souls to a single spiritual principle and then should reconcile the dualism of matter and spirit in God by making them His aspects. Unless this is done, the contradictions n Nyaya would not be avoided. If it wants to be self-consistent, the Nyaya has to give up its atomistic and spiritualistic pluralism and its external theism. Yet in spite of these defects, the Nyaya theism is a step forward. Udayana's arguments for the existence of God have become classical for theism and may be briefly noted here. He gives the following nine arguments to prove the existence of God:

**(1)** The world is an effect and hence it must have an efficient cause. This intelligent agent is God. The order, design, co-ordination between different phenomena comes from God (karyat).

**(2)** The atoms being essentially inactive cannot form the different combinations unless God gives motion to them. The Unseen Power, the Adrsta, requires the intelligence of God. With -out God it cannot supply motion to the atoms (ayojanat).

**(3)** The world is sustained by God's will. Unintelligent Adrsta cannot do this. And the world is destroyed by God's will (dhrtyadeh).

**(4)** A word has a meaning and signifies an object. The power of words to signify their objects comes from God (padat).

**(5)** God is the author of the infallible Veda (pratyayatah).

**(6)** The Veda testifies to the existence of God (shruteh).

**(7)** The Vedic sentences deal with moral injunctions and prohibitions. The Vedic commands are the Divine commands God is the creator and promulgator of the moral laws (vakyat).

**(8)** According to Nyaya-Vaishesika the magnitude of a dyad is not produced by the infinitesimal magnitude ofthe two atoms each, but by the *number of* the two atoms. Number one' is directly perceived, but other numbers are conceptual creations. Numerical conception is related to the mind of the perceiver. At the time of creation, the souls are unconscious. And the atoms and the Unseen Power and space, time, minds are all unconscious. Hence the numerical conception depends upon the Divine Consciousness. So God must exist ( san-khyavishesat).

**(9)** We reap the fruits of our own actions, Merit and demerit accrue from our actions and the stock of merit and demerits is called Adrsta, the Unseen. Power. But this Unseen Power, being unintelligent, needs the guidance of a supremely intelligent God (adrstat).

But all these proofs are ultimately unavailing. Reason, as Kant points out while criticizing Descartes' arguments for the existence of God, leads to antinomies, which are insoluble. The Vedantins, Shankara, Ram'anuja, Madhva, Nimbarka, Vallabha and all, have rejected the Nyaya arguments and have fallen back on the Shruti alone for the existence of God. Kant in the West and the Vedantins in India were `forced to destroy reason in order to make room for faith'.

The chief value of Nyaya lies in its epistemology, logic and methodology, which have influenced all schools of Indian philosophy. But its ontology of atomism, pluralism, realism, theism and spiritualism huddled together in one mass is effective. The logic of pluralistic realism is a common-sense view of the world. If liberation means negation of all qualities including consciousness and bliss, the soul liberated is the soul petrified and Gotama by propounding such philosophy, says Shiharsa, is justifying his name Gotama'-an Excellent Bull.

## Buddhist Literature

Lord Buddha did not compose any book or scripture by himself. His followers compiled his thoughts in the form of scriptures and wrote commentaries on them. It resulted into a large religious literature, many of which scriptures are considered to be the best ones of the world. The followers of Lord Buddha compiled his preachings by the names of *Tripitakas,* the three in number, namely *Vinayapitaka, Suktapitaka* and *Abhidhemmapitaka.*

The *Vinayapitaka* prescribes the rules of conduct for the monks by which they abide by.

The *Suktapitaka is* the compilation of Lord Buddha's preachings and illustrations, which are further divided into five sections or *Nikaya,* namely: *Digha nikaya, Majjhima nikaya, Samyukta nikaya, Anguttara nikaya,* and *Khuchhaka nikaya.*

The *Abhidammapitaka* contains the detailed description of chief preachings and philosophical ideologies of Buddha.

**Lord Buddha's Preachings : The Four Noble Truths**

As we have delineated earlier, the essence of Buddha's preachings are contained in the four noble truths and they form the basis of Buddhism or Buddhist philosophy. What he discovered was "The Four Noble Truths" : *"Dukkha"* or sufferings, *"Samudaya"* or the causes of suffering, *"Nirodha"* or the extinction of all sufferings, and *"Magga"* or eightfold path to eradicate sufferings and experience salvation.

Buddha clarified that this world is full of suffering of various kinds. There are certain causes of man's sufferings and these sufferings can be got rid of, and there are means to eradicate sufferings. In his early life in the worldly embrace, he was pained to see the mankind suffering from age, death and ailments. He saw these sufferings as the nature of man, as man's life is inevitably related to sufferings related to age in which he has to face adulthood, old age and death at last. Whatever experiences of pleasure are in the world, finally get converted into suffering. It has been described that suffering is experienced in many forms - at the time of birth, suffering during old age; old age and death too are sufferings; grief, sadness and indifference too are sufferings; interaction with grievous things and objects begets suffering; parting from the loved-ones begets suffering; not attaining desired thing begets suffering. Thus, every part of our life is full of suffering. According to Buddhism, if man is able to understand this fact, then he becomes disinterested from life and consciously attempts to get rid of that suffering.

The next question arises about the cause of suffering. If we are undergoing suffering without any cause, it will be difficult to find relief from it. However, if we know the cause of our suffering, we can attempt to get rid of the cause to cease the process of suffering. Lord Buddha has enunciated this fact in his second noble truth. He says that the cause of the world's suffering is ignorance. There is a sequence of twelve causes between physical deaths and suffering, which can be called twelve-fold diagnosis. If man frees himself from this sequence, he can be emancipated from the cycle of birth and death. About the second noble truth, Lord Buddha says that man takes rebirth due to desire out of ignorance; and as a result of this desire he looks for pleasure everywhere.

Lord Buddha is of the view that the worldly suffering can be eradicated. Suffering can be eradicated if the desires arising out of ignorance are eradicated. If man is able to conquer his love, enmity, desire and anger, his inner self will not have any more desires and he will become. emancipated from the cycle and bond of birth and death. This stage of emancipation has been termed as *"Nirvana"* or salvation. Lord Buddha says that the cause of suffering rooted in ignorance or *avidya* should be eradicated, which can finally lead man to emancipation or salvation.

There is a way to eradicate suffering. Lord Buddha points out about how to eradicate suffering, for which he prescribes *Ashtangik, marga* or eightfold path, which we have delineated earlier.

Buddhism is of the view that if man leads life according to the above four noble truths, he can attain salvation. Lord-Buddha clearly says that the man who accepts the refuge of Buddhism and embraces the four noble truths by his own free volition, the Almighty looks after his welfare. It is the only path for welfare by which man gets rid of all kinds of griefs.

**The Middle Path**

During the period of Buddha, there was prevalent means for attainment of salvation, which was hard penance or *tapasya.* Having undergone penance for six long years, Buddha felt essenceless. According to Buddha, hard penance is as useless and detrimental as are the worldly desires and wishes. So, Buddha propounded the opinion that those who want to be emancipated of the worldly bonds should give up both ways and follow the middle path. This first alternative is that of giving up; that is, to give up the useless desire of worldly desires; and the other alternative is the provision of hard penance according to the utility of the body. Both these alternatives, if applied independently and in isolation, do not serve the purpose of attainment of salvation. So he advised for following a middle path, or *Samyukta nikaya,* or the eightfold path following which man can attain Buddhatva or salvation.

## Philosophical' Ideology of Buddhism

**1. Pratityasamutpada**

We have described the four noble truths of Buddha, the second of which is *Dukkha samudaya, which* is also called *Pratityasamutpada.* The cycle or bond of birth and death is called by the name of *Pratityasamutpada.* It is considered to be the basis of all Buddhistic philosophical thinking. Its meaning is that there is always a cause or concept behind every production or origin of everything. A cause or concept can be said to be the factor that is helpful in production or origin of something. It is almost necessary for production or origin to occur in the presence of a cause or concept; and as such, there can be no production or origin in their absence. Birth takes place if desire to take birth exists; and it will not occur if desire does not exist. This is the essential principle of *pratityasamtpada.* It can be called the causative factor. It entails that in the presence of a cause or concept, there will be every possibility of occurring something; that is, it will certainly occur. It is the relationship of cause and effect. If there is *avidya* or ignorance, the trait will be moulded accordingiy. If man takes birth, he will have to face weakness, old age and death. thus, there is nothing which occurs without a cause. The occurrence of everything or occurrence is governed by a cause. The occurrence or origination, which occurs due to the existence of a cause or concept, means its necessary possibility. On the other- hand, origination or occurrence is also possible due to the existence of another thing. Thus, it follows that a thing can be produced only when there exists a cause for it.

From the concept of causativeness, Lord Buddha teaches us the lesson of the middle path. He says that the middle path is the synthesis of two extremes - atheism and theism. The former considers that all occurrences in the world occur without any cause behind them, all occurrences are incidental or accidental and occur all of a sudden without any cause behind their bliss or grief; on the other hand, the latter considers that the functions of birth and death are Godly functions who is our creator and determines our destiny. Man leads a happy or sad life according to the wish of God.

Lord Buddha is of the view that we should keep away from these two extremes. He says that birth, old age and death do not occur without a cause; but its cause does not lie in any invisible God. It occurs due to a cause or concept, and it does not occur in its absence. It follows that everything is produced or occurs due to a cause; and nothing occurs without a cause. The present life is the cause of the past life, and the future life will be the result of the present life. Thus; the cycle of past, present and future goes on.

Lord Buddha had renunciated the worldly pleasures in the search of this universal truth. *Pratityasamptpada is* considered to be the fundamental philosophy of Buddhism. Man takes birth and dies, and this cycle goes on and on. Man takes birth only to die; and dies only to take birth. The cause of birth and death is no invisible power or God. We desire to take birth, so we take birth. We cannot take birth if we do not desire to take birth again. Lord Buddha emphasised on the philosophy that the desire of man is the root cause of man's taking birth in the world. Thus, he considers man as the creator, master and owner of himself.

## 2. Kshanikavada or Momentarism

*Kshanikavada* or momentarism is also an important philosophy of Buddhism. We have learnt under *pratityasamptpada* that everything originates due to a cause or desire.

According to *kshanikavada* everything in the world is temporary, that is, it exists for a few days and then it gets destroyed. As one current gives birth to the second, and the second to the third, so the process goes on and on. In the same way, one birth gives rise to the second, the second to the third, and so on. This process goes on unceasingly. This regularity or repeated occurrence is taken as universal or immortal in illusion. In fact, there is nothing which is immortal or universal. Change is the nature of everything, and it changes its form and attributes every time. Thus, we can say that the very nature of matter is momentary.

### 3. Arthakriyakaritvada

*Arthakriyakaritva* signifies the power or energy to do something or produce something. The present have come into existence out of the past, and the present has the power to produce the future. Every moment of time is the result of the preceding moment. It is in the context of this thinking that the Buddhists believe that the existence of everything is momentary and changeable. It follows that the power to change resides in everything. A seed sprouts because it has the power to change. It then gets destroyed entailing that it is momentary or destructible. This, this philosophy is dependent on the momentary existence of matter. It signifies that the reality, activity and changeability are the attributes of matter.

### 4. Anatmavada

The Buddha philosophy is not in agreement with the Brahmana philosophy as far as the attributes of the soul is concerned. The latter considers the soul to be permanent, immortal, immobile which does not change with the change of the body. The different forms of the body continue to be the impression of the soul, according to the latter. So, it finds ease in analysing the existence of the worldly bond and salvation, in which the soul gets emancipated from the worldly bond to blend with the God or supreme soul.

The Buddha philosophy, on the other hand, does not accept birth and death, bond and salvation of the soul; nor does it accept the immortality of the soul. Thus, we can describe it to be *anatmavadi.* However, it has not shied away from discussing the concepts of action or *karma,* bond and salvation in a simple and straight way. Lord Buddha does not consider that the soul is the basis of all things, or the supreme knowledge, or immortal. He says that man desires for woman, man, son, money, etc., so does he desire for soul. He says that all desires will have to be renounced for attainment of salvation. If man renounces all worldly things but does not renounce the desire for the soul, he cannot attain salvation. It is clear that, according to Lord Buddha, the desire for the soul is like the desire for worldly pleasures. Lord Buddha believes that the soul is the collective form of five elements which are *coop* or form, *vedana* or experience, *sangya* or name, *sanskara* or ritual and *vijnan* or science. Man does not live in isolation of these five elements. He is a collection of two conditions of the body and mind.

**5. Pancha-skandha or Five Elements**

As we have discussed that Lord Buddha described the soul as the collection of five elements which are *roop* or form, *vedana* or experience, *sangya* or name, *sanskara* or ritual and *vijnan or* science. Let us discuss these concepts in brief

**(a) Roop or Form :** All forms born of earth, water, fire or air are included under it. These form the body composed of bone, muscles, meat, skin, etc in the form of ether or sky.

**(b) Vedana or Experience** : Happiness or bliss, sadness or grief, and the condition of absence of both bliss and grief, have been called. If something goes according to our mind or feeling, it is bliss, else it is grief. When we are beyond the realms of bliss and grief, we feel a kind of bliss in the lack of either of them, and the *vedana* or experience is that moment.

**(c) Sangya or Name :** We recognise a thing on the basis of its name, and we name something for our convenience of recognising it. Thus, naming a person or thing is included under *sangya* or name.

**(d) Sanskara or Ritual :** When we come into contact with something, we become conscious regarding its efficiency or inefficiency. With prior experience, a man feels affection or enmity, bliss or grief with a thing as attached to its name. The consciousness of this feeling is called *sanskara* or ritual. It is of three kinds-kama *sanskara* or physical ritual, *vak sanskara* or speech ritual, and *chitra sanskara* or picture ritual. The body is the *kama sanskara,* the speech is the *vaka sanskara* and the nomenclature or experience is the *chitra sanskara.*

**(e) Vijnana or Science :** We perceive the external or material things by form, taste, touch or smell. In the same manner, we perceive the inner-self in the form of 'self. *Sangya; vedana* and *vijnana* are interrelated. The experience of sweet or sour is *vedana* or experience, and we are introduced to a thing by its *sangya* name, while *vijnana is* its perception.

**6. Karmavada or Action Philosophy**

The concept of *karma* has been discussed above in brief under different nomenclatures and sections, such as under *Partityasamutpada,* but we deem it prudent to throw more light on it. According to Lord Buddha, the good or evil is the result of man's actions. If a man performs evil actions, he experiences evil or grief in this and the other world. On the other hand, if a man performs good actions, tie finds solace or peace in this and the other world. Thus, a man experiences bliss or grief according to the result of his actions. We can see that this thinking of Buddhism is in consonance with the principles of the *Upnishads* regarding actions and the principles of birth-rebirth. Of a man to be rich, poor, weak, strong, healthy, sick, foolish, intelligent, is not the result of God's desire but the result of man's own actions.

Lord Buddha had belief in *partityasamutpada so* he accepted that there exists one or the other cause behind every phenomenon. The diversity of the world is the reflection of man's own actions. The clear message that he gave to the world is that everything occurs as a result of actions, thus man is the maker of his own destiny. However, one thing must be noted that Buddhism does not think that the soul transits; these are the actions that transit. After death of a man, the soul is destroyed, but his actions remain indestructible; and the second body is formed due to these actions. Thus, we can see that Buddhism accepts the chief principles of *karmavada.* It is in consonance with Jainism and Brahmanism when it. says that every action has its result or effect, whatever may be its kind. This result has its effect on the doer. Buddhism is of the view that the result is not under the God's wish. Action is capable of producing the result.

From the above discussion, we can see that the Buddhist *karmavada follows* a middle path. It accepts three kinds of actionsphysical, speech and mental. A man becomes ready to do something due to a motive. Man does *a* physical action by body or physical limbs, speech action by speech or tongue, and the motive as the mental action. That is to say, if a man thinks about committing thievery, he does a mental action, even though he may not actually do it.

**7. Bodhisatva or Enlightenment**

Salvation is considered to be basic principle. A person who attains salvation meets with the supreme spiritual form, which is also called the God's form. Thus, salvation is the highest or supreme ideal for anyone. Such a man is full of spiritual powers and is as important as the God himself. Thus, a person who desires to attain verbal knowledge, is called *bodhisatva.* It is believed in Buddhism that the tales pertaining to the past lives of Lord Buddha are the tales of *bodhisatva.*

In various scriptures, such as in the *Heenyana,* it is described as a principle or philosophy. According to it, there are four spiritual levels, with three levels of mediators-shravaka, *pratyekabuddha,* and *bodhisatva.* The *shravaka* crosses four levels of mediation, but stops short of attaining full salvation. The *pratyekabuddha* is the one who is desirous of his or personal welfare. While the *bodhisatva is* the one who wants the welfare or good of all people of the world, and is not desirous of personal bliss or grief. He finds pleasure in the welfare of all beings. He determines himself to beget salvation to all beings, and engages himself in the social service. He is liberal and kind, and renounces his own comfort for the sake of others. We can see that there is a blend of sociality in the spirituality of Buddhism. It stands for others' welfare. It finds joy in others' service. A follower of Buddhism should be committed to sacrifice his own good for others' welfare. The life of Buddha is. an illustration of his philosophy in which he roamed from one place to another to preach and do others' good.

Buddhism is of the view that a man should have feelings for others' welfare in his heart. That is, he should be mentally prepared to do the welfare of others. Besides, the education or instruction of Budhism is composed of exercise of the good deeds.

## Provision of Worship

In Buddhism, the provision of worship has seven parts. His day starts with prayers, and he hands over himself to the God's refuge. He looks into the evil deeds he has done and is desirous of begetting salvation. He admires other mediators' efforts and attaches importance to their tasks. He prays Lord Buddha for preaching. He wins over his own 'self' and makes it negligible. Then, he dedicates his life to the welfare of others.

A bodhisatva is considered to be the supreme being because of his conduct and thinking. His life is considered to be sacred and pure. His conduct is flawless.

## Two Schools of Thought of Buddhism-Mahayana and Heenayana

Lord Buddha dedicated all his life to find out the root cause of ail suffering in the world and to provide solace and guidance to people. He provided advice and suggested ways how to attain salvation to get emancipated from the cycle of birth and death. His advice or preachings cannot be bound in any limits or community. It is beyond all kinds of limits of time, place, thinking and philosophy.

However, after the life of Lord Buddha, Buddhism too got divided into two branches or chief schools of thought. The formation of two branches was due to the argument and difference of thought among monks, as different commentaries and views were expressed. Presently, Buddhism flows into several branches, the chief of which are two- Mahayana and Heenayana. Heenayana is prevalent in countries like Sri Lanka, Myanmar, Thailand, etc; while Mahayana is prevalent in countries like Japan, Korea, China, etc.

**Distinction between Mahayana and Heenayana**

The word Heenayana signifies small vehicle or path, while the word Mahayana signifies large vehicle or path. The chief distinction between them is of the part and the whole. We can enumerate the distinction between the two under the following points while remembering that Heenayana is the oldest concept or form of Buddhism.

| **Mahayana** | **Heenayana** |
|---|---|
| 1. It lays emphasis on the welfare of all or the whole, as Buddha lived his life for others good, and nor for his own | 1. It lays emphasis on personal welfare. It says that man should attempt for his indi vidual salvation. |
| 2. *Its aim is the bodhisatva or* good of all, which sees the good of others as its own good. It overlooks its own salvation to facilitate others' salvation. | 2. The ideal of Heenayana lies in the fact that it looks for attainment of personal salvation. |
| 3. It considers that Lord Buddha had three bodies-the form body which he wore; the religious or spiritual body which is not physical; and the blissful body in which he resides in the heaven. | 3. It considers Lord Buddha as an ordinary, historical man who attained Buddhatva by continuous meditation. His life was that of a common man from birth to childhood, marriage and procreation |

| | |
|---|---|
| | of offspring. |
| 4. It considers Buddha as a god of the world and his idol is worshipped. | 4. Heenayana does not follow this practice. |
| 5. It considers the practice of six exercises as necessary. | 5. It considers the practice of ten exercises as necessary. |
| 6. It emphasises the practice of following the ten principles even after attainment of the supreme. | 6. It considers that the attainment of *arhata* or eligibility as the supreme or final point. |
| 7. According to it, the attainment of salvation is possible by meditation, own good and universal good. | 7. It says that attainment of salvation is possible by meditation under the guidance of the teacher. |
| 8. It accepts the reality of matter as science. It believes in the extension of the world from vacuum, the knowledge of which can be attained by prudence and wisdom. This knowledge is not possible by mind. It is beyond it. | 8. It believes that everything is temporary, mortal, momentary, destructible and resulting phenomenon and considers God as the illusion of mind. It considers man as the master of himself. |

From the above points of distinction, we can say that Heenayana is the initial stage of Buddhism, while Mahayana can be called the developed stage. These two schools of thought are only two classes. They are based in the preachings of Lord Buddha. Both of them are essentially found in each other, which are more like a tree and its seed, or the whole and the part. They are more like two branches of the same tree, than being two different trees altogether.

### 9. Shunyavada or Philosophy of *Vacuum*

Lord Buddha did not want to remain in isolation from the world in a forest, nor did he want to live entangled in woe idly things. He wanted to make use of his knowledge for the welfare of the people. It was the reason that he followed a middle path. His philosophy of the *middle path is known by the name of Shunyavada or the philosophy*of vacuum.

*Under this philosophy, the shunya or vacuum is considered to be* the supreme truth which is beyond all basic elements, and is also beyond all arguments. It is beyond all alternatives as well as logics. It is the basic vacuum, We can accept the existence or the real form of a thing by logic, or we can accept the existence or non-existence of a thing to take its reality. However, it is not possible to understand an element or matter by its existence or non-existence. If we try to reason out a thing, we get entangled in the argument deeper and deeper, because there is no end to argument. If we want to get beyond this worldly entanglements, we shall have to go beyond the arguments and logic; as such the only way left out is that of the *shunya or vacuum. It was the reason that Lord Buddha preached to* get rid of all worldly entanglements and traps and logic. If we succeed, it is similar to going to the refuge of vacuum.

Excessive logic of a thing takes us out of the realm of truth. The meaning of vacuum is taken as 'absence', however, the scholars do not consider it to be so; they say that it is something which is indescribable, of which characteristics cannot be described. The world cannot be described as either mental or external. It cannot be described either as 'existence' or 'non-existence'. It is beyond the realm of intellect and speech. The scholars consider two forms of vacuum-truth as well as false.

Thus it is seen that vacuum is a relative principle. All religions of the world are dependent on' one or the other philosophy: all religions are dependent and changeable, and are indescribable too. At the base of all of them is the vacuum. The opinions of the scholars professing either existence or non-existence of vacuum have not been accepted; the opinion with the blending of these two extremes is accepted. What is beyond the realm of mind and speech and what cannot be analysed is the supreme being, and it would be appropriate to call it vacuum.

## Educational Thought Inherent in Four Noble Truths

As we have discussed earlier in the chapter, Lord Buddha saw various suffering of mankind in the form of first noble truth. If a man awakens to the fact that his deeds beget the result of his suffering or joy, he will not do anything which will beget him suffering later. He will also guide his life in a manner as not to trouble anyone. He will govern his conduct in a manner in all aspects of life - physically, mentally, morally and spiritually - that he will be decorated as an ideal citizen of the society and country, and of course the world.

Buddhism is of the view if the parents, teachers and guardians bring up the child keeping in view various facets of physical, mental, moral and spiritual life, the child will certainly rise to the ideals of life and become a noble man in his future life. It will improve upon the educational system which is desired the most in present day society.

Lord Buddha says in his second noble truth that *avidya* or ignorance is the cause of suffering of mankind. A man gets trapped in the worldly traps due to ignorance. The' function of education is to eradicate this ignorance so that man can work toward his spiritual development.

The fact of eradication of ignorance or *avidya* is given by Lord Buddha as the third noble truth: He has compared this task to the attainment of salvation. He says if desires arising out of ignorance are destroyed or overcome, man will be able to conquer over love, desire, enmity and anger.

In the form of. fourth noble truth, Lord Buddha has prescribed the eightfold path to get rid of all worldly suffering. He has prescribed following of the middle path. He was against seclusion when undertaking hard penance. He has said that if the eightfold path is followed by the teacher, his objectives of education can be met.

## Educational Thoughts Inherent in the Eightfold Path

As described earlier, the noble eightfold path has eight steps. These eight steps have adequate educational thoughts inherent in *them. The first of these steps is the Samyaka drishti or Sammadithi,* meaning right view. It signifies prudence, by which man can avoid to be entrapped in the worldly traps. Having attained the right view, the *next step is necessary to have Samyaka Sankalpa or* Sammasankappor, meaning right motives. It is on the basis of these motives that man will proceed further for attainment of salvation. The third step is the Samyaka *Vani* or Sammavaca, which implies right speech. Man should keep his speech and tongue under control. We can lose and win others' hearts with the help of our speech. The next *step is the Samyaka Karmanta or Sammakammanto, which signifies* right action. This control signifies that we shall have to keep our mental and physical actions under control. Under it is included keeping away from all kinds of violences performed by mind, body or speech; it also follows that man will have to do away sensual consumption. The fifth step under the noble eightfold path is Samyaka*Ajiva* or *Sammaajivo* which implies employing right means of livelihood. Man should firmly believe in earning his means of livelihood by adopting justifiable means. The next step is the Samyaka *Vyayama* or *Sammavayamo,* which means right effort. It lays stress on keeping good thoughts in the mind and eradication of evil thoughts from the mind. The seventh step is the *Samyaka Smriti* or *Sammasati,* which means right mindfulness. This step implies that man should always keep in mind the various elements of the acquired *knowledge. And the last step, namely the Samyaka Samadhi or Sammasamadhi, which implies the right concentration, requires man* to engage himself in penance, but not in isolation ın the fearsomer forests, but in the lap of society, at the same time keeping aloof for it but meant for its welfare.

From the above discussion, we can see that the noble eightfold path is replete with noble guidance which is capable of purifying the heart and mind of the man fully. It makes possible for man to attain right concentration, as implied in its eighth step, which finally leads to the attainment of salvation, or the supreme peace as envisaged by most scholars and sages. Thus, we can see that the noble eightfold path has deep educational thoughts inherent in it.

## Educational Thought Inherent in the Pratityasamutpada

As we have discussed earlier, *Pratityasamutpada* signifies cause and effect. This path was propounded by Lord Buddha as the middle path which signifies the blending or ssimilation of two extremes theism and atheism. He believes that the present life is the effect of the past life, and the future life will take form according to the actions of the present. He is of the firm view that the cycle of past, present and future goes on continuously. He has described man as the maker of his own fortune and has described action as the root cause of birthrebirth. It implies that man should shape his own destiny and he can improve upon his present and future life by suitable actions. It makes man optimistic. The teachers should learn from this philosophy and teach the students right kind of optimism which will further social welfare; and it will help eradicate many problems-from the country.

## Educational Thought Inherent in Karmavada

Lord Buddha says that man faces the fruit of his own good and evil actions. The man who indulges in evil actions faces grief and suffering in this and the other world. On the other hand, the man who does good actions finds solace, happiness and joy in this and the other world. Lord Buddha is of the view that man becomes rich or poor due to his own actions, so is the condition of ailment or health, or knowledge or ignorance. God does not play any role in shaping man; it is the man who has shaped himself in such manner as he finds himself to be in today; and it is his present action that will shape his future in this and the next life.

Lord Buddha says that man is fully able to eradicate the suffering he is likely to face; from it springs forth the philosophy of *karmavada* or action. It is not God who gives the fruit of his actions, it is the action which gives the result of its occurrence done by man. Thus, we see that this philosophy has educational thought inherent in it. It lays emphasis on man's actions which should be worthy, true and good. If teachers and students follow this belief, they will not only improve upon themselves, but also help make society a better place to live.

### Educational Thought Inherent in the Concept of Bodhisatva

Lord Buddha says that the highest objective of man is to attain salvation or bodhisatva; and it should function like an ideal for man. The man who sacrifices his life for others' good, ascends the steps to salvation and brings about social welfare. He becomes the epitome *of* kindness and others' good. It implies that education should be so imparted as to enable the student to realize the ideal. If it becomes possible, all beings in the society and world will become free of pain and suffering; and education can play a great role in it.

## Jain Philosphy and Education

In this chapter, we shall briefly discuss the chief factors of Jainism or Jain philosophy. These factors are - *aniswarvada* (no faith in the existence of God), *anekanta-syadvada* (liberalism), *ahimsa* (nonviolgence), good conduct, *jeev ka bandhan* or *karma* principle (action principle), imagination of *moksha* (salvation). After we have discussed these factors in a little detail, we shall discuss the thoughts in Jainism concerning education. In the above we have discussed with particular analysis of their chief fundamental elements; since our discussion is primarily meant of the students of education, so we have left out the analysis of Jain philosophy, Jain literature and principles of Jainism; of course, a mention has been made toward their fundamental elements.

### Jainism

The word 'Jain' has come into being from 'Jin'. The meaning of the word 'Jain' is 'one who has conquered the senses', that is a person who has natural control over all kinds of defects. Thus, all those lectures or precepts given by those who conquered all kinds of defects are called Jainism. The people who take birth just like any other common man, but conquer over desires, love, anger and other defects and experience immortality, the precepts given by such great people form the background of Jainism.

## Birth of Jainism

Jainism considered that this world was a place where people indulged in consumption; that is, all people engaged themselves in consumption of different kinds. With the passage of time with the increase of population, many kinds of needs were felt when the people renunciated 'consumption' and took over the ideal of 'karma' or action. At this time 14 Kulkars or Manus were born. These Manus developed social order, conduct, tradition and tradition for that welfare of the family. Because of their contribution to the factors, these people came to be called 'Kulkars'. The Jain literature mentions a total of 14 Kulkars or Manus. Of them, Nabhiray was the last Kulkar. His son was Rishabh Dev. Rishabh Dev is considered to the first Pravartak or founder. The Jain religion developed from him. The Jain literature considers Lord Rishabh Dev as the Jin or Tirthankar. Jainism is a collection of precepts given by twenty-four such Tirthankaras. Lord Rishabh Dev is accepted as the first Tirthankar and Lord Mahavira as the last Tirthankar. Lord Mahavira was born in a village named Kundagram 600 BC. His father's name was Siddhartha and mother's name was Trishala. The region of Vaishaili is considered to be his birthplace. He could not bear with the killing or slaughter of the animals in yajna. He got disinterested in the worldly life and undertook hard penance *(tapasya)* for 12 years. It begot him *jnan* (realisation). Later, he preached religion for 30 years. He achieved final emancipation at the age of 72 years.

## Jain Literature

The followers of Lord Mahavira collected his various precepts. This collection took the form of an epic and is considered to be the chief literature of Jainism. This literature has been arranged in various parts, the two chief ones of which are - Digamma literature and Swetambara literature.

## Principles of Jain Philosophy

According to Jain philosophy, there are three chief elements of each matter-production, consumption and stability *(dhrovya).* These three elements or characteristics can be considered to be the three indicators of production, destruction and stability. The process of the production and destruction does never cease. On its basis, Jain philosophy considers that the world is changeable, though the unity of the world remains in the same manner; for example, a man grows from infancy to childhood, to adulthood to old age; however, the unity of man is retained during all these ages; despite changes he continues to be man.. Thus, the Jain religion believes that changeability retains its characteristic in the proximity of unchangeability.

According to Jainism, the world is without any beginning or end. It believes that no one created the world. The world is formed of two kinds of matter-live and not live it mentions of five kinds of non-live matter-Pudgal, *Dharma, Adharma, Akash* and *Kala.* These matters continue to remain without any change, they neither increase nor decrease. Jainism does not believe in the existence of God. God neither creates nor destroys, because the concept the God by itself is without basis.

## Jainism has no Faith in the Existence of God

Jainism has no belief in the existence of God. The teachers of Jainism consider the imagination of God as illogical. They contend that a proof is needed to prove the existence of anything, so a proof must be needed to prove the existence of God. If 'direct' is considered to be the proof, then it can be said against it that direct is perceived by the sense organs, while God is beyond the knowledge of sense organs. He cannot be seen. So, it is clear that we shall have to estimate or guess about the existence of God.

## Anekanta-Syadvada

Jain philosophy looks at a thing from different angles and perceives many forms in one thing. According to it, a true follower of Jainism is neither adamant on a thing nor quarrels with anyone on any point, nor does he stick to his viewpoint in logic. His viewpoint is liberal and generous. He believes that everything can be perceived from many angles. Because of this viewpoint, a true follower of Jainism is able to adopt equal-feeling under all circumstances. This viewpoint is called syadvada.

Some people think that the meaning of syadvada is 'perhaps', but it is not correct. The word 'perhaps' points to the uncertainty. Some people think that the meaning of this word is 'possibly', but again there is a feeling of uncertainty or doubt in it. In fact, syadvada does not point toward a doubt. It is an indicator of a true and definite principle. Syadvada indicates relativity. There is one or another expectation included in relativity. So, the Jain religion believes that a thing can be both true and untrue. A thing can be considered to be true from one's viewpoint; but the same thing can be considered to be untrue when considered without its form. No thing is either completely true or completely untrue. We look at a thing from different viewpoints of true and untrue out of some expectation. The two forms of true and untrue are included in everything. For example, an earthern pot is true in its form, but it can be considered to be untrue when broken. In the same way, everything is true in its form, and can be considered to be untrue against its form. True and untrue seem to be contrary terms. The synthesis of such contradictory facts under Jain philosophy is called Anekanta principle.

## Education and Anekanta Principle

Liberalism is included in Anekanta principle. If we analyse this principle further, we reach the conclusion that only one aspect or side of an argument or topic cannot hold true of its own. There can be two or more sides or aspects of a topic. To reach a definite and just conclusion, we shall need to look at a subject from more than one angles and look at their natural aspects. It is but natural to have contrary views in the prevailing democratic society. It is not necessary for all students to agree with the contention of a teacher or any other student. Everybody has his different opinion. So, there should be established synthesis of different opinions in the classroom in the light of different aspects. The students should feel satisfaction in the process of reaching a conclusion. Such an experience will bring about development of personality of the student and will enable him to adopt a liberal viewpoint. We should endeavour synthesis of different opinions in the modem education in the context of mutual and collective exchange of thoughts. It would be pertinent to say that it will be undemocratic to impose any one thought on all students which will hinder the development of their personality.

**Non-violence**

Non-violence is the chief conduct or behaviour philosophy of the followers of Jainism. Non-violence has been accorded a very high place in Jainism. It has been very minutely analysed in this religion. It prohibits the slaughter or violence against an animal or creature. Non-violence keeps happening in our bodies when we are engaged in various activities such as eating, sleeping, sitting, etc. According to Jainism, we should keep making efforts from saving ourselves from violence in all its forms. It prohibits both 'physical violence' and *'emotional violence'; that is, we should not indulge in physical violence* as well as make someone suffer with mental agony. It may be known that the Jains do not take dinner with the fear of violence. Many minute creatures can go into our body through nose with inhalation, and it is a kind of violence of the minute creatures. So, the staunch Jains cover the nostrils with a light cloth which filters the air going into the nose with inhalation, which they consider that obstructs the minute creatures from going in and thus save them. Jainism believes that all creatures can be saved by following non-violence and beget happiness.

**Educational Thoughts Included in Non-Violence**

Today the world is subject to various kinds of violent activities in all countries. A country wants to subjugate a part of another country. The citizens of a country are competing against one another which has given rise to terrorism. The women are susceptible to various kinds of violent activities when they are out of their houses, especially after their coming out of homes after sunset. The teachers and students of different schools and universities fail to show sympathetic conduct toward others of their own flock. All people are engaged in selfish activities. Even the members of one and same family are not immune from ill-wills against one another. It is clear that we have gone beyond the concept of non-violence and our duty of non-violence. The Jainism teaches us that we must not hurt anyone with our activity or speech. It would be a golden concept for the teachers to teach the ideals of non-violence to the students and carry out all activities accordingly. It would give birth to ideal citizens in our schools. If we succeed in our this aim, the whole society will turn out to be idealistic and we shall be able to lead a happy life.

### Penance and Good Conduct

The Jainism has given an exalted place to penance or tapasya. Excessive emphasis has been laid on both internal and external penance. No one can indulge in good conduct without self-control and non-violence and penance is possible with only good conduct. It is necessary to have love for all creatures. If someone happens to commit a crime, we should forgive him. We should not keep a feeling of enmity against anyone. It is irreligious to have the feelings of cheating, anger and proudness. We should speak the truth and should not steal. It is necessary to follow celibacy. It is not possible It to follow the true religion by depending on anyone else. If we take up a thing from somewhere, we should replace it in the same condition again. We should not spoil a place with our faeces, urine or spitting. We should order our mind, speech and body such that we may not commit a sin. We must respect a person greater than us from any viewpoint. We must try to help out the grieved people as far as possible. We must not show anger against the people with contradictory conduct, rather we must remain neutral or indifferent to them. The Jain religion considers the three chief ratna-(1) *Samyak darshana* (true philosophy having love in true principles), (2) *Samyak jnan* (complete knowledge), and 3. *Samyak charitra* (complete good character).

### Educational Thoughts Included in Penance and Good Conduct

The thoughts of penance and good conduct as propounded by the Jain religion point toward the fundamental ideals of education. We desire that education should make a person with good conduct in all respects and methods. Self-control and non-violence are the chief thoughts of Jain religion. If a person becomes self-controlled and nonviolent by the medium of education, all disorderliness of the society will be eradicated and all people will have love for one another. This thinking will result in the feeling in every person that we should not commit any sin or crime. It will help fulfill our educational ideals and the people will move toward the complete development of his personality. It would make people endeavour, to make others happy and it would eradicate the griefs of the poor and suffering, thus making them happy. The ideals of complete truth, complete knowledge and complete character will produce the true teacher, true God and true scriptures and love for them. The true knowledge is the complete knowledge and good conduct, is the complete character. Devotion or complete truth and complete knowledge is dependent on good character. Complete truth and complete knowledge cannot be realized without good character.

Jainism lays special emphasis on penance. Hard work is necessary for solution of a problem or attainment of an objective. The students in the modern schools do not want to undertake hard work, rather they want to pass by hook or by crook. Due to this tendency, they do not go into deep study of a subject and acquire only superficial knowledge. It has resulted in the falling standard of education with every passing day. If the ideal of penance of the Jain teachers is placed before them, the students can come to believe that such a hard work or penance is necessary for success and attainment of ideals in life. Good conduct should be the basis of penance. Good conduct emphasises on five points which are-ahimsa (non-violence), satya (truth), *asteya* (non-stealing), *brahmacharya* (celibacy), and *aparigraha* (lack of hoarding things). We can propagate an education based on these high ideals as propounded by the Jain religion. Its execution into practice will enable eradication of many ills of society which includes violence, telling a lie, stealing or grabbing others' rights, violation of celibacy, hoarding of money, etc. If we succeed in injecting the feelings of these high ideals, we can inculcate the feelings of hatred toward the ill-feelings and make the society devoid of any of these evils. It will make the earth as lovely as the paradise.

The Jain religion emphasises on sweet and just speech, and bars the feelings of anger, proud and cheating. It teaches us to have the feelings of friendliness or ownness with all creatures and respect for all elders. It also teaches to help the poor and grieving, staying neutral against a person of contradictory nature, etc. It lays emphasis on complete philosophy, complete knowledge and complete character. Complete philosophy points to the true knowledge and true principle. Complete knowledge means the true knowledge of a thing. Complete character indicates good character. All these factors remain character and one cannot remain in isolation of others. The attainment of these aspects can enlighten the path to salvation. Thus, we can see the educational thoughts as included in the above precepts.

## Karma Principle in Jain Philosophy

Indian philosophy has analysed the 'bounds of life' or `salvation' in different *ways*. However in Jain philosophy, the relation or binding between the soul and body has been considered to be a bond. Jain philosophy considers the creature as conscious. The creature is composed of infinite knowledge, infinite philosophy, infinite virility and infinite bliss. These powers of the creature are lost due to ignorance of karma. If the creature is able to gain knowledge, he would regain these powers. The creature is emancipated or gains salvation on gaining these powers. When he is emancipated, he regains his infinite knowledge, philosophy, happiness and virility and his form is illuminated. Now the question arises how the 'living' is joined with the 'non-living'? according to Jain philosophy, this bond is due to karma. When the creature establishes its relationship with karma, their real form is changed and affects one another. We perform various actions due to love and enmity. Whatever is the mental, speech or physical activity of the creature, it blends in a liquid creature or 'living'. As a result of which the creature is bound in it. Now a natural question arises - Why has the creature relation with karma? The Jain philosophers have opined that the relationship between the creature. And action is infinite and endless. Doing action produces love and animosity and actions continue due to love and animosity. New births are taken due to karma. New births beget body. The body begets sense organs and sense organs produce desire. This kind of awakening continues to produce different kinds of loves and animosities. Thus, the *sansar-chakra* (wheel of the world).goes on and the feelings of the creatures continue to produce actions which in turn produce love and animosity. The *pudgal is* attracted toward the creature due to actions. In other words, action is the cause of the blending of creature and *pudgal*. When each action of the creature is because of the result of love and animosity, he continues to be stuck by the bounds of karma or action.

According to Jain philosophy, karma signifies action-atom or *karma-parimanu.* Action atoms draw the creature toward *pudgals. A* creature is attracted toward *pudgal* due to love, enmity, affection, desire, proud, etc. These have been termed as passions. These passions are the chief cause of bounds. Jain philosophy mentions the bounds of the creature in four parts. These are-natural bounds, place bounds, situational bounds, and love bounds. The nature or conduct formed as a result of several action atoms is natural bound. The definiteness of action *pudgals* is the country or place bound. The time prescribed of the actions with the creature are the situational bound. And the results or fruits got by action *pudgals* are considered the love bound. It is clear that all these bounds are the result of action, so action is considered to be the cause of bounds.

Jain religion considers that whatever a creature gets is the result of his action. The colour, shape, form, age, sense organs, etc. are the result of our actions. Analysis and elaboration of action is a specific part of Jain philosophy. According to Jain philosophy, God is not the maker of luck or fortune. In fact, Jain philosophy does not believe in the existence of God. Whatever a creature gets in his life is the result of his actions, and not due to the gift of God. Man by himself gets the fruit of his actions. He is the maker of his own good or bad. We must not take it as the control of an invisible person or power. Jain philosophy classifies action into two *kinds-ghati karma* and *aghati karma.* The *ghati karma includes jnanavarana, darshanavarana, mohaniya* and *antaraya* karmas. Age, caste, name and *vedaniya karmas* are counted in the *aghati* class. Thus, there is a mention of a total of eight karmas in Jain philosophy

*1. Jnanavarana karma,* or the actions which cover knowledge. Such actions cause more or less knowledge of a person.

*2. Darshanavarana karma,* or the actions which cover philosophy. Such actions cause hindrance in knowing the truth.

*3. Mohaniya* karma, or the actions which attract a person.

4. *Antaya karma,* or the actions which do not beget the desirable results.

5. *Vedaniya*-karma, or the actions which beget happiness or grief.

6. Age karma, or the ations which determine the period of life of the creature.

7. *Nama karma,* or the actions which beget good or bad physique to the creature.

8. *Gotra karma,* or the actions due to which a person takes birth in a high or low caste family.

All the above karmas are included in the natural bounds and on the basis of these action-atoms, the nature of a man is determined.

**Educational Thoughts Included in Karma Principle of Jain Philosophy**

The above discussion clarifies that Jain philosophy gives prominence to action in a person's life. Even **Tulsidas**, a great poet, has said that a person gets the result according to the actions he performs. This principle teaches us that. a person should be action-oriented; that is, he should continue to do good actions in a planned way for his progress and emancipation. It is- cowardly to rely on luck or fortune. The poverty in India is the result of our inaction. Many people sit idle and cursa their fate. In all the countries of the world, education is being formulated as vocational. If our education too is made vocational or professional, our poverty will be eradicated. Many of our young people continue to study in the universities and colleges just for passing a few more years without indulging in fruitful activities in their lives. Such education can get them nothing but unemployment. They become inactive and education fails in its task of making them action-oriented. The need of the hour is how to relate education with the realties of life so that the students become active in the practical life, and not sit idle cursing their fate. It is a matter of pleasure that now employment-oriented education is being given prominence in our country. If this awakening is properly executed in ou- country, most of our young people will become active and hard working and will contribute greatly in the prosperity and progress of the country. It will not be out of place to say that the action principle of Jain philosophy is a great ideal which needs to be put into practice.

## Imagination of Salvation in Jain Philosophy

According to Jain philosophy, the breaking away of the relationship of soul and body is salvation, that is, the non-relation between 'living' *(pudgal)* and 'non-living' (body). If a person gets rid of such actions, he gains salvation. How is the relationship between creature and *pudgal* broken away? It takes two things-one, that the new *pudgals* are not given refuge, and second, the old *pudgals* are destroyed. These two processes have been termed as *sanvara* and *nirjara.* Sanvara means 'stopping them'. It means that the paths by which the actions are exited, should be hindered. The meaning of *sanvara* is to safeguard. It is *sanvata* to hinder actions by mind, speech and action. If a person succeeds in these mental and physical activities, his *sanvara* becomes possible. If he succeeds in it, new *pudgals* will not be bom in him. It will also eradicate the old *pudgals* in him. *Nirjara* is of two kinds-avipak and savipak. If a person finishes the result of his actions on the basis of his penance, it is called *avipak.* And the eradication of the result of actions is called savipak *nirjara.* Thus, according to Jain philosophy, sanvara and *nirjara* eradicate the result of all actions which beget salvation. On attaining salvation, the relationship between the living and non-living is broken completely and the creature is established in the emancipated world. On breaking away of this relationship, he experiences infinite power, infinite knowledge and infinite virility. Thus being established in the emancipated world is called the attainment of *'siddha shila'.*

According to Jain philosophy, the attainment of the supreme bliss is acquired in the state of salvation and the creature gets rid of all kinds of griefs. After this, the emancipated soul becomes fully aware of complete knowledge. This condition of complete knowledge is full of infinite knowledge.

### Means of Salvation

According to Jain philosophy, five means are considered necessary for attainment of salvation. These are:

1. Non-violence, that is, not doing anything violent by mind, speech or action against anyone else.
2. Renunciation of untruth, that is, not telling a lie.
3. Not stealing others' property.
4. Celibacy, or the renunciation of desires.
5. Not hoarding money and other worldly things.

### Educational Thoughts Included in Jain Philosophy Pertaining to Salvation

It is not difficult to understand the educational thoughts contained in the above salvation-related thoughts. In fact, it can be said that the supreme goal of attaining education is salvation. In this sense, `salvation' and 'education' become synonymous. Salvation does not desire for the worldly things and attainment of infinite knowledge, infinite power and virility.

If we are not interested in worldly things, many of our useless or meaningless desires will be eradicated. Then we shall proceed toward a situation of 'siddhi'. Due to this, all our actions will be guided for the welfare of others. If it so happens, this earth will turn into a paradise for all creatures. The five means of non-violence, renunciation of lies, not-stealing, celibacy and not-hoarding have been propounded and can be considered the chief means for attainment of salvation or emancipation from this world.

# UNIT-2

## LEARNING OBJECTIVE

**Western Philosophies: Major Schools:-**

**Naturalism**
**Idealism**
**Pragmatism**
**Realism**
**Logical**
**Positivism**
**Existentialism**
**Marxism**

**Their educational Implications with special reference to epistemology, axiology and the process of education.**

# THE SCHOOLS OF PHILOSOPHY

Having explored the relation of education to the different philosophic categories, let us now focus attention on the major schools of philosophy as they affect education.

Philosophers themselves disagree as to how many philosophic schools there are and of what they consist. For present purposes we may distinguish three: *idealism, realism,* and *pragmatism.* This division, however, though convenient, is certainly not complete, and in Chapter 3 we shall examine some newer philosophies: *existentialism,* which has yet to establish itself in this country, and *philosophic analysis. All* these terms represent broad classifications, each embracing a variety of philosophic attitudes.

It is not enough to locate a philosopher in a particular school, however; he must also be studied as an individual. The great eighteenth-century French philosopher and man of letters, Jean-Jacques Rousseau, was not simply a "romantic naturalist"; he was a unique and fascinating thinker in his own right. Some philosophers have been classified in more than one school. Locke and Kant, for instance, were "idealists" in some respects and "realists" in others. More confusing still, it is by no means easy these days to find an existentialist who admits that he is one!

We can understand a philosophic school only if we know the contributions that it has made to the different categories of philosophy discussed in Chapter 1. We must, therefore, consider "idealist metaphysics," "realist epistemology," "pragmatic axiology," and so on. In order to attain a clear grasp of what follows, it might help to construct a chart in which the key ideas of the different philosophies may be entered as they are met.

# Naturalism and Education

## What is Naturalism

| | Meta-physics | Human Nature | Epistemology | Values | Education |
|---|---|---|---|---|---|
| Naturalism | | | | | |
| Idealsism | | | | | |
| Realism | | | | | |
| Pragrmatism | | | | | |

Naturalism considers that matter is the basis of the world. It considers even the mind as a form of matter, that is, it is an element of matter and they are closely related. Naturalism as a philosophy considers that nature is everything, there is nothing beyond it. So, man should endeavour to discover nature which can be done with the help of science. The naturalists believe that the present civilization and social development has taken man away from nature. If he comes back in the proximity of nature, it will make possible his natural or spontaneous development. Naturalism emphasises on causal relationship with power, dynamism and natural laws. Thus, naturalists believe in the ultimate power of nature. They do not have faith in the rule of God or spirituality, immortality of the soul and freedom of desire. Ward has written in this connection : "Naturalism is a doctrine which separates nature from God, subordinates spirit to matter and sets up unchangeable laws as supreme." Thus, naturalism believes as the subordination of mind to matter, and has faith in physical world as against the spiritual one.

Naturalism came to be considered from the beginning of the world. The natural things and matter have given man an inspiration to think about it in various manifestations. So different scholars and thinkers considered water, air, fire, earth, etc as the fundamental elements of nature. Later, the four fundamental elements considered necessary for existence were air, fire, earth and water, and some of them included the fifth element as sky or ether. The Indian philosophers have included these elements in their study. Thus, we can find a glimpse of naturalism in both western and Indian philosophies.

Though naturalism can be said -to exist from ancient times, yet we can attribute its development to the revolution caused during the eighteenth century in the modern education.

This was the time when freedom of man was not given an important place in the governance system. The higher classes exploited the lower classes, so did the strong to the poor or weak. However, the progress of science brought an awakening in the mind of the downtrodden and they came to think that their freedom could be got by nature. This thinking came about in the form of renaissance in the earlier thirteenth and fourteenth centuries, which was later followed by various movements regarding social reforms, realism, Puritanism, etc. All these movements concentrated on the eradication of absolutism and formalism from the social and religious life. This movement reached its peak in the eighteenth century, especially in France where Voltaire and Rousseau contributed much to this thinking. Of course, it resulted in mass exploitation and violence, but the wave of awakening started by these two thinkers aroused the French people. The people were fascinated when Rousseau informed that there was no inequality in nature and it was without any bounds. He also exhorted that man could get emancipation from his bounds and pathetic condition only if the social order was based on the principles of equality, freedom and brotherhood. Thus, we can see that the thoughts of Rousseau awakened the people and brought about the philosophy of naturalism into being.

## Definitions of Naturalism

The following definitions will go a long way in clarifying the concept of naturalism

"Naturalism is not science but an assertion about science. More specifically it is the assertion that scientific knowledge is final, leaving no room for extra-scientific or philosophical knowledge."

**R.B.** ***Perry***

"Naturalism ... is a term loosely applied in educational theory to systems of training that are not dependent on schools and books but on the manipulation of the actual life of the educated." -

**J.S. Ross**

"Naturalism is a system whose silent characteristic is the exclusion of whatever is spiritual or indeed whatever is transcendental experience from our philosophy of nature and man."-***Joyce***

## Classes or Forms of Naturalism

There are four classes or forms of naturalism-atomism, scientific naturalism, mechanical naturalism, and historical naturalism. Among them, atomism was the initial naturalism and historical naturalism has no philosophical significance. So, there remain only branches of naturalism-scientific naturalism and mechanical naturalism. Scientific naturalism is divided into two branches-naturalism based on physical sciences and naturalism based on biology. Thus, there are three important branches of naturalism-(1) Naturalism based on physical sciences, (2) Naturalism based on biology, and (3) Mechanical naturalism. We shall study these three classes or forms in some detail.

**1. Naturalism based on Physical Sciences**

Naturalism depends a great deal on physical sciences. So it is also called physical naturalism. Physical science accepts both nature and atom. According to it, nature is what really exists physically, can be experienced by sense organs and can be gained as a subject. Physical science does not accept what cannot be experimented and tested. There is much difference of opinion in the old and new form of atom. According to old thinking, atom was indivisible, solid with shape, quantity and activity. According to modern thinking, .atom is divisible which is divided into electron and proton. Electron goes round proton. The physical scientists consider atom as energy, which move in the form of waves. These waves create the world. Atom is not found in nature in an independent form.

According to naturalism, there is not difference between matter and conscious. These are merely two conditions of nature. There is a specific order of incidences and speed. According to natural laws, consciousness is contained in consciousness, and it is not found in matter. Life can sprout out of matter any time all of a sudden. John *Stuart Mill lays emphasis on causal relationship of physical naturalism. He says that nothing occurs without a cause. There is a* certain order for every action or incidence, which occur one after the other. He does not consider the existence of natural matter as the cause, but he considers some incidence or activity as the cause. The wave of energy is the cause of incidence or activity. Energy does not reduce or increase, it is constant. Only its form is changed. Incidences or activities take place in the order of this change in the form of energy.

## Physical Naturalism and Education

Naturalism considers that matter and conscious are two things, both of which are situated at two different levels. Life has sprung from matter, and consciousness from conscious. Naturalism considers matter as the basis of energy. Energy is such a fundamental element, which is not developed. This branch does not give any significance to consciousness. Thus, this possibility is reduced from educational viewpoint. Both life and consciousness are the gift of nature. These are temporary and sudden. So the aim of education is to develop life and consciousness develops mind. This branch has no utility for education.

## 2. Naturalism Based on Biology

This branch of naturalism is the gift of progressivism of Darwin. The history of western philosophy tells that one or the other science has always had an influence over philosophy. Philosophy in the seventeenth century was under the influence of mathematics. It was the time when great philosophers and mathematicians did their work such as Libiniz, Spinza and Descartes. In the eighteenth century, psychology had influence over western philosophy and experientialism viewpoint came into being. At this time the philosophers such as Hume, Berkeley and Locke etc., prevailed. In the nineteenth century, progressivism of Herbart Spencer and Darwin influenced western philosophy.

The influence of biology over western philosophy was seen due to **Charles Darwin. Charles'** father, **Irasmus Darwin** wrote two books on the development of creatures and affection of plants. These books illustrated similar things to progressivism. Before **Charles Darwin,** the name of **Lamarke** too is worth mentioning. **Lamarke** established deep relationship between environment and creature. He said that the cause of diversity in the environment was due to the diversity of creatures. **Lamarke** said that due to natural environment, the creature uses his/Its parts for maintaining its existence. The parts which are not used disappear, and the parts which are used for excessive work become strong and sturdy. This form is handed down to the progeny by the medium of hereditary.

According to the progressivism theory of Darwin, the creatures will be able to develop more only when they are capable. They are engaged in a struggle to maintain their existence. This struggle is collective. The capable and able creatures live on, while the weak ones are destroyed. He also says in relation to the change of behaviour, use and disuse of the parts of the creatures that sudden change in the environment also brings about a change in the behaviour of the creatures. The same is true of the limbs. The limbs which are used become strong and developed, while the limbs in disuse become weak and get destroyed. **Darwin** imagines of two qualities-acquired and hereditary. According to him, along side the hereditary qualities; the acquired traits too are transmitted to the next generation. From the viewpoint of sexual attraction, **Darwin** says that the males or females are attractive in their own right. The selection of different colours for wings, neck, homes etc. are the result of sexual selection. This imagination of **Darwin** seems to be true even though it is not. In naturalism, even creatures have been included in the category of non-living. With this view, how can we imagine of sexual consciousness or consciousness toward the environment? **Darwin** gives more significance to chance factor in his principle. Both these points have been chief points of criticism of his principles.

## Biological Naturalism and Education

The naturalism based on biology is the modern naturalism. Darwin was a scientist so he paid more attention to the past, than the future. So he considers man an animal by nature. He gives significance to natural feelings and powers of man. It has reduced the possibilities of human development. Due to the influence of science and psychology, progressivism of Darwin could not gain much importance and extensiveness. Science is centred round the past, it does not look into the future. Psychology considers the original or essential behaviour of man as important; it does not pay attention to acquired nature and remains indifferent to the possibilities of the future.

The endeavour of education is to bring about all-round development of man. The possibilities of development under naturalism are certainly less, so much benefit could not be accrued in education. Still, we should make education as child-centred to find out his fundamental nature, ability, interest and need and should conduct education in that direction.

### 3. Mechanical Naturalism

Mechanical naturalism considers the whole universe, including the conscious beings as mechanical. It has found support from **Herbart Spencer** and **Laplas.** They have said that the creation of the world was the result of dust from the sky, which we call nebula. According to it, the atmosphere was filled with dust and water particles. These particles got separated from the center due to the activity or speed of the solar system and began to form new axis round which they rotated now. Due to decreased temperature, these particles solidified and began to go round the sun as the basic center. This development was purposeless and mechanical. Thus the creation of the universe was the result of particles, speed and energy without any purpose which occurred accidentally. Naturalism wants to find out those universal laws which determine the creation of the world. The idealists study the future circumstances while the scientists study the past circumstances to study the relevant laws. The supporter of naturalism, **Herbart Spencer** wants to follow the scientific methods to discover the mystery.

Some of the concepts in naturalism are self-contradictory; such as it accepts the existence of speed or activity, but does not accept its purpose or aim. If we accept this concept in this form itself, we can conclude that these activities and systems have been continuing from the beginning. Naturalists consider the body as a machine which is subject to change according to nature. However, the body is not a machine, but is a conscious creature which has prudence. Baby is born from a body; it is an automatic machine and develops in a natural way. There is no independent significance of the limbs of the body. These cannot be used for any other body. The body arranges and reforms the limbs of the body by itself. This thing is not applicable to a machine. Machine depends on others and cannot improve upon itself, nor can it maintain its form. So, it is erroneous to consider man as machine.

## Mechanical Naturalism and Education

Education is a process with specific aim. Means are arranged with the aim in view and suitable programmes are made. There is no place of purpose or aim in mechanical naturalism. It considers the body and world as mechanical, so it has no utility in education.

**Ross** considers mechanical naturalism as more useful to education than physical naturalism. Due to physical science, naturalism considers the world as non-living and mechanical naturalism considers it a machine which has coordination, relationship and system among parts or limbs. A machine is an organisational system. It has some reality. Mechanical naturalism gave rise to psychological behaviourism. It has always been influenced by mechanical naturalism.

## Principles of Naturalism

The chief principles of naturalism are as follows

1. Life comes into being from lifeless matter and it is a collection of physicai and chemical influences.

2. The world is a large machine. Man too is a part of this machine, while being complete in his own right.

3. Reality is only external nature. Everything is born from nature and gets assimilated into it. The external laws of nature do not change.

4. Reality can be truly analysed by natural sciences.

5. All powers of man are limited according to his nature. He is nothing but a collection of his hereditary powers and instincts.

6. Man is the highest creature or animal according to his nature. So, the essence of his life is animal instinct, and not spirituality.

7. The present life is the real life. There is no other life or world beyond it. So, man should make the present life happy and peaceful.

8. The unchangeable natural laws clarify all incidents of the world.

9. The credit for bringing about revolutionary changes in the physical conditions of the worldly life goes to scientific discoveries and inventions of machines. It is absolutely necessary to gain the knowledge of natural sciences.

10. Thoughts depend on natural environment. They are born when stimulation is felt in a nerve, vein or muscle.

11. The final existence is that of physical elements. God, soul, mind, desire for the other worldly pleasures, moral instincts, prayer, superhuman activities and phenomena -all are illusion.

## Characteristics of Naturalistic. Education

Naturalistic education might be partial and not capable of developing all-round personality of man, however, it has excessively influenced western education. **Rousseau's** compilation in *Emile* and *Education* of **Spencer** have contributed significantly to the expansion of naturalistic education. The famous naturalists before sixteenth century were **Demacrites, Lusius, Thales, Apicurus, Lukaritius,** etc. Between sixteenth and eighteenth centuries, **Rousseau** and **Hobbes** were famous. The naturalistic philosopher of this era was also Bacon. Naturalistic education has the following characteristics

**1. Follow Nature :** The fundamental principle of naturalistic education is to follow nature and naturalistic teaching methods. According to it, if a child is taught to become civilised and cultured in ways other than natural, his personality will not remain spontaneous and it will disintegrate. The child will lose nutrients for want of taste, he will be deprived of natural sun, air and light by living in artificial air and light and ultimately become sick which will need costly treatment. This treatment will destroy natural health of the child and his natural development will get impeded. It is -the reason that Rousseau emphasises on nature in his compilation by the name of *Emile*. The child should be educated in the natural environment, by the medium of nature, using-natural terminology and words, using simplest of methods and means. The child should be given maximum opportunity of being in the proximity of nature in which he can read, write, play, sleep and eat. He should be given access to natural food with adequate amount of nutrients and vitamins, natural air, rain and water. Only then he will remain healthy and will evolve a habit of forbearing the environment. Nature by herself is a good teacher. So the educational system in the schools should be in the lap of nature, away from artificiality.

**2. Freedom to Child:** Rousseau considers the big cities and towns as cremation grounds, because they lack natural facilities of air, water, light, food and living. It makes the people living there unhealthy. Their life is depressed and under control. The environment there is not free and independent. The teachers, preachers and social leaders teach and educate in such an artificial atmosphere. Man is, born independent according to natural circumstances and he should be given an opportunity to lead a free life. Rousseau felt sad that man is carrying the burden of dependence and slavery away from the life of nature. He said : "God makes all things good. Man meddles with them and they become evil." A child's personality can develop in a natural environment. For him to be able to develop an independent personality, he should get natural environment where he can develop with the help of free expression and activities and thus tread the path of natural development. If he is given guidance and opportunity to find out his way independently, he will certainly have better life. Thus, Rousseau desires the child to lead a life in the lap of nature with adequate freedom.

**3.Prohibitive Education : Rousseau** was not in favour of artificial environment and education. He said that education should be against the modern education which makes the child evil because it teaches to admire evils and despicable acts. So, we must remain away from such an education. According to Rousseau, the elementary education of the child should be completely prohibitive. Attempts should be made to keep him away from bad qualities; social traditions should not be imposed upon him. The society itself is evil, then what else can it teach to the child? What is termed as civilisation and culture is in fact backwardness. The child is susceptible to loss instead of any gain. So, the child should be given prohibitive education in place of traditional education in vogue.

**4. No Book Knowledge:** According to naturalistic-philosophy, book(ish) knowledge is artificial, imaginative and useless. It is burdensome, difficult and practical, so it is meaningless. Naturalistic philosophy considers that the knowledge of the physical objects contained in the books is dependent on words and indications which is not useful. The child should be given freedom that they come in direct contact with physical objects, study their attributes and name the things on the basis of the qualities. This will become a realistic, active and natural education. Adman and Rousseau consider such an education as useful and encourage Teaming by doing.

**5. Progressiveness:** The naturalists think that the mental development of the child should take place in synchronization with physical development. Rousseau is the symbol of progressivism. He divides the life into four parts from educational, viewpoint-infancy, childhood, adolescence and youth. He wants ordered and progressive education, in all the four parts. He does not consider it fit to burden the child with the load of books. He wants to restrict the burden of curriculum according to the age, intellect, interest and emotions of the child, and that curriculum should be increased with the passage of time with the development of the child in age, intellect, interests and ability. He contends that only then the child will be able to gain permanent, useful and meaningful education. **Rousseau** divides education into three classes from the; purpose of viewpoint of progressive education-teaching of man, teaching of behaviour and teaching of the whole. The teaching of the whole implies giving adequate opportunities to the child for development of his sense organs and natural instincts equally for the complete and balanced development of his body, mind, intellect and soul.

**6. Emphasis on Sense Organs :** The naturalistic education lays emphasis on the training of sense organs. The naturalists are against the viewpoint of forcing knowledge into the child. They think it necessary to train the sense organs for them to assimilate knowledge effectively, for it considers sense organs as the entry points of knowledge.

Laying emphasis on the training of sense organs, Rousseau has written : "Education should prepare the way for reason by the proper exercise of senses.'

**7. Child-Centred Education:** According to naturalistic viewpoint, education should be made child-centred, that is, undeveloped, immature, natural, spontaneous, hereditary qualities of the child should be found out and education should be accordingly systematised. The term of 'child-centred education' was used by **John Adman** for the first time. It was taken as the fundamental basis of natüralistic education. According to this thinking, everything in the field of education aims of education, curriculum, classification, discipline, teaching, teaching system - should be according to the needs of the child. Earlier, education was not imparted by taking the child at the core. Now education is arranged keeping in view the child's present condition, ability, need and qualities. It is no more considered good for the teacher to impose anything on the students.

The above discussion reveals the educational characteristics of naturalistic education. It tells that naturalistic education is child centred, progressive and useful which encourages spontaneous, natural, practical education in place of bookish knowledge. It also supports prohibitive and progressive education. Due to the demand of this education for gaining knowledge by sense organs, various scientific methods have been included in the field of education and due to child-centredness psychology too has found a place in it. The various kinds of vidya mandirs, shishu shiksha niketans, nursery schools, Montessori schools and kindergarten schools have sprung up everywhere with this education in their fold.

## Aims of Naturalistic Education

The philosophers have demanded various aims of education from naturalistic viewpoint. They are not uniform in their views. **Darwin** considered to make' the child ready for the future struggle in life, and it was his primary aim of. education. On the other hand, **McDougal** considered amendment of instincts of a child. So diverse views were expressed by different philosophers. We shall sum up the chief ones here

**1. Present and Future Bliss** :Various schools of thought in naturalism have different views. According to biological naturalists, the aim of human life is to attain present and future happiness, so they consider it to be the aim of education as well which should help man in realisation of this aim. However, **McDougal** is not in favour of this aim as he considers that happiness or sadness are the result of natural processes. So he emphasised that amendment of instincts and change toward proper direction and their synthesis should be the aim of education.

**2 Natural development: Rousseau** was of the view that to make the child healthy and energetic., we should keep in view his natural instincts, physical ability and individual differences. According to him, the sole aim of education is to develop the child according to his nature.

**3. Preparation for Struggle for Existence :** Darwin believed *in the principle of struggle and survival of the fittest. According to this* principle, the development of man has started from the lowest levels and he has to continuously struggle with environment for existence. The fittest wins the battle and the weak is eliminated. So, he considered that the aim of education should be to develop those abilities in the child, which will make him capable of taking on the struggle in life.

**4. Perfection of Human Machine :** According to mechanical naturalism, the whole world is like a great machine. Man is a part of this machine and is also complete by himself. So the primary aim of education should be to develop such behaviour, which will help him work like a good and effective machine. **J.S. Ross** has written in this *regard : "Education should make the human machine as good a* machine as possible by attending to its constitution, by elaborating it and making it capable of more and more complicated tasks." Of course, this view has not found favour from other great philosophers.

**5. Adjustment with Environment :** It is considered that the development of life has started from the lower levels and man is able to improve upon himself, his physical constitution and habits according to the circumstances. According to-neo-Lamarchians, education is such a process, which helps man to adjust with the circumstances and environment around him.

**6. Natural Development :** Rousseau has clearly said that we should develop the natural instincts independently of the child for making him healthy and powerful keeping in view his limitations, physical capacity and individual differences. They think that the sole aim of education is to help the child develop according to nature.

**7. Unhindered Development of Personality :** T.P. Nunn was .of the view that the aim of education should be scientific and natural which should aim at development of personality in an unhindered way.

## Naturalism and Education

The word 'nature' implies two senses: child's nature and physical nature. Physical nature can be considered to be the external nature while the child's nature is the internal nature which is signified by instincts, emotions, abilities and; capacities with which a child takes birth. Naturalism is of the view that the external laws of nature should be made use of development of child's internal nature.

Naturalism in education implies such an education which enables the child to develop himself in a natural way. Though the credit for starting the naturalistic movement in education goes to **Bacon** and **Comenius**, but it reached its logical peak with the guidance of Rousseau. Various other philosophers are also considered naturalists, among which the names of **Herbart Spencer, Basedaw** and **Campe**, etc. are important.

Stagnation came into education when excessive emphasis on book(ish)knowledge and language came to be applied, thus hindering the natural development of the child. As a result, educational naturalism came into being in the form of a teaching method which was not dependent on books and schools. It aimed at providing a suitable and adequate base to the child's life. Comenius was against the use of any such means which was used for Torcing knowledge into the child's mind. He said the following nature in imparting education was the best means. Rousseau went a step further and termed this world as fully artificial and laid emphasis on breaking away all the bounds to give importance to natural instincts and desires so that he is able to freely express himself and develop fully.

In his compilation, *Emile,* **Rousseau** considered nature as the best teacher and declared it as the natural process. He said that education was internal development and not a thing to be forced into the child's mind. He was of the view that education was the development of instincts and not attainment of external knowledge. He supported imparting education in a natural environment keeping in view the child's interests, instincts, abilities, aptitudes, abilities and capacities. He considered education as absolutely necessary and said that the all related factors should be developed first before imparting education: according to him, the true education consisted of development of sense organs, private abilities and instincts. The aim of education, according to **Rousseau,** was not restricted to preparing the child for adulthood, but the complete development of man and his personality, which was possible only on learning by doing. **Herbart Spencer** too was of the view that the aim of human life was self-preservation which can be attained by emphasis on natural education. Thus, we can say that naturalistic education is a revolution in its own right against the prevailing and traditional education which hinder the independent and natural development of the child.

## Naturalism and Curriculum

Naturalistic education does not give significance to education by subjects. The naturalists want to make curriculum as composed of. only direct natural knowledge and natural activities, which should have the following characteristics

1. It is against the curriculum based on subjects and attaches importance to natural abilities and coordinated development of the child.

2.It favours to make education practical and useful for life, and accordingly does not attach any significance to those subjects: which have no relation with human life. It wants to include only those subjects which concern human life.

3. It gives place for skills and other useful educational activities. It considers literary subjects as useless and gives no place in the curriculum.

According to **Rousseau,** the curriculum should be constructed according to the physical and mental development needs of the child and his interests. The mental condition of the child is instable in the beginning, so he should be saved from book knowledge and moral education. He should be given opportunity for physical activities and other activities concerned with natural development. The teacher should act as a guide; he should only guide and see that the child is making progress toward desirable natural direction. According to **Rousseau,** curriculum should be constructed according to the age of the child. Education in childhood should include the education of physical development; education in childhood should include the education of development of sense organs; education in adolescence should include limited subjects and moral education. **Spencer** considers the education related with life as useful. According to him, the activities included in the curriculum should be of five kinds:

1. Physical cducation for direct self-preservation, healthy education, physics and chemistry, etc.
2. Educational activities for other science subjects for indirect self preservation.
3. Education of home science, health science, child psychology, etc. for nutrition.
4. Education of history, economics, civics, sociology, etc. for the development of citizenship.
5. Activities related with leisure time.

We can see that he accorded a secondary importance to literary and other artistic subjects, while gave prominence to physical sciences, health science, mathematics, chemistry, biology and home science, and other science subjects.

## Naturalism and Teaching Methods

Naturalistic education is a child-centred educational system, so it is also called child-centred teaching method. This method is chiefly activity- and emotion-based. According to **Rousseau,** the child should be taught with the ,help of activities so that his emotional, interest and activity development can be effected. This thinking considers direct knowledge and useful knowledge as important. This knowledge is gained naturally. It is gained by sense organs and is direct. The child is inspired by nature to gain useful knowledge. Free environment is needed for the spontaneous development of the children, which purify instincts.

According to naturalism, teaching should be psychological, so the principles of child psychology are used in it. Such opportunities should be made available to the child in which he is able to perform natural activities and progress independently. The teacher should act as a guide and keep an eye over the child's progress while making natural environment available to him. He should not interfere in his activities. Book(ish) knowledge should not be imposed on the child because it hinders natural development. Teaching should fully attend to child's ability, capacity, activity, interest, etc.

The chief characteristics, as we have delineated earlier, are emphasis on activity instead of knowledge, natural activity in the lap of natural environment, direct gaining of knowledge by sense organs, making the present more important than the future, activity-based education for fulfilling the present needs, etc. However, such education can also not be imparted in the absence of teachers. Naturalistic education is not in favour of imparting collective teaching, so it recommends to restrict the number of students to the minimum.

## Naturalistic Education and Child

The chief emphasis of naturalistic education is on the child. According to **Rousseau,** a child is gentle, without any evil and innocent. He has no concern with any class, community or tradition at this time. An adult person is opposite to the child's nature because he has grown among social vices. As a child comes into the contact of adult people, his innocence is eliminated and his natural form is eclipsed. The child learns evils, uncivility and untruth from the adults. So **Rousseau** desires that the child should be kept in a natural environment separate from society. Only then, he can be saved from social evils.

The statement of **Rousseau** seems to be true from this viewpoint that a child learns all vices from society and he is susceptible to the traditions, goodnesses and evilnesses from society. He is helpless but to take over and learn all evils which make his personality narrow and complex. Our educational system includes our social traditions and policies, and no educated child remains aloof from them. Society is the future reality of a child's life and it fails to pay attention to the present. Natural education should be such which keeps the child away from the vices of society while continuing to develop his instincts and hereditary qualities without any hindrance. The system which is according to the conduct, nature, need, ability imparted in a natural environment will prove to be the best for the child. Naturalism also wants to make education more useful and meaningful with the use of child psychology and educational psychology.

## Naturalism and Teacher

Naturalistic education considers the teacher as unrelated or unnecessary to the educational process. He has no place in the educational system He is expected to be present before the child but without doing any kind of hindrance or disturbance to the child's activities. Some of the naturalists have gone to the extent of saying that the teacher is not required even as a guide. The teacher should remain mute in the classroom and should speak the least possible. He must interfere in the educational process of the child to the minimum.

Naturalistic education gives secondary place to the teacher. He is like a gardener who prepares the ground for the development of the plant, but does not hinder in its development. He does neither help it nor touch it. The naturalists say that the teacher should be like such a gardener who should prepare background and environment for the child's development, but without interfering in activities. He should keep an eye over the child's activities as does a gardener. According to naturalists, the teacher should have personal, social, psychological and humanistic qualities so that he is able to know about the interests, attitudes, natures, abilities and capacities and needs of the child and is able to adopt a cooperative and affectionate nature. He should be able to entertain the child, play with him, do physical exercise with him and take interest in his natural and spontaneous activities. It would enable the child to undertake his natural activities.

## Naturalism and School Organisation

According to naturalism, the school organisation should be flexible and according to healthy atmosphere and natural rules. Though nature by itself is a school, but social viewpoint can be adopted to some extent to maintain social order. This social environment should be free. The school should be in the natural environment, and should have natural sunlight and pure air. The organisers or administrators should be such who are free from social control. There should not be strict rules of punctuality and system should be flexible. According to **Dalton,** the school organisation should be like a laboratory where freedom to work rules. The time limit is often an impediment in the development and freedom of the school. The school system should be based on self-administration so that self-administration and leadership can be taught to the students. The students should be held responsible for its administration. According to naturalism, there should be separate arrangements, curricula and teaching for the students in infancy, childhood, adolescence and youth.

## Naturalism and Discipline

According to **Spencer,** nature punishes those who do not follow the rules of nature. If the students too disobey the rules of nature, they will be punished. A child conducts himself according to his instincts and hereditary attitudes. If he does not behave accordingly, nature will punish him, only then he will learn to lead a disciplined life. So nature also acts like a punisher. No other thing than nature can punish a child. According to **Herbert Spencer :** "When a child falls, or runs its head against the table, it suffers a pain, the remembrance of which tends to make it more careful, and by reflection of such experiences, it is eventually disciplined into proper guidance of its movements." A child should not be imposed a burden of external discipline. We cannot call some thing discipline which makes the child a mute, inactive and peaceful child. External discipline eradicates the activism of the child. Naturalist punishment has come under severe criticism because it imposes such a heavy punishment, even to the extent of peril to his life, for a simple incidence of indiscipline. It is not justified.

## Naturalism and Types of Education

According to naturalism, education cannot be classified into specific classes. Naturalism desires that all opportunities for development of the whole personality of the child should be provided, only then hereditary capacities will develop. So, the naturalists do not recommend any single type of education. They only recommend general education. It also does not recommend imparting of any specific professional education too.

**Rousseau** too has not expressed any specific thoughts about the type of education to be prescribed. He only desires that education should be free external influences . Education should be so freely imparted by self-activities that the child's natural activities and internal capacities should continue to develop without any outside interference. He calls such education as prohibitive or negative. **Rousseau** considers religion as the subject of heart or emotion, and not that of intellect or mind. So, moral or religious education should not be imparted using intellect, the child should rather try to learn it by self realization or experience. The naturalists lay special emphasis on physical development and training of sense organs, but do not speak of any separate educational system for it. They want to make it a part of general education. In their view, the universal education is the best kind of education.

## Naturalism, Formal and Informal Agencies of Education

Formal education agency is the one under which the child is imparted education with specific aim in view by teachers at a specified place and time. The modern system of colleges, universities and schools is one such arrangement.

Informal education agency is the one which is independent from the above bonds of time, system, time and teachers, and educates the child in an irregular way unknowingly. Such institutions such as family, neighborhood, society, religious community, music club, etc are such informal agencies of educating the child.

Under the educational thinking, naturalism accords significance neither to formal agencies nor informal agencies of education. It wants that the child should be free from the influence of both of them. He should learn in an independent environment without any external discipline or system by his natural activities. Naturalism considers natural system and environment as most suitable agencies of imparting education.

### Naturalism and Modem Education

Naturalism has had good impact on the modem education. As a result of this, education has become child-centred. Now the child is no more considered a blank slate in which anything can be written; now his hereditary powers are given due significance and accordingly education is arranged for.

Attempts have been made to universalise education under the influence of naturalism. It has encouraged democratic principles. Naturalism has also influenced greatly the curriculum of modem education. Now a child's interest, hereditary faculties, aptitude, nature, etc. are kept in view when determining curriculum. Thus, psychological viewpoint is being followed in the construction of curriculum.

From educational system viewpoint too, modern education has been much influenced by naturalism. From the training of sense organs viewpoint too, various systems such as nursery, Montessori, kindergarten, balvari and basic education have developed. Taking the self-activity of the child as the core in the educational system is the gift of naturalism. Now the teacher lays importance to activities instead of oral teaching. Now, various means of audio,_ video, audio video and other entertaining programmes are being arranged for attainment of direct knowledge to the child. Teaching by play way methods, physical activities is the gift of naturalism.

Due to the influence of naturalism, the provision of severe punishment has been removed from the modern education. Now encouragement to impart education in the natural set up has been provided.

## Naturalism and Indian Education

The ashrama system prevalent in ancient India was conducted in the lap of nature in the beautiful, green forests, where the teachers and students lived, taught and learnt according to the natural laws. This viewpoint resembled the naturalism of Rousseau. But Indian education was not based on naturalism, it was basically idealistic. The Indian sages had arranged for imparting welfare-oriented and impractical education for moral upliftment by learning from merits and demerits of nature. This system continued in the middle ages and some of the institutions even today follow this system. Some of the modern symbols of such education can be Shanti Niketans, Vanasthali Vidyapeeth, Gurukuls, Sanskrit schools, Pondicherry Ashrama, etc.

Modern Indian education has certainly been influenced by naturalism. Like western countries, here too different kinds of nursery, Montessori, kindergarten schools have been established for children. These educational systems are being encouraged too. Much natural decorative, efforts are being made in these schools. Attempts are being made to educate the children using play, toys and independent activities. The children get adequate opportunities for expression of their thoughts and feelings. They are given opportunities to speak, question, and speak up their minds. The children also get opportunity to express themselves on the platform of their unions or committees. The curriculum is constructed according to their interest, aptitude, capacity and attitude. Education has become child-centred. The teacher too follows the democratic principle and acts like a guide. The teachers are trained in useful teaching methods with the help of child psychology and psychology.

## Merits of Naturalism

The above discussion has centred on various factors of naturalism. We shall sum up its merits in the following few lines

**1. Study of Society Scientifically:** Naturalism has scientifically studied society and has given rise to pragmatism.

**2. Experience-centred Curriculum:** Naturalism chiefly emphasises on experience-based curriculum according to which the experiences of the child are included in it. Much significance is given to co-curricular activities; the modern education should feel indebted to naturalism for it.

**3. Absence of Repressionistic Discipline:** Naturalism is against the use of repressionistic disciplinary measures as it accords freedom to the child to develop his personality without any outside obstacle. It disciplines the child on the maxim `let the child face the consequences of his doing'. Freedom to the child is the gift of naturalism to modern education.

**4. Development of Child Psychology :** Naturalism is childcentred education system. Much emphasis is laid on the development of his natural instincts, emotions and feelings. Child psychology came into being from it and modern education adopted the psychological and social attitudes.

**5. Revolution in Invention of Teaching Methods**: Naturalism has laid emphasis on developing the child according to his nature, as such revolutionary changes could be seen in the field of teaching methods in education. Various teaching methods like Huristic method, Dalton method, observation method, play way method, Montessori method, etc. are the contribution of naturalism to modem education.

## Demerits of Naturalism

**1.Excessive Significance to Science Subjects in Curriculum**: Naturalism lays emphasis on the study of science subjects to a great extent. It gives secondary significance to literary and art subjects. The scholars are in agreement with its preference of science subjects, but they severely criticise its non-inclusion of art subjects from the curriculum.

**2. Excessive Emphasis on Physical Education**: The naturalists say that mental and moral development of a child cannot take place without physical development. Due to this thinking, Rousseau is of the view than a child should get only natural education up to the age of 12 years. The purpose of this education is to impart training to the sense organs and physical education. It, however, neglects social education and moral development. Pestalozzi too has said : "Specialised development of one side of human nature is unnatural and false... To consider any one capacity exclusively is to destroy man's natural equilibrium." It has been criticised for its undue emphasis on physical activities. All-round development of the child can be attained only by an attempt made to develop all of his attributes.

**3. One-sided Aim of Education :** As discussed, naturalism wants the child to develop in the natural environment. The scholars opine that if a child is developed in the lap of nature, social and human qualities will not sprout in him and he will remain just like an animal, as some cases of wolf-children have shown. If the animal instincts of a child are to be got rid of or socialised, his education must be conducted in a social environment. Thus, the aim of education of naturalism is one-sided:

**4. Ignoring Books :** One of the points of criticism against naturalism is that it undermines the significance of books saying that the child's education should be based on physical activities and life experiences. But education cannot be completed only by activities and experiences. How can we leave alone the books which are the treasure house of knowledge and wisdom of our culture, tradition and custom? Learning by self-activity can be an effective method to learn, but the books and guidance can also not be ignored. In other words, the suitable method of imparting education should include all activities, books and guidance.

**5. Unfounded Thoughts on Discipline :** Naturalism expects that the child will have to face the consequences of his doing. This principle cannot stand the test of time and experience. Such a thinking can beget the child: severe punishment for a small error, or a negligible punishment for a great error. It is injustice and should be eradicated.

**6. Unsocial Thinking :** Naturalism is of the view that the child should be given an opportunity to develop individuality. This thinking can prove to be unsocial, because the social ends are more important than the individual ones. Naturalism neglects all environment-related aspects and bases education on only natural attitudes. It is not proper.

**7. No Role of Teacher :** Naturalism looks upon a teacher in the form of a friend and guide whose duty is to overlook and inspect the present environment and child's development. The scholars opine that this view is not proper in the modem democratic world. The teacher occupies an important place in the educational system as without his presence the social qualities of cooperation, sympathy and forbearance cannot be developed in a child, and without these qualities he will not be of any use to the society, country and the world.

**8. Excessive Freedom to Child :** Naturalism provides excessive and uncontrolled freedom to the child for treading the natural path. This uncontrolled freedom will only develop the feeling of self-assertion, but he will remain devoid of self-realization.

**9. Significance of Present:** One of the major drawbacks of naturalism is that it advocates laying emphasis on the present utility of the knowledge. It does not attach any significance to the future or past significance, and such subjects such as spiritual aspects or other world. Education should also have a final aim without which a child's thirst for knowledge in the fields of intelligence, art, thinking and spirituality will not be quenched. It will spring up dissatisfaction in the child.

**Idealist Metaphysics, Reality, and Education**

We have defined metaphysics as the study of "ultimate reality. The idealist claims that this reality is spiritual in nature rather than physical. He does not deny the existence of the world around us-the world of houses, hills, stars, and of all the objects and events with which science and our senses acquaint us. But he maintains that real as these things are, they are not *ultimate* real. They are manifestations of an underlying spiritual reality for instance, believed that all material thins were imperfect copies, of certain eternal Ideas or archetypes. Hence, the Fu nature of a thing was to be found not in the appearance it presented to the senses but it in the Idea from which it sprang, and this was accessible to the reason alone Berkeley mutinied that material things were ideas in Te mind of the beholder. Hegel declared that this world was the evolving expression of a Mind or Spirit, which was striving to embody itself ever more completely in material form.

Contemporary idealism seeks to unite the child with the spiritual reality to which he belongs. It teaches him to cultivate the soul as that part of him which is closest to this reality. It also attempts to create a closer intimacy between the child and nature. The child should not regard the world around him as an enormous machine functioning soullessly and without purpose. Nature is more than merely matter in motion, for even the *ultimate* constituents *of* matter are spiritual and, hence, akin to himself.

## Idealist Metaphysics, Human Nature, and Education

T o the idealist man is a spiritual being who exercises free will and is responsible for his actions. Because man is free and spiritual his essence eludes us if we study him simply as an object to sees the soul as emanating from the world of Ideas and imprisoned temporarily in the body, returning after death to its former habitat. Berkeley takes the orthodox Christian view that the soul is immortal, having been created by God to enjoy eternal life with Him after its probation on earth. According to man is both free and determined, free insofar as he is a sprit and determined to the extent that he is also a physical subject to natural law. Hegelian idealism regards man as a fragment of the Absolute, a spark as 't were, of the Eternal Spirit into which he is to be reabsorbed Thus, we see that idealists are united in their acceptance of man's spiritual essence, but they disagree as to how exactly he is related to the ultimate spiritual reality from which he spring

The pupil, therefore, is a spiritual being whose chief end in life is to express his own nature. The purpose of education is to help him do this. We harm the child if we regard him primarily as a mind or nervous system that stores information; we must see him, instead, as a person with a spiritual destiny to fulfill. Consequently he should be taught to respect the spiritüal worth and dignity of other people, not so that he may conform successfully to what they expect of him, but rather out of a high regard for human personality as such. Personal idealists in particular, who emphasize the importance of The individual personality, maintain that the significant thing for the child is not that he "gets along" well with everybody-although this, too, is good, provided it does not lead to the development of a false personality-but that he matures genuinely in accordance with his own inborn potentialities

Because, in the long run, the state is a personality greater than any individual and is, in fact, a whole more important than its parts, the student must learn to respect his country and the community into which he is born. He should study the cultural foundations of the nation, as well as the locality in which he lives, in order to develop a strong sense of loyalty to the political ideals of his nation and his community

The idealist teacher presides, like Socrates, over the birth of ideas, regarded not as things external to the student but as possibilities within him, which need to be realize He does not expect the student to mature in accordance with rules of development that have been decided by other people but seeks to awaken within him his own latent capacities The idealist teacher also believes with Kant that knowledge is best "wrung out" of the student rather than "poured into" him, although the content of education is not something that the student decides for himself. It is only the appro*ved* subject matter that the teacher may "wring out.' Finally the idealist teacher is supposed to be a person whom the student may emulate: In idealism, then, the teacher is accorded e than he is in any other educational Philosophy.

***Idealist* Epistemology *and* Education**

Within idealism different philosophers have proposed different theories of knowledge Plato to maintains that-knowledge acquired through the senses must always remain uncertain, since the sensory world itself is only partially .real. True knowledge is the product of reason alone for reason turns from the confusion-of matter to contemplate the order and clarity of the pure archetypes. Truth, therefore lies in the ideas of the reason and not in the physical world.

For an absolute idealist like. Hegel, knowledge is valid to the extent that it forms a system. The more comprehensive the system and the more consistent the ideas that it embraces, the more truth it may be said to possess. This principle is generally known as the *coherence theory* of·truth. It is based on the view that knowledge is not fragmented but unified, since reality, which knowledge reflects, is itself a whole Any particular item of knowledge Becomes significant only o the extent that it is seen in its total context. Hence, all ideas and theories must be validated according to their coherence within a continuously developing, unified system of knowledge.

The school curriculum should reflect the wholeness of knowledge and reality. It should widen the child's understanding of .the universe and of man himself. Hence, it should pay greater attention-to such subjects as history, philosophy, the fine arts, and religion, which tend to be neglected in the contemporary school. Science should be taught less as factual information than as a way of thinking.

Influenced especially by Kant, idealists state that the mind actively imposes meaning and order on the information of the senses. Therefore, the purpose of teaching is not so much to familiarize the student with a mass of information as to stimulate him to discover the meaning of this,, information for himself. Since what is known depends; in part, upon the knower, the student must relate his information to his own previous experiences, so that what he learns becomes significant to him personally Learning, therefore, does not consist of absorbing elected items of knowledge but of personally exploring the reality that is around and within us.

Idealists reject the claim that scientific methods are the only way to truth. They maintain that in personal life especially, intuitive thinking is as important as scientific thinking. Hence they recommend the study of art and literature both to foster and to discipline the intuitive faculty. At the same time, they caution that intuitions should be tested rationality and experimentally wherever possible.

Idealists also believe that the teacher should judge the different needs and abilities of his students by blending scientific knowledge with personal insight. Psychology can measure something of the child's intelligence, but it must be supplemented by the teacher's own intuitive grasp of the child's personality.

## Idealist Values and Education

Idealism declares that values are absolute and unchanging. Goodness and beauty are not man-made but rather part of the very structure of the universe. School policy must, therefore, be founded on enduring principles.

The child should learn to live by permanent values, which' put him in harmony with the spiritual whole to which he belong He should understand that certain actions are fitting for him a; a member of a spiritual order, whereas other actions profane this relationship He should realize further that evil offends, no merely himself or society or even, mankind as a whole, but also the very Soul of the universes .His values become reliable and significant only as they relate to this pattern of reality, which the teacher can define. ',

Contemporary idealism explains evil in terms of the disorganization and lack of system still present in the universe; evil i an incomplete good, not an entity in itself. As the underlying .Spirit expresses itself more and more fully, the universe become more systematic and less imperfect, and evil and ugliness diminish. , To the extent that the child acts morally, he is in harmony, with the nature of things; but to the extent that he acts immorally. he jars that concord. In any school system there are, for the ideal Ist teacher, no really bad children but only those who have strayed away from or do not yet fully comprehend the fundamental moral order of the universe.

Both Plato and Hegel emphasize that the good life is possible only within a highly organized society. In *The Republic,* Plat describes an ideal society in which each individual has his special function. This society is ruled by an elite of philosopher-kings. Hegel declares that, since anything existing is real to the extent that it participates in a whole greater than itself, the individual realizes himself only insofar as he is a participating member of society. Man owes society his complete allegiance, he says be cause from it he derives his moral nature and his freedom Kant however, proposes a less totalitarian ethic, urging men to-treat one another as ends rather than means. His famous *categorical imperative,* or moral law, states that we should act always a though our, actions were to become a universal law of nature; binding on all men in similar circumstances.

Assuming that no one would wish to see his own wrongdoing universalized, we could expect anyone following Kant's maxim always to refrain from evil actions. When a pupil becomes a disciplinary problem, the idealist teacher tries to show him the effect of his misconduct on the rest of the class. The teacher asks the wrongdoer what would happen if *everyone* behaved as lie does. Is he setting a good example for his classmates to follow? (The teacher might also ask himself whether he is a good example for his students to follow.) Wherever a student goes and whatever he does, he should remember what he owes to his community. He should bear in mind always the obligations he owes to' his fellows, without whom he would be nothing. Infractions of discipline are conceived, therefore, as demonstrations of selfishness and willfulness to be punished in accordance with the moral principles that have been incorporated in the common, or religious, culture over many generations.

If we leave idealism without criticism, it does not mean that idealism is necessarily the "perfect" philosophy for a teacher to' hold. But an adequate critique of idealism would take us too far a field. It is better to read the arguments of competing philosophies, which establish their own positions partly by refuting those of their rivals. Philosophical realism is one such rival. It is another absolute system, but one based on a theory of reality entirely different from that of idealism. By studying realism we shall, in fact, be reading an implicit, and sometimes explicit, attack on idealism, as well as an alternative philosophy to it.

# Idealism and Education

## Meaning of Idealism

Idealism and naturalism are two mutually contradictory or opposing philosophies. While naturalism wants imparting of education by taking man as the creature of his natural instincts; idealism considers man as a spiritual man composed of mental strengths such as good thoughts, prudence, wisdom, logic, imagination, decision, etc. Some people prefer to call idealism as the philosophy based on ideas, because idea is thought for them. Idealism can be called 'idiaism' but there is a difference between the two. Idealism accords importance to mind and God instead of body, while in thinking, the truth and meaningfulness of idealism is contained.

As a philosophic principle, idealism accepts the significance of thoughts, emotions and ideals, and accepts the development of personality and spiritual values as the aim of life, so that unity (God) in diversity is known. It is the concept of idealism that it considers the spiritual world as more significant, important, permanent, better and truer than the physical world. Its cause is that the physical world is susceptible to destruction and mortal. On the other hand, spiritual world is composed of thoughts, emotions and ideals by which the knowledge of mind and soul is begot, as such idealism considers it as true and immortal. It does not consider anything beyond its realm. It lays emphasis on the study of man and his mind.

This philosophy says that the nature of man is spiritual which finds expression in intellectual, aesthetic 2nd religious fields. It does not apply to lower animals and creatures because man is greater than them. It also lays emphasis on the study of mast because he ,has mind, intellect, wisdom and prudence. He does not remain a slave to his circumstances, but overcomes them and changes them, e- n occupies the place as possessed by gods. He creates various mental, artistic and spiritual activities. None else than man made the prevailing cultural and spiritual atmosphere.

In other words, idealism gives importance to man and his feelings, emotions and ideals. Man can attain these ideals and values to know of the real God and true knowledge and thus develops his personality. We can say that idealism considers that the ultimate reality is spiritual, not physical. In the words of **Horne** : "An idealistic philosophy of education, then, is an account of man finding himself as an integral part of universe of mind." According to this philosophy, the order or place and time goes on according to the manifestation of spiritual truth regularly. Thus the field of idealism is the infinite and unending, regular reality. It does not believe in neutral or opposing world.

## Definitions of Idealism

The following definitions make the concept of idealism clear

"Idealistic philosophy takes man and varied forms, but the postulate underlying all is that mind or spirit is the essential world stuff, that the true reality is of a mental character." **-J.S. Ross**

"Idealism holds that the' order of the world is due to the manifestation in space and time of an eternal and spiritual reality." **-H.H. *Home***

"Idealism holds that ultimate reality is spiritual." **-D.M. *Dutta***

"Idealists point out that it is mind that is central in understanding the world. To them nothing gives a greater sense of reality than the activity of mind engaged in trying to comprehend its world. For anything to give a greater sense of reality would be a contradiction in terms because to know anything more real than mind would itself have to be a conception of mind." ***-Brubacher***

## Idealism and Naturalism .

Idealistic philosophy considers matter and creature as true and real, and considers mind as secondary and result of the creature or living being. The universe has been born from mind. Matter and consciousness are not one. Naturalists consider matter as real while idealists consider mind, consciousness, spirituality as real, permanent and true. According to idealistic philosophy, self-being or consciousness is the essence of nature or material world. Matter or nature can be understood only after proper analysis of mind or consciousness. Thus, idealism is different from naturalism.

## Characteristics of Idealism

The characteristics of idealism can be enumerated in the following points

1. Consciousness is the primary and chief source, and is the basis of the universe. The imagination of the universe became possible only due to consciousness. Matter came into the universe only after consciousness existed.

2. Consciousness is conscious, not mechanical. It is composed of life of man.

3. Consciousness has its own independent reality, it is self-existing, and is not a part or reflection of the mind or a part of body.

4. Nature has no any independent reality. The activity or nature of consciousness is the nature or matter. There exists coordination between nature and man; the universe is the manifestation or expression of consciousness; there is deep relationship between human mind and the process of world.

6. We cannot know about the entire world with the cooperation of only the material or physical sciences; because analysis of the universe cannot be given without consciousness.

7. The creation of the universe was done with a purpose; every activity or process occurring in it has a specific purpose. These values can be determined with the help of aesthetics, ethics and logic.

8. Consciousness provides meaning to the physical world; the world has no meaning without consciousness. The whole creation of the world is contained in the creation and activity of the consciousness.

9. The human life is a purposeful activity, and not mechanical. There is a great purpose behind this creation.

10. The state has no physical reality without consciousness. The state is only an imagination of consciousness. The basis of imagination of the state is the contribution of moral precepts. The state is not a group of individuals, it should be considered as consciousness. The state is not an artificial institution; it has been created with the willingness of man. The unity pervading in the state is the result of consciousness which is born conscious.

**Basic Principles of Idealism**

The basic principles of idealism can be enumerated in the following headings

**1. Significance to Personality Development :** Idealism is of the view that the personality of man forms the core round which all his activities rotate, so they lay emphasis on this aspect. According to the idealists, the purpose of man's life is to attain the complete spirituality. Plato was of the view that man has inherent ideal character in his personality to attain which he continues to work tirelessly. Some of the idealists are of the view that self-realization is attainment of this personality which takes to the knowledge of the soul. The scholars are of the view that the knowledge of the soul can be begot by living in society. It concludes that education come to help man in achievement of those aims which take man nearer to self-realization. It should also develop such qualities in man, which fills him with non-partisan interests, non-discrimination against one another, love, kindness, sympathy, etc. for others. J.S. Ross has correctly written: "Thus the grandeur and worth of human life at its best are emphasized by idealism. Human personality is of supreme value and constitutes the noblest work of God." Idealism opposes the concept of the education of a few people; it supports general education for all so that personality development of maximum number of people becomes possible.

**2. Significance to Spiritual Values :** Idealistic philosophy believes in spiritual values and attainment of the truth which are considered immortal. The attainment of these high ideals is the attainment of God in itself. The idealists also believe that these values are comprehensive and can be attained in proximity of one another, and not independently; for which the three activities of knowledge, feeling and willingness are needed. J.S. Ross has said : "Goodness, truth and beauty are seen to be absolutes, each existing in its own right and entirely desirable in itself." Thus the idealists say that man should endeavor to attain truth by knowledge, beauty by desire and goodness by attempt; and man should make his life according to these ideals where lies his final emancipation.

**3.Bi-fonms of the World :** The idealists divide the world into two distinct, yet inter-related entities-physical world and spiritual world. The idealists lay more significance to the spiritual world as they believe that the physical world is only a glimpse of the spiritual world. The physical world is mortal while the spiritual world is immortal; the former is untrue while the latter is true. The study of the latter begets knowledge of self and soul. According to **H.H. Home** "Idealism holds that the order of the world is due to the manifestation in space and time of an eternal and spiritual reality." So the chief aim of human life is to attain the knowledge of the spiritual reality or world, as against attainment of the physical matter.

**4. Unity in Diversity :** Idealism believes that all matters of the world are different yet there exists an underlying unity in them. The idealists have termed this unity by different names such as consciousness, God, soul, etc. They believe that this unity is like the central energy of a machine which makes the whole system work, so is the case with this unity in the form of consciousness, soul or God. H.H. Horne has said : "An idealistic philosophy of education, then, is an account of man finding himself as an integral part of the universal mind." According to idealists, the task of education is to make the child realize the underlying unity or God or the supreme energy, because its attainment leads him to spiritual entirety and complete development of personality.

**5. Idea Vs. Matter :** Idealistic philosophy lays more emphasis on idea than matter. It considers idea, feelings and emotions as more important than the physical world. The idealists believe that the physical matter is irrelevant and untrue, while the thoughts and ideas are true, all-pervading and unchangeable. In the words of Plato "Ideas are of ultimate cosmic significance. They are rather the essences or archetypes which give form to cosmos. These ideas are eternal and unchanging." The idealists are of the view that the whole universe is composed within these ideas.

**6. Man over Nature** :Idealistic philosophy lays more significance to man than the material nature. The idealists argue that man has power to think and experience and thus man assumes more importance as the unit which experiences himself. Man is a prudent and intelligent creature, unlike animals, who does not remain slave to the nature or environment. Rusk has said : The spiritual or cultural environment is an environment of man's own making, it is a product of man's creative activity." Man not only thinks and experiences, he also makes necessary changes, occupies exalted places, creates literature, takes part in religious and spiritual activities, and develops various mental and aesthetic activities.

## Indian Idealism

Indian idealism is considered to be the oldest one. It had influence on the common people and makes him take interest in philosophy. Indian philosophy has sprung forth from the Vedas. The sages have engaged themselves in thinking and learning God and soul. According to Indian philosophy, each creature is composed of God. If God is seen as a subjective identity, it is the soul; and if it is seen in an objective perspective, it is the God. Our body is changeable and mortal, while God is unchangeable and immortal. Sage Yajnavalkya says in the *Brahadaranyaka Upnishad* : "We must perceive the soul, must listen to it and must pay attention to it always; because, perception, learning, thinking, attending and knowledge of the soul can make us understand anything."

The Vedas are the chief lectures of advaita. They term God is the supreme being, truth or the essence, which is true, mind and bliss. God is all-pervading. Indian philosophy is full of idealism which has been recognised from times immemorial. Shankaracharya's philosophy is still illuminating Indian philosophy. According to him, God is true while the matter or world is untrue. The difference perceived between soul and God is illusion; the eradication of this difference begets the true knowledge of God. We can achieve God on the basis of this knowledge.

The dualism of Ramanujacharya too finds an important place in Indian philosophy. According to him, the three fundamental elements are consciousness, unconsciousness and God. The former two are the parts of God.

Monism-dualism philosophy of Sage Nimbakarcharya is also important which considers God, soul and nature as three fundamental elements. God pervades all matters and creatures.

In a similar way, Madhavacharya also considers the existence of creation, God and soul as distinct. Ballabhacharya said that God is truth and regular, no matter is different or separate from God. Thus, the world can be considered to be immortal and regular. .

The thinking of Shankaracharya was made a basis of thinking in Kashmir which gave rise to Shaivism. According to it, when knowledge descends on the earth, illusion disappears and the supreme element is saved.

Besides the above philosophers, there have been many Indian philosophers who have analysed Indian philosophy in a practical perspective. The names of those worth mentioning are **Swami Dayananda, Aurobindo Ghose, Srinivas Bhattacharya, Dr. Radhakrishnan,** etc.

## Indian Idealism and Education

According to Indian philosophy, there is no difference between salvation and attainment of God, so the highest ideal of Indian education has been attainment of salvation or emancipation. Various philosophers opine differently in problems such as the means of attainment of salvation, the condition of the creature after attainment of salvation, etc. However, all of them are of the same view when it comes to the aim which is final emancipation. Imparting education and gaining education are considered sacred duty and considered to be the best kind of donation. It is the duty of the society to arrange for education.

Indian idealism considers that personality is prominent and the body is secondary. The level of personality is much higher than the physical element, because it is composed of thoughts and ideals. It is very necessary to give place to Indian ideals and related practical thoughts in education. We cannot change heredity but we can provide such an environment in which the hereditary attributes can be developed according to suitable ideals. Will power of man is very useful in gaining knowledge. If will power is composed of good and positive thoughts, ideals, virility and suitable environment, education will result in the development of personality to a great extent.

Education, according to Indian ideals, is which takes man toward spiritualism and finally toward emancipation or salvation. According to Indian philosophy, education provides man with a welfare-oriented personality and assists in attainment of the aims of religion, economy, desires and salvation.

## Idealism and Aims of Education

From idealistic viewpoint, education is what makes man self experience. It the duty of every man to self-realize and self experience. We can enumerate the aims of idealism under the following headings

**1. Spiritual Development :** The idealistic philosophers give more importance to the spiritual world as compared with the physical world. In the words of Rusk : "Education must enable mankind through its culture to enter more and more fully into the spiritual realm, and also to enlarge the boundaries of the spiritual realm." It considers that the aim of education should be to attain spiritual development. Education should be arranged in such a manner as to realize this aim.

**2. Transformation of Instincts into Spirituality :** It is a commonly accepted fact that a child is born with certain inborn instincts. The idealists believe that the aims of education should be to transform the instincts of the child into spirituality; that is, purification of the instincts for attainment of higher goals of life, keeping pace with cultural, social and environmental atmosphere.

**3. Development of Intellect and Prudence :** All material things in the world have come into being with a specific purpose and can be understood because they are well organised and arranged, governed by certain principles and laws. The idealist philosopher is always in search of such principles which maintain the analysis of the world on the spiritual basis. It follows that the aim of education is to develop intellect and prudence of the child. **Adams** takes lead in this role. **Froebel** too has said : "In all things there reigns an eternal law... this all-pervading law is necessarily based on an all-pervading energetic, self-conscious and hence eternal unity. This unity is God. Education should lead and guide man to face with nature and to unity with God." The idealists give more importance to the principle of unity in diversity. They consider it such a central power or energy which governs or operates all other ancillary parts or the whole machine. They contend that every man should be in know of such central energy, and this knowledge can be had only by those who are intelligent and prudent. Adams is of the view that all things of the world are purposeful and meaningful, and man needs intelligence and prudence to have authority over them on the way to his final emancipation.

**4Preservation of Culture :** Idealism considers that man is not enslaved by his environment, rather he is an intelligent creature who moulds everything according to his needs. He has taken active part in the development of culture, society, and aspects related to spirituality, mental, intellectual, aesthetic and religious. We can find its existence in the form of various subjects such as mathematics, religion, morality, art, literature, science, etc. All men have equal right over all these. So it is the duty of every man in the world to be acquainted with all these and also to contribute to them for their progress and preservation. From this view, the idealism considers that the aim of education should be to preserve our cultural heritage and enable its transfer to the progeny in a better-developed form.

**5. Goal of Self-Realization :** Idealism considers that man is the supreme creature of God and his personality is unique in every way. Personality of man can be further exalted by self-experience and self-realization. In the words of J.S. Ross : "The aim of education specially associated with idealism is the exaltation of personality, or self-realization, the making actual or real the highest potentialities of the. self." The meaning of self-realization is to gain knowledge of the soul while living in social and cultural environment. So the aim of idealistic education is to make man able to realize this exalted aim so that he achieves salvation.

**6. Inspiration for Sacred Life :** Idealism considers that a child should develop love for spiritual values and such circumstances should be produced in which he can achieve his spiritualism fulfillment. According to Froebel: 'The object of education is the realization of a faithful, pure, enviable and hence holy life." So the aim of education should be to enable the child to lead a sacred life.

**7. Attainment of the Supreme Qualities :** Idealism has deep faith in the values of truth, beauty and goodness, and lays emphasis on their development. It is the duty of every man to develop these high values, without which attainment of spirituality is difficult. Spiritual development is subject to the achievement of spirituality in the social environment, and education must come forward to achieve this aim.

## Idealism and Curriculum

If human development, civilisation and human experiences are included in the curriculum, it will help make human personality more useful. The naturalists are of the view that only present human experiences be included in the educational curriculum and do not give any importance to the past experiences. On the other hand, idealism desires to include all those experiences in the curriculum which man has earned from the time immemorial. Man has created social and cultural environment and he should be fully acquainted with it. The teacher should find out the needs of both society and child and arrange such knowledge keeping in view the interests, capacity and nature of the child. It will be prudent and justified to choose the curriculum in accordance with the needs of' society. The achievements of. the society and man should be included in the curriculum under all circumstances.

Curriculum should include all three aspects of child's personality which are knowledge aspect, emotional aspect and activity aspect. Knowledge aspect develops perception power of the child; emotional development is effected by aesthetic subjects such as art, literature and poetry and bring him unique experiences; while activity aspect brings in him skill and professional proficiency.

Idealism is of the view that knowledge can be gained from physical environment or in the company of friends. It is with this view that idealistic curriculum includes both scientific and humanistic subjects. Plato wanted to make curriculum equipped with three kinds of activities-intellectual, aesthetic and moral. His intellectual activities were included in such subjects as language, literature, history, geography, mathematics and science; his aesthetic activities were based on art, music and poetry; while his moral activities included the study of religion, metaphysics and ethics. Herbart was of the view that the aim of education was morality and he favored to include such subjects as literature, history, art, poetry, music, etc,in his curriculum. Nunn divided the subjects to be included in the curriculum into two classifications: the subjects which can safeguard or preserve life, and the subjects which can make or construct human civilisation. In the former he included the subjects as physical, social, moral and religious subjects while in the latter category were included aesthetic and literature subjects such as literature, art, handicraft, history, geography, science, mathematics -and music. Ross too divided the curriculum into two parts which composed physical or health related activities and spiritual activities. His physical activities included skills and health education; while spiritual activities included the study of literature, language, history, geography, science, mathematics, ethics, fine arts, religion and metaphysics.

**Idealism and Teaching Methods**

Having determined the aim and curriculum of education, we should proceed toward discussion of teaching methods, so that the curriculum can attain its purpose of teaching the child. Idealism is liberal from teaching method viewpoint. According to it, teacher and child are independent and they can adopt any teaching method according to their needs. Socrates considered the question-answer method as suitable, Froebel thinks that play way method is suitable; while Pestalozzi talks of a teaching method according to mental and intellectual development of the children.

According to idealism, inductive and deductive methods are the best suited to education. The inductive method proceeds from specific examples to the general rules, while in the deductive method, we proceed from general rules to specific rules.

Idealism lays emphasis on ideas because only ideas have existence in the world. The idea is subjective, so it is not necessary for all to agree to anyone idea. Science is considered to be objective. It is not true and universal to have faith in matter, while having faith in knowledge and idea is more real and true. So any teaching method which exhorts the child toward thinking is a good one.

Idealism is not opposed to direct knowledge, but does not approve of it. Direct knowledge is based on self-experience for which there are hardly any opportunities. So we must benefit from others' experiences. Lecture is a good method to acquaint with others' experiences.

Idealism wants to be related with unbiased, universal and immortal reality. Man should endeavour to attain it by education. Education is a continuous lifelong process. Man learns every moment of his life and still wants to learn more. Whatever the method, it should be convenient to learn keeping in view, the needs of the child and society. Any common method can be beneficial according to the prevailing circumstances.

## Idealism and Child

The body is composed of five elements, but is a light of consciousness in which spirituality resides. Consciousness is more powerful than the body. Consciousness does not reside in any particular part of the body, not even mind. It is present in every part of the body in the form of consciousness; for example, as power is imagined in the physical world, consciousness is imagined in the body.

The purpose of education is to make consciousness of man awakened and active. Man's consciousness is creative. The child should also be seen and tested in that perspective. Development of the spiritual aspect of the child is the aim of education. So, from idealistic viewpoint, the child is not a body, but consciousness with private and important personality. He brings with him such hereditary attributes which are susceptible to spiritual development. So it would be prudent to arrange for education keeping in view his hereditary attributes, consciousness and the nature of his mind.

## Idealism and Teacher

Idealism gives supreme importance to the role of a teacher in the process of education. The teacher is the source of knowledge and ideal personality for the children. It is the reason that idealism calls upon bringing the child in the company of the teacher where both teacher and child are influenced by each other's personality. The child is not a mere body, 'but is consciousness incarnate. The strong personality of the teacher influences the personality of the child to take him toward spirituality. **Ross** has correctly written in this regard:" The naturalist may be content with briars, but the idealist wants fine roses. So the educator by his efforts assists the educand, who is developing according to the laws of his nature to attain those that would otherwise be denied to him." Indian idealism too has accorded a high place to the teacher terming him as one who helps meeting with God and salvation, and without whom the road to enlightenment cannot be illuminated.

## Idealism and Learning Process

Idealism does not consider learning process a mechanical or physical process. It is not the conditioning of stimulation and response, either. It is the total sum of mind and body. Consciousness is the reality, and body has no significance before it. The mind is not dependent on the body for its functioning. It is independent in its own right. Learning cannot be effected without the presence of mind and activity.

According to idealism, in the learning process we proceed toward an idea or thought. Consciousness is the complete whole in itself, that is, it is thoughtful and is not required to be learnt. However, personal consciousness is that part of the whole consciousness which cannot establish contact with the whole without undergoing a learning process. Our attributes are the result of our past activities, and learning according to them improves upon our personality in a true way; that is, it is helpful in reaching the consciousness.

**Idealism and School Organisation**

Establishment of school is sought by society in order to educate man to make him useful for society. Good attributes of man should be imparted with the help of education. The idealistic viewpoint of education is to construct consciousness and personality of the child. Our school should provide such means, premises and environment in such manner which will enable man to gain thoughts or ideas.

The school environment should be according to the ideals sought to be achieved. The principal and teachers should be such who influence the child's personality positively. School should have residential arrangement where teachers and students live together. The students should live under the guidance. of -the teacher. There should be arrangement for games and;, play within the school premises, and the school should be armed with library having good books and literature. There should also be a place in the school where teacher and student can' interact, hold meetings and conferences, and organise debates. The daily routine of the students should be well-regulated and disciplined with laid down rules. School rules should be changed from time to time with the passage of time and change of situation. The school organisation should be flexible, in which the child should be given freedom so that he is able to adjust between discipline and freedom.

## Idealism and Discipline

Unlike naturalism which provides uncontrolled freedom to the child, idealism lays emphasis on discipline with. particular stress on self-control. Idealism wants the child to follow rules not out of fear but willingly. He should be given freedom but it should be. subject to certain restrictions so that the child is able to establish coordination between discipline and freedom. It will make him self-disciplined. The fundamental aim of idealist education is to realize self-discipline willingly. For it, it is necessary to give him freedom to self-experience and develop his personality and interests. A child will attempt to form his personality with the help of art, music and literature, etc and his interests gradually develop. Such self-discipline will guide the child toward betterment without any greed of a reward, nor fear. The child can also be punished if he commits a crime willingly or knowingly; but it is aimed at making the child realize his crime. Punishment is not aimed at repression or redressal of grievances, but meant for the welfare of the child. The child should not be rewarded so as not to make him greedy.

## Idealistic Education and Society

An educational institution is society in its miniature form. It fulfils the needs of society. If there prevails any evil in the society, it can be eradicated with the help of education. It is the duty of school to prepare able citizens for society, only then the society can become progressive. If the school is awakened to this need, the society should help it with necessary means but without undue interference. The society wants to make the school according to its ideals. Idealism does not only consider the school as the miniature form of society, but also considers it a tool for social reform. The school should do its duty in carrying out its responsibility faithfully. The people who become social reformers, thinkers, able citizens, leaders, etc. all are made in school. The school should lead the society effectively.

The school not only develops the personality of the child, but also undertakes the task of social and cultural development. It can lead and guide in all fields of human life. If the school prepares able leaders in all walks of life, it will be easier to bring about reforms in the society and the schools will be able to carry out their responsibility.

The school is the place where social problems can be resolved. The school should bring such changes in educational system where the ideals, thoughts and traditions are not lost. Thus, we can see that the school can play a leading role in the development of society.

## Impact of Idealism, on Modern Education

Idealism is very old thinking in which immortal and universal elements have been studied and contemplated. It has been a source of inspiration for the development of human civilisation. Idealism determines the educational aims. The ideals of self-realization, beauty, truth and goodness are given by idelism. The development of human qualities and welfare was the responsibility of such educational system. It includes the subjects such as literature, art, history, music, etc. with certain aims in mind. Idealism lays emphasis on morality and its education, the ideal which all countries of the world have accepted.

Idealism gives highest importance to teacher. The personality of the teacher should bc high and ideal so that he is able to influence the child in the desired direction. When we arrange for the training of the teacher, we look into the aspect of his personality.

The teachers and students should come into one another's contact. According to idealism, we should pay attention to individual training. We make an attempt to reduce the student-teacher ratio. Idealism teaches self-discipline by influential discipline. It does not want to make the child frightened by punishment or greedy by reward.

## Merits of Idealism

The above discussion has centred round various aspects of idealism in detail. We can sum up the merits of idealism in the following points

1. Idealism alone has analysed the aims in detail.

2. Idealistic education lays emphasis on the development of such attributes such as truth, beauty and goodness which determine moral inclination of the child.

3. Idealistic education favours self-realization and universal education.

4. The teacher occupies an important place in idealistic education who attempts to influence the personality of the child in a positive way.

5. Idealism respects the personality of the child and emphasiseson his creative powers.

6. Idealism is in favour of the principies of self-discipline and self control.

7. The school has become a part of society due to the efforts of idealism.

## Demerits of Idealism

Idealism is composed of multi-layered benefits and advantages for the child, teacher and society. However, certain demerits can be attributed to it, which can be recounted under the following points

1. The ideals of idealism are abstract, which prepare the child for the spiritual existence, as against the ideals of practical life in the present times.

2. The ideals of the spiritual development fail to realise the aims of present day society in which the child will have to face many kinds of problems.

3. Idealism lays more emphasis on thinking and mind, which lays undue emphasis on intellectuality.

4. Idealism favours learning by rote which are not considered good teaching methods.

5. The teacher is given a prominent place in idealism while the child is receded to the secondary place. It does not conform to the present ideals in which education has become child-centred.

6. Idealism forgets the reality that we presently live in a scientific era. The mere study of humanistic subjects for spiritual development cannot take us anywhere in the modem world.

## Limitations of Idealism in Education

The demerits of idealism are clear from the above demerits. However, it deserves a discussion. Idealism considers God's and spiritual reality as regular, universal and absolute, gives prominence to consciousness and considers everything else as secondary. It is difficult to understand this ideal. This purpose is so minute that a child will not be able to understand it. Similarly, the aim of education as self-realization is also very difficult for a child to understand. The students can only gain knowledge of the direct matters, understanding abstract thoughts is difficult for them. The path from personal experience to social experience under idealism is so complex that the modem teacher thinks it improper and impracticable, besides being imaginary.

Idealism has placed great ideals before us in a logical way, but has not spoken much on how to attain them. It is the reason that idealism has occupied the highest place in determination of aims but lowest in the field of teaching methods. Some people opine that idealism is only a preaching or lecture in which the child remains a mute spectator. Though idealism speaks of coordination between man and society, yet gives more importance to man over society. Society and man are complementary to each other and both of them should get equal importance. Under this ideology, the teacher has occupied a prominent place, but has made the student dependent on him; how *then can the student learn to be independent? Idealism is criticized* from this viewpoint too.

Idealism has its own limitations. It is a good and effective philosophy from the viewpoint of aims, coordination of man and society, self-discipline, doing away of evils, neglect of reward, eradication of social evils, purpose of social good, etc. We should accept its good points and assimilate it into our system as far as possible for effecting prosperity of our education, culture, man and society.

**Idealism in Indian Education**

In Indian educational system under idealism, spiritualism has been given prominence. India has adopted the viewpoint of an idealist from the beginning. The aim of education in the ancient times was attainment of God or salvation. The teachers and students in the Vedic period emphasised on self-experience and self-realization. The students used to be self-controlled, self-disciplined, with simple living and high thinking. Education was completely idealistic and teacher student enjoyed good mutual relationship.

Indian education remained under the influence of ancient idealistic education even during the medieval period. The gurukuls, schools, and madarasas of the Muslims continued to be on the ancient ideologies. Modem Sanskrit schools and gurukuls too are trying to follow this tradition. Though our schools, colleges and universities are adopting realist attitude these days, yet they respect idealism. The influence of idealism over our education is decreasing. We have to inspire those prevalent essential elements which can encourage idealistic attitude and can make Indian education idealistic.

Our thoughts have changed into western materialistic thoughts. Self-realization is no more the aim of our education. The humanistic qualities are being neglected. Spirituality is taking the back seat. The students are giving preference to professional education. Industrial revolution has turned our viewpoint materialistic. There is no system of discipline. Many evils such as corruption, immorality, dishonesty are finding new meanings. There is much need of ideals and educational efforts in the Indian society today. We shall have to bring about coordination between man and society to enhance the determination of consciousness and adopt suitable mental aptitude so that we are once again able to establish the ancient Indian idealism.

# PRAGMATISM

Pragmatism is popularly regarded as an indigenous American philosophy. In fact, it is related to the British empiricist tradition, which maintains that we can know only what our senses experience. In its doctrine of change it looks back to Heraclit a Greek philosopher who lived before Socrates. Its leading exponents, Charles Sanders Peirce, William James, and John Dewey, differ considerably in their methods and conclusions. Peirce's view of pragmatism is oriented toward physics and mathematics, and Dewey's toward social science and biology. James's philosophy, on the other hand, is personal and psychological, and is motivated by religious considerations. To a greater extent than realism or id ism, pragmatism has been influenced by contemporary events. During the Depression, for instance, it muted its earlier emphasis is on individualism and called for a greater social consciousness.

The principal themes of this philosophy are (1) the reality of change over permanence; (2) the relativity of values; (3) the social and biological nature of man; (4) the importance of democracy as a way of life; and (5) the value of critical intelligence in all human conduct. Pragmatism has been known by a variety of names, from *pragmaticism,* used by Peirce, to *instrumentalism, functionalism,* and *experimentalism.* The last of these terms has found particular favor with recent commentators on the relation of pragmatism to educational methodology. n his later years, Dewey preferred experimentalism to instrurumentalism, on the grounds that the latter sounded too materialistic.

## Pragmatism, Reality, and Education

Pragmatists agree with realists that the material world exists in its own right and is not just a projection of the mind. They maintain, however, that the world is neither permanent nor independent of man. Change being the essence of reality, we cannot be sure that anything will endure forever. Moreover, reality itself is not simply external to man but is created by the interaction of the human organism with its surroundings; reality is the sum total of what we experience. Man and his environment, Therefore are coordinate Both are equally responsible for what is real.

The world is only meaningful to the extent that man is able to read his own meaning into it. If the universe itself possesses some deeper purpose, it is hidden from man and cannot be part of his philosophy what man cannot experience cannot have reality for him. Pragmatist in humanist temper, to the old Greek maxim that "Man is the measure of all things." The difference of between Jamesean pragmatism and the pragmatism of Peirce and Dewey is that James emphasized the individual's right to create his own reality, whereas the latter declared that the facts of reality were established primarily by the scientist.

If like the pragmatist, we believe that change is the essence of reality, we always must be prepared to alter the way that we do things. The ends and means of education must be flexible and open to constant revision. They should also be adopted scientifically in the light of all relevant facts and values rather than speculatively on the basis of reason alone. There is also an intimate connection between ends and means; ends and means are reciprocal. Means are indigenous to their ends, and ends may derive from their means. Thu in education interest is not opposed to discipline, but rather discipline grows out of interest. Similarly, the psychological method of learning complements the logical organization of subject matter.

Since reality is created by the interaction of man with leis environment, we must learn to study the world as it affects *us. The* child should regard reality, not as impervious to man, but intimately responsive to him and capable of serving him in countless ways. Just as man is not a being apart from his environment, so the school is not separate from life itself. 'Education is life and not a preparation for if " School should use real-life situations rather than depend primarily on formal academic studies.

## Pragmatism, Human Nature, and *Education*

With the notable exception of William James, most pragmatists reject the view that man is a spiritual being. On the other hand, they insist that he is far too complex a creature to be nothing more than a highly intricate mechanism,-as-some natural realists have maintained, In fact, they say, man is a natural organic living in both a social and a biological environment. They emphasize the social side of human nature and the extent to which the individual may be formed by thoughtful interaction with others, *sustained by effort*

Unlike realists and idealists, pragmatists consider human nature to e fluid and plastic. They believe that education entails the total development of the individual. We should educate the child as an active, thinking organism, w rich science and observation reveal him to be, by persuading hi continually to reconstruct and interpret his own experiences Because he grows only by associating with o not only to cooperate but also to compromise. He must be taught how to live in a community of individuals and how to adapt himself intelligent to their needs and Ideals. Therefore, those who teach him should know more about the nature of group behavior and the part, played by individuals in group processes than they do at present.

## Pragmatist Epistemology and Education

Pragmatists consider the mind to be active and exploratory rather than passive and receptive .Man does not simply receive knowledge; he *makes* it. Truth-does--not lie solely in correspondence With external reality because reality for man is not independent of the ideas. that he proposes in order to explain it. Knowledge is *a transaction* between man and his environment.

Pragmatists have been accused of maintaining that an idea is true if it "works." This charge is misleading. James, it is true, regarded an idea as true if its consequences were favorable for the person who held it. On the other hand, Peirce and Dewey have maintained with most other pragmatists that an idea is true only if it has favorable consequences when scientifically tested. All pragmatists agree, at ]cast, that the meaning of an idea lies in its consequence after it has been tit into operation.

However, pragmatists deny that man invents whatever truths he wishes. Truth may not be something-outside -man awaiting his discovery, as the realist would put it but neither is it something willfully manufactured. Truth is what man concludes after he has carefully investigated the evidence. Because truth depends on the data investigated and the methods used to investigate them, it is necessarily revised and expanded as better methods are used and more data discovered. Truth, then, is relative and change -able.

According to pragmatism, the "method- of intelligence" is the ideal way to acquire knowledge under any circumstances. We grasp things best by locating and solving problems. Faced with a problem, the intelligence proposes hypotheses to explain or handle it. The hypothesis that explains the facts or solves the problem most successfully is regarded as true. It results in what Dewey called a "warranted assertion," one that is useful for testing further hypotheses.

The pragmatist teacher, therefore, constructs learning situations around particular problems, which he regards as truly significant for his pupils and likely to lead them to a better understanding of their environment and of one another. Rather than teaching traditional subjects directly, the teacher tends to draw on them only as they contribute to the solution of the problems at hand. As we shall see in Chapter 3 when we come to progressivism, these problems may be topics of both general and immediate interest, such as "transportation" and "life in an Indian village." To understand such topics or to complete a project related to them, the pupil draws on those aspects of knowledge that are pertinent to his particular task. Reading, writing, and arithmetic become more meaningful and more easily mastered, declares the pragmatist, when they help the pupil to fulfill his purposes. The child studies best when he grasps the relevance of what he lea as to what he *intelligently* needs.

Thus, the pupil's interest and curiosity principally motivate his learning. Instead of feeding the pupil exclusively with information selected or him by others on the grounds that these arc the things an "educated person" ought to know, the teacher should allow him to learn what he personally is curious about The teacher's function is to assist the child when he is in difficulty and to guide his general development in the light of a superior wisdom, which the child does not yet possess. This does *n'of* mean that pupils can be capricious about their schooling bet rather that their studies should be related as closely as possible to their own *examined* interests.

The pragmatist does not reject the study of logically organized subject matter, but he maintains that this should come late rather than early in the pupil's school career. The intelligence is best trained by being applied to what interests it. When it is trained or comparatively so, the pupil can turn to the study of organic' knowledge as such) His studies, then, should grow by degree more abstract and more demanding, his topics more general their implications, until he is ready to tackle the major intellectual disciplines in their own right.

For the pragmatist abstract knowledge is not something hard ' understand or remote from life. It consists of any experience idea that has-been-emancipated from its limited context and given a wider-reference for further use. The process of abstraction indispensable to any reflective activity. Abstract thinking a' implies that the student not only has learned the specific physic symbols of a problem but, more important, has grasped its meaning and is 'able to transfer that meaning to other and similar problems. In Dewey's words, abstract thinking "signifies conscious transfer of a meaning embedded in past experience for use in new one. It is the very artery of intelligence, of the Intention rendering of one experience available for guidance of another. Thus, abstract thinking is an active educative experience: and ;active educative experience, contrary to popular opinion, is not limited to muscular exercise. It includes intellectualizing, conceptualizing, imagining, or anything that helps us to sense the *meaning* of what is going on

## Pragmatist Values and *Education*

For the pragmatist, values are relative. There are no absolute principles on which we can lean, irrespective of their consequences for others. All moral and esthetic canons are liable to alteration in the course of a culture's development. This is not to claim,' that morality must fluctuate from day to day. It is to maintain that no particular moral precept may be regarded as universally binding, irrespective of the circumstances in which it is exercised. The Fifth Commandment, for instance, is not an absolute principle; on occasion it may be right to kill, as, for example, ii a just war, or to defend oneself, or to save the life of another. The values to be taught in school are those that advance human welfare. The child should learn how to make difficult moral decisions, not by falling back on rigidly prescribed principles, but rather by determining which course of intelligent action is likely to educe the best results in human, finite terms.

Men should establish their values in the same way that ;they shod establish the truth of their ideas They should allow the intelligence to consider impartially the proms of human affair Pal to select the values that seem most likely to resolve them These values should not be imposed on us by a higher authority .They should be agreed upon, if possible, after open and informed discussion:

Only a democracy permits the expression of all points of view and the establishment of free consensus. Hence, in the pragmatist view, democracy and intelligence imply each other. ,Only within a democratic environments can intelligence attain the freedom of thought and action that, ideally, it requires. The school should actively foster the democratic spirit and all v its students as much scope as possible for governing themselves

Dewey's view of "growth leading to more growth and his definition of education as a "process of continuous reconstruction of experience emphasize two very important points education is not a thing but a process, and it never finish .These is a tendency is a to refer to education as something we have "had," such as four years in college or a course in physics, as though we le experienced something final, something that we never are liked to experience again. Yet, in reality, education never ends. It not a product taken home, like *a* bundle of groceries after leaving school, but a process that goes on partly in school and partly in informed social intercourse throughout a lifetime.

For the.pragmatist, self-realization constitutes the supreme end, of *all* men. Society sees to it 'that this goal is achieved through education. As the social group becomes more complex, it exerts; greater demands upon the individual .Its aims, skills, and value are incorporated into the school instruction.

But Dewey never posed the Individual against society or society against the individual. His social morality rejected any sort of rugged individualism that supported exploitation of others and any social arrangement that submerged the unique reality of the person Dewey envisioned the blending of individual thought and group sanction marked by what he called a "critical engagement The utopian community, which Dewey espoused, is established by people who have the courage to think independently and yet relate themselves to the group. This is a society that nourishes irate tualism, creativity, and a truly humanistic spirit.

All this and more constitute the pragmatist contribution to education. But to see this contribution spelled out in greater detail we must wait until we discuss in Chapter 4 the educational movement known as progressivism.

Let us now turn to two new philosophies, which largely disclaim the traditional categories in terms of which the three philosophies in this chapter have been expounded. Both philosophic could, it is true, be pressed into these categories, but it is fail' to let them speak for then selves.

## Definitions of Pragmatism

The following are definitions of pragmatism in vogue

"Pragmatism offers us a theory of meaning, a theory of truth, of knowledge, and a theory of reality."-***James B. Prett***

"Pragmatism is essentially a humanistic philosophy, maintaining. that man creates his own values in the course of activity, that reality is still in the making and avails part of its complexion from the future, that to an unascertainable extent our truths are manmade products." **-J. S. Ross**

## Principles of Pragmatism

The following are the chief principles of pragmatism

1. According to pragmatism, truth undergoes a change according to time, ideal and place; so the truth is not eternal, whole and definite. According to it, truth takes us forward to creation and is changeable.

2. According to. pragmatism, anything can be considered to be reliable and useful only by looking at its result or outcome. What begets pleasure, peace and satisfaction in doing, is practical and useful. Anything is good in the measure of its utility. It is the reason that it recommends inclusion of useful arts and skills in the educational curriculum.

3.The truth being changeable, so the aims and values are also changeable. Our ideals of life keep changing according to time, place, situation. If we do not change our ideals, we shall not be able to progress.

4. It is necessary for us to create a suitable atmosphere keeping in view the present situations. It should change according to the i utility of the ideal. Man should make use of his intellect and ability in preparation of suitable environment.

5. Performing activity on the basis of knowledge is the quality of pragmatism, and cannot be termed as blindly following.

6. Education should inculcate social virtues, because man's progress is inherent and possible within society. Developing social ability is the aim of education.

## Forms of Pragmatism

The following three are considered to be three forms of Pragmatism

1. **Humanistic Pragmatism :** The chief objective of humanistic pragmatism is to satisfy man's desires and needs. Whatever fulfils the purpose, satisfies the desire, develops the life, is true.

2. **Experimental Pragmatism :** The thing which can be proved true, useful and practical by experiment, rather than observation, is useful. Whatever can be experimentally verified as true, or what works is true

3. **Biological Pragmatism :** Biological pragmatism considers that man should prepare suitable atmosphere for fulfilling his needs. John Dewey has said in this connection : "By this type of pragmatism test is found in the function of thought in adapting the human organism to its environment.'

## Pragmatism and Faculty Psychology

Faculty psychology does not consider the centric power of the mind, while pragamatists consider the mind as the force behind the objective and energy. It is for this reason that pragmatism does not have faith in faculty psychology. Pragamatists do not have any faith in fruitless activity.

Pragamatists consider behavioural psychology as useful; so they give preference to practical and useful activities to thinking and knowledge. According to them, knowledge, thinking and feelings are secondary while activity is chief factor. Though pragamatists also give importance to emotions, yet their emotions have the clear reflection of their knowledge and activity.

Both Pragmatism and progressivism believe that the child is the future man. The aptitude of the child and adult are not similar. They have sufficient difference. It is the reason that the pragamatists consider me child as a child, and not as a small adult. They recommend that we should educate the child according to his aptitude. They want that the child should be given activity-based education according to his interest, attitude and needs. They want to eradicate all those things which are not useful, practical and according to the life of the child.

**Pragmatism and Idealism:** Pragmatism and idealism can be compared and contrasted on the following points

| Pragmatism | Idealism |
|---|---|
| 1. According to pragmatism, the truth is changeable, so it does not consider spiritual elements, such as thinking and eternal truth. The only individual consciousness. pragamatists have belief in | 1. Idealism considers nature soul and God as spiritual reality and have belief in them Idealists believe in spiritual consciousness. |
| 2. The pragamatists consider situation, feelings, activities as the basis of morality and civilisation. | 2. The idealists consider now ledge, idealistic behaviour and intellect as the basis of civilisation and morality. |
| 3. Pragmatism considers the physical world as true and the fulfilment of physical or material needs as the basis of happiness and satisfaction.. It gives prominence to activities of physical pleasure. | 3. idealism considers physical happiness and world as mortal, and considers spiritual pleasure and the other world as true. It considers the existence of ideas or thoughts as true. It is chiefly composed thoughts. of spiritual pleasure and ideal |
| 4. Pragmatism considers that truth keeps changing according to place, time and ideal. | 4. Idealism considers that the principal of truth is internal and permanent |
| 5. Pragmatism wants the development of useful -qualities by education. | 5. Idealism wants education to beget ideal aims and spiritual pleasure by emphasising on means and methods of teaching and teacher. |

| | |
|---|---|
| 6. Human civilisation keeps changing due to changeability of the world and so does the truth. Pragmatism wants to adopt useful activities for fulfilment of physical or material pleasure. | 6. According to idealism, truth is not enslaved to circumstances, ideals, time and place. We should influence situation according to truth and ideal. We have not to change the ideals and truth, but the circumstances. |

**Pragmatism and Naturalism:**

Pragmatism and naturalism can be compared and contrasted on the following points

| Pragmatism | Naturalism |
|---|---|
| 1. Pragmatism lays emphasis on the proven ideals and values on the basis of experiments | 1. Idealism does not accept any ideal or value. |
| 2. Pragmatism gives much importance to emotions. It does not consider human a machine. It considers man as the inspiration of the thinking mind. All necessary elements for human life have been accepted under it. | 2. Naturalism does not lay any emphasis on emotions. According to it, man is a machine and all his activities are mechanical. |
| 3. Pragmatism has provided good teaching methods but not good ideals and aims. Thus, it is not a complete philosophy. | 3. Like pragmatism, idealism too has not provided us with good ideals and aims. So it is also not a complete philosophy. |
| 4. Pragmatism is positivistic and supports society. | 4. Naturalism is negativistic, and is mutually opposite to pragmatism. It also opposes society. |
| 5. According to pragmatism, rules keep changing according to circumstances and are not universal. The rules are subjective which keep changing according to man's needs. | 5. Naturalism considers rules asuniversal and permanent. |

## Evaluation of Pragmatism

Pragmatism philosophy has direct relationship with man and his life. The necessary condition of human development is that he keeps changing his values and ideals under the pressure of circumstances, but the rules and principles determined earlier no more remain useful to him. If some thing is useful and pleasurable for us, is true as well and accepted. Pragmatism does not consider any predetermined ideal, value, truth or activity as true. According to it, everything changes according to the prevalent circumstances. Man is such a conscious and intelligent creature who brings about change in the environment for fulfilment of his needs. He finds solution to his personal and social problems in such changed circumstances. So it recommends that the form of our education should be individualistic which meets all human needs.

## Mertis of Pragmatism

Pragmatism has the following merits

1. Pragmatism frees man from orthodox traditions and makes him progressive and lays emphasis on the "establishment of his independent personality. He gives prominence to personality and activities and does not give importance to book knowledge.

2.Pragmatism lays emphasis on activity-based education for developing creative aptitude of the child. It is the reason that this philosophy has given birth to project method.

3. Pragmatism desires to discipline the child with activities. It lays more emphasis on activities than thoughts.

4. Pragmatism nurtures democratic administrative setup. It begets man opportunities for free thinking, independent working and development.

5. Pragmatism wants to educate the child in social environment.

### Demerits of Pragmatism

Pragmatism can be attributed the following demerits

1. Pragmatism neglects educational aims, while no activity or work can be proper without any aim. Not accepting the significance of aim is a shortcoming of this philosophy.

2. Human intellect contributes in the development of civilisation a great deal. This makes man as the superior creature. It is incorrect to enslave man under

instincts and emotions. Pragmatism considers intellect as secondary and imposes uncontrolled instincts, emotions and activity on it. It is not proper.

3. Some truths are universal and eternal. It is not good to negate them. The truth is always stationary; it does not change with the change in time, circumstances, place or anything else.

4. The basis of human consciousness is spirituality. Neglecting it means strangling humanism. Pragmatism does not approve of spiritual thinking. All-round development of human personality is not possible. It does not seem proper for pragmatism to overlook spiritual aspect of life.

People have come to like pragmatism because it emphasises on practical and learning things; but it does not consider the truth as eternal and permanent. We cannot think it proper from farsightedness viewpoint. The major shortcoming of pragmatism is neglect of aims, values and permanency of truth. It is helpful only for material development of man, it does not help in any way in spiritual development. Despite its shortcomings, it is useful for social development and activity-based teaching.

## Pragmatism and Education

According to pragmatism, change in life also brings a change in the truth as well. So, it is not justified to consider the predetermined truth as truth. With a change in the environment, many problems arise. Pragamatists use education to find out a solution to these new problems; so our education and educational system should be such which can provide solution to our personal and social problems.

According to pragmatism, the form and order of education and educational system should be useful as to effect the welfare of both man and society in physical or material terms. With this ideology in view, **John Dewey** has made education as pragmatic. Pragmatism and modem education are closely related with the concept of change at its core. It considers that the world as changeable, and nothing can be considered as eternal or permanent truth. The agricultural countries of the past have turned into industrial countries of the modern times. Even India has changed its face from a country completely based on agriculture to industries and computer revolution. Our economic, political and social conditions have undergone enormous change since we gained freedom; so have our needs. It is likely that this change will continue in the future too. The scholars are of the view that only those things and people can survive which change with the change in circumstances; and no educational system can be said to be the final form. Educational system has to be flexible which can change with the changing circumstances and provide real life experiences to the child and make him adaptable and socially efficient.

**William James** and **John Dewey** were exponents of pragmatism. According to them, the purpose of education is to bring about such ability in the child through intellectual, emotional, activity based and aesthetic experiences that he can establish new values and fulfill the social needs. It is the reason that they consider that education does not originate from philosophy. In fact, it is philosophy which comes from educational practices. **John Dewey** too has said "Philosophy is the theory of education in its most general phase." Pragmatism has brought about a new consciousness and awakening in the educational field, due to which many orthodox problems, traditions, ideals and beliefs are being eliminated. It lays emphasis on inductive method to impart education so that the child becomes an explorer treading the path of discovery of new ideals, values and truths. His personality is emphasised upon along side his independence, activity, experiment, flexibility of experiences, adjustability and utility.

## Features of Pragmatism

We can enumerate the features or characteristics of pragmatism in the following points

**1.Education as a Means of Newer Experiences :** Pragmatism considers practical utility and development as the aim of education and not book knowledge. According to its followers, knowledge is not predetermined; rather it undergoes a change with a change in the circumstances. So the pragamatists dismiss 'knowledge for knowledge' and oppose forcing of knowledge into the child. They are of the view that true knowledge can be gained by the child through his experiences. Experiences effect a change in his behaviour. In the words of **John Dewey** : "It is a process of reconstruction or reinstitution of experiences." In its essence, education is such a process which brings about enhancement and change in the child's experiences and reconstruction of his new experiences.

**2. Education for Development :** Pragmatism considers that the society is always undergoing the process of change, and education too should change with this change. Now the rate of progress has become tremendous; and the sociologists sometimes find it difficult to cope with the change. It has become difficult to predict what shape will the society take after a few years from now. In such a case, it is useless to educate the child using traditional education. The times have gone by when the child of a farmer became a farmer and the son of a goldsmith adopted his father's profession. Pragmatism has laid emphasis on the fact that education is for the child, and not vice versa. The pragamatists do not accept that the child is like a plain slate on whom anything can be written or like an empty vessel in whom anything can be forced into. It considers that the child is bom with certain innate and hereditary qualities, and education should employ its power to develop such qualities which can be done by keeping in view his interests, aptitude, attitude, abilities and capacities. This child should be enabled to take on the practical life in a fruitful way and effect his all-round development.

**3. Education as a Social Process :**'Man is a social being, and in the words of John Dewey, 'Education is the social continuity of life'. Man is closely related with the members of society as well as with the family members. It is in the contact with the society and family that he gains more knowledge in comparison to his contact with books. So pragmatism considers that a child's education should be conducted within society so that he develops social qualities and live a successful life.

**4. Education is Lively :** Pragmatism considers that traditional education is lifeless as it tries to transfer the old obsolete knowledge to the child. This ideology considers that life is activity-based and the child can gain knowledge only by activity. It is necessary to give him ample opportunities for activities for his all-round development so that he can adjust himself according to the new values and truths of the society.

**5. Responsibility of Education Lies on State :** In a democratic society like ours, the state should take over the responsibility of education on itself. Democracy will not be successful if the child remains ignorant and illiterate. Only then education will spread to every nook and corner of the country and do its duty of all-round development of the child.

## Pragmatism and Aims of Education

Pragmatism is of the view that it is not proper to predetermine the educational aims. The old values cannot determine the aims of modern education. Educational aims should be constructed keeping in view the needs of man and society. The child should be kept in such natural circumstances that he is able to determine his own values and ideals. External values and control should not be imposed upon the child. In the words of **John Dewey** : "Education, as such, has no aim. Education is an abstract idea. Only persons have aims. And the aim of persons are indefinitely varied, differing with different children, changing as children and their teachers grow. Stated aims, such as we are about to make, will do more harm than good unless they are taken only as suggestions as to how to look ahead for consequences, to observe conditions, and to choose means in the liberating and directing of children's energies.' According to pragmatism, the instincts and interests of the child should be guided toward new values as may be needed. The child should become active and enterprising by natural and social activities. His mind should become dynamic so that he can look for new values. It will do a lot of good to society. The child will be able to fulfill the needs of the society and himself.

The above discussion takes us to the realm where we do not find any specific aim of pragmatic education, as it does not have faith in any of static, predetermined, ultimate and general education. In the words of J.S. Ross : "The most general aims of education of pragamatist is just creation of new values, the main task of the educator is to put the educed into position to develop values for himself." So, if there is an aim of pragmatic education, it is only determining new values which gives birth to several specific and immediate objectives. Such an education aims at providing opportunity to the child according to his interest and abilities such dynamic guidance in social and literary activities in which he continues to develop and become able to face the worldly challenges of the modem world. He should be enabled to solve the problems of his livelihood and respect the others' needs with a flexible, dynamic and adaptable mind.

## Pragmatism and Curriculum

The following principles govern the construction of curriculum in according with pragmatism

1.Principle of utility.

2. Principle of Interest.

3.Principle of Activity and Experience.

4. Principle of Integration.

Now we shall discuss these principles in some detail

**1. Principle of Utility :** This principle supposes that only those experiences, things or topics should be included in the curriculum which are useful. The useful experiences are those which enhance knowledge and skill and are helpful in fulfilling his personal and social needs. Thus, the curriculum should include language, literature, health science, exercise, geography, history, etc. The curriculum for girls can include home science. These subjects will provide the child with abilities to face the realities of the world. The pragamatists want to include vocational subjects in the curriculum because it is very useful for life.

**2. Principle of Interest :** The construction of curriculum should be made keeping in with the nature and interest of the child. According to this principle, importance should be given to dialogue, writing, reading, counting, nature's study, art, handicraft etc.in the primary classes, because the child takes interest in artistic and creative activities and dialogues.

**3. Principle of Activity and Experience :** Education is an activity-based process. So, the curriculum should include such personal, social and purposeful activities which fulfil the personal and social needs of the child. It will help make the child self-dependent, social and moral.

**4. Principle of Integration :** According to this principle, integration of subjects should be effected while including various kinds of knowledge and skills. Teaching various subjects separately will not find any meaningful purpose. So the pragamatists want that the different subjects should not be taught in isolation, but co-relation should be established. The whole knowledge is like a tree with different subjects acting as branches. Similarly, integration should be attempted between knowledge and skill.

**Pragmatism and Teaching Methods**

Pragmatism has greatly contributed in the devleopment of education from the viewpoint of teaching methods. It has given us activity-based and practical teaching methods. The teaching methods should keep changing with a change in time, place and circumstances. The teacher should continue to experiment with newer methods in search of more suitable activity-based teaching methods. All those teaching methods should be adopted which should be suitable according to time and need, and complementary to the needs. The teaching methods should be purposeful and emphasis should be laid on making the child to take on purposeful activities so that he is able to find out solution to the future problems. Pragmatism does not support any orthodox or ancient teaching method. It is of the view that the minds or brains of the children are not similar; how can then a single kind of teaching method be useful and effective for all children? The teacher should use a teaching method which is related to the life of the child and is integrated with activity, practicality and experience.

Pragmatism lays emphasis on activity and experience, rather I than theory. It follows that the child should be given practical training with the help of activities. The pragamatists are of the view that activity creates new thoughts. Such problems should be presented before the child which he can solve using his physical and social abilities. Self experience is a great teacher and provides opportunity for learning. The chief purpose of this principle is to keep the child in a practical It atmosphere where he can solve the. problems to be faced by him as a meaningful member of society.

Thus, pragamatists want to make education and learning process meaningful, practical, activity-based, synthesised and adjustable. With these aims in view, pragmatism has put forward the project method. Under this method, the personal and social problems to be faced in actual life are included as activity and education is made child centred.

### Pragmatism and Discipline

The pragamatists want to bring about adjustability in the child by social thoughts and activities. According to it, the purposeful independent activities should be pleasurable, useful and collective which make the child self-controlled. It begets him a great character and moral life. Such activities do not allow the child to become uncontrolled.

## Project Method

The project method was conceived by **Kilpatrick**, a pupil of **John Dewey**. It was a solid and practical teaching method. This method involved activities at the child's end. The child experiences the things by doing. The function of the teacher is limited to presenting a problem before the child so that he 'is able to recognized it. Now the child attempts solution of the problem of his own, while the teacher acts as a guide. The children take the help of one another in the solution and come to conclusion by independent activity. When the stage of final conclusion is reached, the children discuss the problem and reach the final, definite and solid results and form new values.

### Pragmatism and Teacher

Pragmatism lays emphasis on the teacher as he plays an important role in the whole process of education. In fact, pragmatism came into being due to the practical endeavours of the teachers. William James engaged himself in the search of new teaching methods and principles all his life. He also attempted to establish coordination between religion and science. All these attempts were practical in nature. He used to choose suitable and useful teaching methods for his practical. He considered knowledge as the means by which we can reach the end-the activity. He believed that the human mind chooses out of good and bad, beautiful and ugly, useful and useless. If the mind is fully developed, he will be able select good, useful and beautiful things properly. Man is a practical creature by birth. His mind enables him engage himself in useful, worldly activities which will fulfil his needs. This thinking of **James William** was taken forward by **John Dewey**. He laid importance to the project method.

## Pragmatism and Discipline

Pragmatism bases its educational activities on the interest, attitude and aptitude of the child and makes him engage in activity based learning. It does not favour external control and physical punishment. According to it, discipline is a mental condition which can be attained by social activities. It believes in playway activities and non-interference in the child's activities. It thinks that if a child is not unnecessarily interfered, he will do his work seriously and with interest. The duty of discipline, according to pragmatism, is to inculcate love, cooperation and sympathy. It also lays emphasis on self-control, self-discipline and moral discipline. It is of the view that a child should given ample opportunities to perform purposeful and independent activities so that he develops a social attitude and begets the lesson of citizenship, which will inculcate in him the sense of responsible citizenship.

## Pragmatism and School

Pragmatism is of the view that the school should serve as an institution where the child comes into contact with others to experience collective and social life for inculcation of good moral qualities which will enable him to fulfil his responsibilities in the practical life in the future. The school, according to John Dewey, is the true representative of society where he should get opportunities for gaining experiences according to his interest, aptitude and ability in a collective atmosphere. Thus, pragmatism considers the school as the most appropriate place for preparing the child for the future life. The school not only provides education, but also acts like a centre for social activities.

**Evaluation of Pragmatism**

From the detailed discussion above, we can. evaluate the utility of pragmatism. The emergence of pragmatism in the educational world has done much good to the educational system and society. It has laid emphasis on activity, experiment, experience, utility an development of man and society; and has thus changed the outlook of man. It has brought about a new era in the modern education. 1s/is a revolution which wants to educate and develop the child according to the changing needs of the society and make the society progressive and modem in real terms. In the words of Rusk : "It is merely a stage in the development of a new idealism that will do full justice to reality, reconcile the practical and the spiritual values and result in a culture which is the flower of efficiency." Pragmatism wants to make the child's personality dynamic and flexible so that he can adapt and adjust according to the changing environment and needs, so that he proceeds to make his life rich, happy and civilised. Though this thinking has taken education out of spiritual realm, yet it remains important in the world of modern development.

## REALISM

The basis of realism is a belief in the reality of matter. The universe, for the realist, is not an illusion but rather something that really and concretely exists. Hills, trees, cities, and stars are not simply ideas in the minds of observing individuals or even in the mind of an Eternal Observer. They exist in their own right, independently of the mind. However, although realists agree about the reality of matter, their disagreements in certain other respects have divided them into many different schools. Today the major groupings are rational realism on the one hand and natural or scientific realism on the other.

***Types* of Rational Realism**

Rational realism may be divided further into *classical realism,* sometimes known as classical humanism, and *religious realism, of* which the chief type is scholasticism, the official philosophy c the Roman Catholic church Both schools bear the imprint c the great Athenian philosopher, Aristotle, who founded his own school of thought as an alternative to Platonism. Whereas rational realists look directly to Aristotle, the scholastics do so on˘, indirectly; they base their philosophy on that of **St.Thoma Auinas** the great mediaeval philosopher-theologian. By harnessing the doctrines of Aristotle to the theology of the Church, Aquinas created a new Christian philosophy, later called *Thomism.* in opposition to the modified Platonism espoused by most theologians of his time.

## Classical and Religious Realism-The Nature of Reality

Both classical and religious realists declare that the material world is real and exists outside the minds of those who observe it. Thomists, however, maintain that both matter and spirit have been created by God, Who constructed an orderly and rational universe out oh His supreme wisdom and goodness Spirit, though not exactly more "real" than matter, is nevertheless more important: it is a "higher" mode of being, because God Himself is Spirit and perfect in every way.

How do Thomists know this? By revelation-from Biblical history, prophecy, and the teachings of Jesus Christ, which they affirm to be God's word to all mankind. But their knowledge is also attained by means other than faith, that is, by reason and experience. Among the world-famous spokesmen of modern Thomism are Etienne Gilson and Jacques Maritain. Leading American Thomists include William McGucken, Robert J. Henle, Edward A. Fitzpatrick, and William F. Cunningham. The best known American exponents of the educational implications of classical realism arc Mortimer Adler, Robert M. Hutchins, and Scott Buchanan, whose views are discussed later under the heading of *perennialism.*

**Natural or Scientific Realism-The Nature of Reality**

Natural realism followed the rise of science in Europe during the fifteenth and sixteenth centuries. Its leading spokesmen were the British philosophers. Francis Bacon, John Locke, David Hume, and John Stuart Mill. In the field of education its foremost exponent was Jean-Jacques Rousseau, founder of romantic naturalism, although some people prefer to classify him as an idealist. In this century natural realism led to two American schools, neorealism and critical realism, whose differences are largely epistemological. According to neorealism, we perceive objects directly; according to critical realism, we do so only at second hand through certain intervening media that are not in themselves physical. Among the leading neorealists are Bertrand Russell, Alfred North Whitehead, and Ralph Barton Perry. The best known critical realist is George Santayana.

Skeptical and experimental in temper, natural realism maintains that philosophy should seek to imitate the rigor and objectivity of science. Since the world around us is real, it is the task of science rather than philosophy to investigate it; philosophy's function is to coordinate the concepts and findings of the different sciences. The most significant feature of the universe is that it is permanent and enduring. Change is real certainly, but it takes place in accordance with the laws of nature, which make the universe a continuing structure. Many natural realists deny the existence of spirit or else maintain that its existence cannot be proved.

**Realism-and- Human Nature**

Realists are divided in their conception of man. Rational realists. regard man as a spiritual being. Classical realists maintain that rationality is man's highest attribute, but they reject the view that he has been divinely created. Thomists declare that man is a fusion of the material and the spiritual, with body and soul forming one nature. lie is free, they say, and responsible for his actions. He is also immortal, having been placed on earth to love and honor his Creator and to live with Him after death in perfect happiness. Since all men are implicated in the sin of their progenitor, Adam, each individual is prone to evil unless he is aides by Divine Grace.

According to natural realism, man is a biological organism with a highly developed nervous system and a naturally social disposition. His supposedly mental or spiritual activities are, in fact, highly intricate physical processes, which science has not yet been able to explain satisfactorily. Most natural realists *deny* the existence of free will; they argue that the individual is determined by the impact of the physical and social environment upon his inherited genetic structure. What we call freedom of choice is apparent only. We *think* we choose, but actually we do not.

**Realist Metaphysics and Education**

The realist maintains that, since the universe exists independently of us and is governed by laws over which we have little control, it is necessary to know certain definite things about this universe in order to adapt to it. Education must have a central core of subject matter that will acquaint the pupil with the basic physical and cultural structure of the world in which he lives. The Catholic realist adds that the order and harmony of the universe must be seen as the result of Divine Creation' therefore, he says, we should study nature as God's handiwork. In his view,. the prime purpose of all education is to prepare the human being for life in the Hereafter The earth is a testing ground. God has put us on our own e and has given us a conscience and free will. But He also has established the Church as the supreme educational agency; if we are wise, we will accept her Guidance and learn her doctrine. For classical realists there is no personal God or heaven. Hence, other factors, whose nature will be explained in due course, must become the determinants of education. t For the realist the purpose of education is not primarily to con: H each child into something rare and individual. It is to enable aim to become a tolerant and well-adjusted person, in harmony mentally and physically with his physical and cultural environment This view does not mean that the realist underestimates to value of individual. creativity. In

Whitehead's view, in particular, all nature is creative, and 'Iltdi6dual creativity is a manifestation of a universal creative fore When we speak of adjustment, therefore, we also mean justment to the individualism, creativity, curiosity, and personal enterprise that really are present in human nature. The realist conception of adjustment is not hostile to spontaneity and individualism.

**Realist Ejistemology and Education**

Realists assert that objects exist independent of perception. Furthermore, we make direct contact with them. What we see, hear, taste, touch, and smell are not ideas or impressions but rather things themselves. Instead of actively creating or recreating its own world, as the idealist suggests, the mind receives information *from* the world. The mind no longer dictates to reality; reality dictates to the mind.

For the realist an idea is true when it "corresponds" with those aspects of the world that it claims to describe ''A theory about the world cannot be true simply because it "fits in" or "coheres" with other existing theories. In order to interpret the world validly, a theory must *correspond* to it.

It is the pupil's responsibility to master those elements of knowledge that have stood test of time. Before deciding what can be done with the world, he should learn what experts say the world really is like. The teacher must not be diverted by temporary fads from accomplishing his true task, which is to impart substantive knowledge of the actual world. Nor should he allow the pupil to find out for himself whatever he wants to know, since what lie wants to know is often less important than-what. he should know.

Classical realists insist that, since man is a rational. being, the school should give priority to the cultivation of reason. This emphasis on intellectual training is one that has been shared by most educational philosophies in the past. The classical realist school, therefore, will tend to be traditional in its choice of methods and subject matter. Despite the school's concentration on subject matter rather than on the personality of the individual child, it is not the purpose of education to turn out pedants and professors but individuals who are well rounded in the Aristotelian sense-moderate and temperate in all things.

Natural realists maintain that physical science provides man with his most reliable knowledge. Hence, next to the three R's, science should have the most important place in the school curriculum. Natural realists advocate the application of scientific methods to the study of all aspects of human life. They deny. however, that the behavioral sciences-psychology, sociology, anthropology-are reliable enough as yet to major attention in the school.

For the realist, initiative in education rests with the teacher. It is his responsibility to decide what knowledge the child .should learn. If he can teach in such a way that the child's own interests and intellectual curiosity are satisfied, so much the. better. but pupil desires are not of primary concern. Intelligence demands discipline-the discipline imposed both by awareness of the things in the world that are permanent and unalterable and by our consciousness of the limits of human ability. Knowledge makes us "realists" in the popular as well as the philosophical sense of the term.

**Realist Values and Education**

Although all realists agree that values are permanent and objective they differ in their reasons for thinking so. Classical realists concur with Aristotle that there is a universal moral law, available to reason, which is binding on all men as rational beings. Thomists agree that men can discern this moral law by using reason, but they insist, nevertheless, that it has been established by God, Who has endowed man with the rational faculty to apprehend it. Man can understand the moral law without Divine aid. However, because his nature has been corrupted by Original Sin, he cannot *practice* it without God's grace. Scientific realists deny that values have any supernatural sanction. Good is that which adjusts man to his environment, evil is that which estranges him. Because both human nature and its physical environment are constant, the values that adjust one to the other will be constant also: It is true that social institutions and practices vary considerably; but the basic values t at any society should observe main unchanged.

Realists agree that any educational system should be geared to Main well-defined values. Since values themselves do not vary, neither do the true ends of education. Similarly, the moral standards that we teach the child should be influenced as little as possible by the views of the teacher or the preconceptions of the era. Instead, they should conform to what has proved of most enduring value to man throughout history. The child should be taught to live by absolute moral standards in the knowledge that what is right is-right-for man in general and not simply, for the members of a particular, race or society. It is also important for him to acquire good habits, for virtue does not come automatically; it has to be learned.

Religious realists declare that "natural" goodness is insufficient. They hold that man has been created to transcend what is_ natural and to attain in the_supernatural. The true purpose of morality and education is the salvation of souls. The child should be taught always to keep his soul in a state of grace, that is, filled with Divine Grace and free from mortal sin. He should seek the good and avoid evil, not simply because it is prescribed by reason, but rather because it is God's will.

Education say religious realists, should train man's will ass well as his intellect. Although God offers salvation, man himself must decide to accept or reject it. Hence, his will should be "habituated" to making the right choices. Because human nature has been corrupted by Original Sin, education also has an essentially corrective role to play. Firm discipline is needed to eliminate bad habits and cultivate good ones.

Natural realism teaches that right and wrong come from man's understanding of nature and not from religious principles. Morality should be based on what scientific investigation has shown to be beneficial to man as the highest species of am al: Disease is evil and health is good must favor the good by taking measures to improve our genetic constitution and overcome evil by understanding and improving the environment in which we live.

Many scientific realists are also religious-minded, but they tend to understand religion and science as two different aspects of the same truth. Not necessarily in conflict with each other, religion and science lead to a greater understanding of the ultimate mystery of the universe: "The hëavens declare the glory of God and the firmament showed His handiwork." God has given us the talent to understand Ills Handiwork. He has even endowed us with the reason by which we may reject Him and has said that we have free will to do so. But the rejection of God merely signifies that we have to presuppose some other explanation principle, and there is no reason to believe that the something else will be any more valid than the Christian God.

Like many scientists, too many teachers perform their tasks without feeling the need to make any final decisions in these matters. The problem remains, however: When children themselves look for answers, what will they be offered" How long can the teacher of physics remain neutral in the presence of questioning minds? Is it enough for the student to know the "facts" of physics? To ask the same question as before, in *the long run* why are we teaching and learning physics anyhow, if not to understand the nature of the universe as the physicist sees it? And what good is the physicist's interpretation if it does not take into account the knowledge that has been obtained in other fields?

**Realism and Education**

What we can perceive using our sense organs is real.: he thing we cannot perceive or experience, is not real. The ideology of realism is based on this concept. This ideology is against the ideology .of spiritualism or idealism. The mind can also be true or untrue like all *oilier material things. As the world has ·developed', toe mind toe) as* along side. The ideology of realism is foe gift of science. cording to realism, it is necessary to scientifically analyses the tendencies a interests of the society and child; and those tendencies and *interests should be developed which are in the interest of the society and country. Educational system should be accordingly managed end* arranged. Such education will help development of man, and society. bring about prosperity and happiness.

## Meaning of Realism

The word `real' pertains to an object which can be receive , as such realism is a concept which is related with "he existence of thoughts concerned with things: it takes all things of the worm as real. The proponents of this ideology consider *that the* knowledge gained by sense organ.. alone is true ;only that is true which is physically present before our eyes.

## Definitions of Realism

*"The doctrine of realism asserts that there is a r*eal world of things behind *and corresponding to the objects of our perception* ,**J S Ross.**

"Realism is the reinforcement of our common acceptance of the world as it appears to us."- **Butler**

"Realism means a belief or theory which looks upon the, world as *it seems to us to be a mere phenomenon.* ***-Swami Ramatirha***

### Basic Principles of Realism

The chief principles of realism can be enumerated as follows

**1. Man is a Part of Physical World :** Realism considers man as a part of the physical or material world with possession of mind and sense organs by which he perceives the physical objects.

**2. Sense Organs as the Entry Points :** Realism considers the sense organs as the entry points through which knowledge is gained. The sense organs get sensation on coming into contact with the material things, which are the real experience. Bertrand Russel has written in this regard : "I contend that ultimate constituent of matter are not atoms but sensation. I believe that the stuff our mental life consists wholly of sensations and images."

**3. Significance of Practical Life :** Realism is of the view that spiritual world cannot be perceived by sense organs, so it does not consider them for study. It gives significance to the physical matters in the world, and lays emphasis on the practical life of man and things. The aim of life, according to realism, is to lead a happy life and which can be attained when all facilities of life are available and consumed. Rusk wrote : 'The aim of new realism now expound a philosophy which is not inconsistent with the facts of common life and with development of physical science."

**4. Opposition to Idealism :** Realism is against any concept of imagination. It considers that the words like soul, God and other world are only figment of imagination, so it opposes idealism and accepts the existence of only real things.

**5. Truth of Phenomenal World :** Realism considers only the real world as true and real. So it considers the world which is present and real as really existing. The followers of this ideology are of the view that there is no other world beyond the one before our eyes, and they do not at all have any belief in the indirect world. J. S. Ross wrote in this connection : "Realism simply affirms the existence of an external world and is therefore the antithesis of subjective idealism.'

**6.Theory of Organism :** Realism considers that the conscious and unconscious things make organism. According to Whitehead "The universe is a vibrating organism in the process of evolution. Change is the fundamental feature of this vibrating universe. The very essence of real actuality is process. Mind must be regarded as the function of the organism."

**7. Emphasis on Observation and Experiment :** The ideology of realism lays emphasis on observation and experimentation. It does not accept anything as proven unless it has been observed, experimented and analysed.

## Characteristics of Realistic Education

The ideology of realism came into being as a result of its opposition to idealism. It has left a deep mark on education. It should be necessary to point out the characteristics of realistic education, which are as follows

**1. Emphasis on Experiment and Practical Life :** One of the chief characteristics of realistic education is that it lays emphasis on experiment and practical outlook in life and education. It emphasises on the activism and practicality of the students, so that they are able to lead their life happily by meeting everyday needs.

**2. Scientific in Nature :** The ideology of realism lays emphasis on the scientific outlook of life, as such it says that the study of science subjects is necessary. It is against the study of artificial subjects in school, and says that nature should be studied instead. Being based on science is one of the chief characteristics of realistic education.

**3. Opposition to Book Knowledge :** The proponents of realism say that the book(ish) knowledge merely adds to memory, but it does not impart knowledge of the real; as such it condemned the prevalent book education as meaningless. It lays emphasis on such an education which is able to impart knowledge on both matter and environment. It advocates that education should be such which is able to develop intellect, prudence and other qualities in the students.

**4. Emphasis on the Present :** Realism lays emphasis on the present life, as against the concept of idealism which considers the spiritual life. It says that the sole aim of education is to make the present life of man happy and successful.

**5. Limited Freedom to the Learner :** Realism considers that the students is an important factor in the process of education, and that his desires, feelings, emotions and abilities cannot be ignored. However, it is of the view that the freedom of the student should be accepted but in a limited way because he cannot learn everything of his own, as the purpose of education is to make the student tread from the dark of ignorance to the light of knowledge. It does not advocate freedom of the student in every respect, as does idealism.

**6. Significance to individuality and Sociability :** The realist education lays emphasis on both individuality and sociability. It considers that the aim of education is to meet the needs of both individual and society. **Becon** has said that education must make an individual useful for society. It is clear that realistic education considers the development of individuality and development of sociability on an equal footing.

**7. Training of Sense Organs :** The realist education considers that the sense organs are the entry points of knowledge, wherefrom the student senses knowledge and gains it. It does not consider forcing knowledge into the mind of the student. It says that gaining knowledge is the result of training of sense organs. It thinks that knowledge will not be real if it is not gained by sense organs.

**Aims of Realistic Education**

We can infer the following aims of realistic education

**1. Preparing the Student for a Practical Life :** The primary aim of the realistic education is to prepare the student for practical life. The ideology of realism considers the material and physical world as the real life, and it aims to prepare the student for his future practical and real life.

**2. Knowledge of Nature and Society :** The realistic ideology is related to nature and society. It considers its duty to acquaint the student with the knowledge of, nature and society so that he is able to lead a coordinated life with them.

**3. Vocational Guidance :** The realistic education considers that education should have practical aspect and should be useful for leading a good life. So. it lays emphasis on vocational aspect by which livelihood can be earned, as such one of its aims is to impart professional training. .

**4. Happy and Successful** Lure : The foremost aim of education should be to enable the student to lead a happy and successful life, and the realistic education too aims at it. It considers that education should be such which prepares the students for a practical life essence of real enabling him to meet his needs of life so that he is able to lead a successful life.

**5. Mental and Physical Abilities :** The realist education also aims at physical and mental development of the student, as both these aspects are considered necessary part of matter. It is of the view that developed bodies are able to meet the physical needs, while the developed mental faculties help to utilise prudence, decisiveness, etc. for a successful life.

**6. Training of Sense** Organs : According to realistic ideology, the student gains knowledge using the sense organs, as such the training of sense organs is necessary, without which he will not be able to gain knowledge. As such, training and development of the sense organs is necessary.

## Merits of Realism

The merits or advantages of realism can be enumerated in the following points

**1. Practical Education :** Realism emphasises that education should be practical. Now it is considered that impracticable education is useless.

**2. Realistic Aims :** Realism professes realistic aims for education and thus greatly contributed to the world of education. It lays emphasis that what exists now and here is real and true, all else is only imagination. The aims of education based on this merit are worthwhile.

**3. Significance of Science Subjects :** Realism has laid emphasis on the study of science subjects. It is now the established view that a country cannot develop without the aid of science.

**4. Emphasis on Scientific Methods :** Realism has brought about revolutionary changes in the teaching methods. Induction method has replaced the deduction method, so have come into use the practical, experimental, huristic and co-relation methods.

**5. Effective and Free Discipline :** Realism advocates limited freedom to the students while keeping discipline effective and liberal.

**6. Objectivity :** Realism professes objectivity of view, as the students today study by objective methods.

**7. Effect on School Organisation :** Now the sight of a crying child going to school has become a thing of the past, as education has changed itself to adjust to the psychological needs of the child to make it interesting with the overflowing sentiments of love, affection, cooperation, sympathy and humanity. The students are not unnecessarily given harsh punishments.

## Demerits of Realism

The ideology of realism is susceptible to some demerits too. Here is a brief mention of them.

**1. Undue Emphasis on Material World** : Realism lays emphasis on the present,' real and material world, but finds itself unable to answer the questions which ask about the super phenomenon, other world, soul, God, universe, and many more things. The scholars are of the view how the present world can be considered the end in itself when there are several direct and indirect indicators to show that such `imaginative' things do exist.

**2. Knowledge by Sense Organs** : Realism says that knowledge is gained by the sensation of the sense organs, but it fails to answer how are we subjected to illusion and false knowledge.

**3. Unimaginative** : Realism accepts and approves real needs of life, feelings, emotions; but it discards imagination, sentiments and mood; whereas these too are equally important aspects of human life.

**4. Emphasis on Elements** : Realism emphasises elements or facts and considers them valuable. Many educational problems, such as indiscipline, corruption and injustice are such elements which can be proved, but do they deserve to be called important and valuable?

**5. Emphasis on Real Daily Life** : Realism discards idealism and has faith in daily life, easily forgetting that lack of ideals and idealism in life will make the students dull and pessimist.

**6. Neglect of Art Subjects** : It may be a positive aspect of realism that it emphasises the study of science subjects, but its failure to, pay attention to the art subjects is. unfounded. The art subjects, like art, music, literature, etc., have their own significance in life and cannot be neglected, as they are very necessary for intellectual and mental development.

## Realism and School

All advocates of realism do not hold the same view as far as school is concerned. Some realists consider that school is not at all needed. They have advocated the fact that tour, experience and private tutor are the best means of education. On the other hand, such a thinking has been opposed by other realists. They have accepted the significance of school and opined that school works like a reflection of society. They are of the view that all those activities which take place in society should be included in the curriculum of school, so that the students can be made to experience the real life around them. They opine that the school is the place where individual and social needs can be fulfilled. Secondly, professional and vocational education can also be imparted in school. It entails that all those activities should be included in the activities of school where a child is taught about the real world using love and affection, and where he can experience all those means and resources which are necessary for society.

## Realism and Teacher

Realism does not attach much importance to teacher as does idealism, but it has not receded to a secondary or insignificant place either as naturalism has done. Realism expects of a teacher that he possesses complete knowledge of his subject and also the needs of the students who is going to usher in the society-after completion of his education. Not only this, he should be able to present the subject matter before the student in a scientific manner using scientific and psychological methods. According to realists, it is the duty of the teacher to acquaint the students with science and also tell them the contribution of the great people and scientists in various fields. He should also endeavour to develop the student's mind to the extent that he is able to find out new paths for himself by analysis. The teacher should be able to ascertain which child needs how much knowledge, and it should be given in that ratio. Realism desires that the teacher should be trained according to the ideology of realism before he steps into the classroom.

## Realism and Teaching Methods

The realists have opined that the prevalent education is not suitable for launching the student in the practical life, as it restricts its scope to the teaching of words and theoretical knowledge. It was the result that they put forward their own brand of education and teaching methods which are based on self-experience, self-observation and self-realization using their sense organs. We can say that that the child should be shown the thing first, and the knowledge of the word should follow later.

It is the result of the endeavours of the realists that the teaching methods have begun from the objects, than realists emphasised on the reality of the things while impa.ting knowledge. They are of the view that from the abstract concept, and the use of audio-video means has started in the schools. Some of the realists emphasised on learning by traveling. **John Locke** and **Milton** favoured tour, observation, experimentation and experience as the necessary ingredients of learning. Others, like **Becon,** advocated the use of inductive method in place of the old deductive method as professed by **Aristotle.** This method presupposes the introduction of a thing first and the related words later. It enables the child to learn by his self-experience, self-observation and decision.

Thus, the two chief teaching methods that came into being were learning by doing and learning by experience. The realists have considered knowledge as a unit and have supported correlation method.

### Realism and Discipline

The advocates of realism consider discipline as a necessary attribute in the personality of a child. However, they favour that the child should be able to study in an atmosphere of love and affection where he is in the proximity of material things learning by self observation and self-experience, and is able to coordinate with the real things of the world. Comenius was of the view that the school should be like the lap of the mother where a child takes flights of fancy in the environment of love, affection, security. Thus, the realists favour the use of impressionistic and emancipationistic discipline, and discard repressionistic discipline altogether.

### Realism and Curriculum

Realists have their own specific viewpoint regarding the curriculum. They have accepted the existence of only real physical things, so they emphasise that curriculum should contain only those subjects which are useful for the child in his practical real life. It is this view that they have accorded prominence to subjects like nature, science and vocational subjects keeping in view the real circumstances, problems and needs around in the society; they have accorded a secondary or least-important place to art, literature,language and music, etc. It may be pertinent to note that the realists have laid down about 26-28 subjects and they give freedom to the child to choose from them according to his interest, aptitude and attitude. The realists have propounded that the learning of the mother tongue is necessary for all-round development and vocational training is necessary for progress in social life. As such. realists have recommended inclusion of the mother tongue and vocational training in the curriculum.

## Forms of Realism

The basic aim of realism is how to make man's life happy and prosperous from material viewpoint. The education in accordance with realism prepares the student for a happy future life. It trains the individual to face up the challenges of life and become successful. However, there have been a few forms of realism that it has taken from time to time

1. Humanistic realism,
2. Social realism,
3. Physical realism, and
4. Neo-realism.

Now, we shall discuss them in brief

### 1. Humanistic Realism

Humanistic realism had a belief that education should be realistic and only then it can beget success and happiness to the individual. It advocated the study of Greek and Roman literature as necessary for achievement of this exalted aim; it contended that all knowledge necessary for making the life successful was contained in this literature. It was of the view that there was not a problem on which literature did not throw light and that the knowledge of the real form of society cannot be got without their study. Thus, the advocates of humanistic realism considered the study of Greek and Roman literature as necessary for the happiness and success of life.

The following scholars supported this ideology

**Irasmus (1446-1536) :** Erasmus lived in England. His famous books, in the field of education are : *System of Studies* and *Ciceronianism.* He has propounded liberal education and strongly opposed narrow and unrelated education. He has written: "Knowledge seems to be of two kinds that of things and that of words, that the word comes first that of things is more important."

**Rebelias (1483-1553) :** Rebelias was a French and, propounded liberal education. He opposed the education which taught words and theory alone. He emphasised on the study of physical, social, religious and moral education. Two of his books which highlight his principles are : *The Heroic Deeds of Pantagruel* and *Life of Gargantua.* He was of the view that education should enable a child to solve every problem that he might face in his practical life, so he tried to bring about a change in the curriculum and educational system too. He attempted to remove logic, grammar and literature from the curriculum and provided a scientific basis to teaching in place of exercise and learning by rote.

**Milton (1608-1674) :** Milton was a British poet and writer besides being a philosopher and educationist. He has written his education-related thoughts in his book the *Tracts of Education in* which Fie opposes emotional education and supports liberal and complete education. He writes : "I call therefore a complete and generous education that which fits a man to perform justly, skilfully and magnanimously all the offices both private and public in peace and war." Milton was religious by nature and said that education should enable the student to know about God and his heart should get illuminated with love. He opposed theoretical education and emphasised the study of real things. He also advocated physical education and termed tour as important means of education. It may be surprising to note that he opposed general education. He prepared a curriculum from the students from 12 to 21 years of age and gave prominent place to language, literature and moral education, and gave secondary importance to physiology, architecture and agriculture.

## 2. Social Realism

Social realism seeks to make life successful and happy while meeting the social needs. The proponents of this ideology opposed learning by rote and laid emphasis on the social environment and society for gaining real knowledge. The proponents of this ideology were of the view that bookish) knowledge should be replaced by what is practical and useful in real life so that the person becomes proficient,' skilful and capable. They professed that the subjects' such as geography, history, mathematics, law, political education, use of arms, horse-riding, dance, gymnastic, etc. should find a place in education so that social qualities can be developed in the students. J.S. Ross has written in this regard: "The social realists looking askance at bookish studies, stressed the value of direct studies of man and things, having in mind chiefly the upper class, they advocated a period of travel, a grand tour, which would give real experience of the varied aspects of life." The proponents of social realism also said that the school was not a proper place for imparting education, because it provided only book (ish) knowledge; while they emphasised the need of tour, journey, observation and experience for gaining knowledge and education.

The following scholars are chief supporters of social realism

**Lord Montaigne (1533-1592)** : Lord Montaigne was a famous French essayist. He has written many essays on a variety of subjects. His education-related essays can be found in his three books-Of *Pedantry, Of the Education of the Children,* and *Of* the *Affection of Father to Their Children.* He was of the view that the purpose of education was to inculcate intelligence and prudence in the student so that he is able to live a happy and organised life. He believed that man should never accept anything for granted without giving a thought to it. He opposed 'knowledge for knowledge sake' and emphasised imparting of practical knowledge which is useful for practical social life. He considered the journey or tour as an important means of education, and was against the use of repressionistic measures for imparting knowledge and maintenance of discipline among the students. He said : "A boy should not so much memorize his lesson as practice it. Let him repeat it in his actions." Montaigne was of the view that a child should first learn his mother tongue, than the language of the neighbour and at last attempt to learn Greek and Latin languages.

**John Locke** (1635-1704) : John Locke was a British educationist who emphasised that the aim of education was development of various qualities in the students which included virtue, wisdom, breeding and learning. His education-related thoughts can be found in his book Some *thoughts Concerning Education.* He emphasised on the physical, intellectual, mental and moral development of the students. He was an individualistic philosopher who opposed general education and advocated education for the high and elite. He considered the brain as a plain slate on which anything could be written. He also favoured taking services of a private tutor. He also emphasised interesting and entertaining teaching methods. He favoured imparting education using the mother tongue and argued that those subjects should find a representation in the curriculum which were socially useful and practicable, and helped the students in settling down in practical social life.

### 3. Physical Realism

Physical realism, or realism concerned with sense organs came into being in the seventeenth century in which the educational principles of the modern education can be found. The proponents of this ideology claim that knowledge is gained primarily using sense organs, and not by words. It says that a child will not begin to learn unless he has felt by skin, smelt by nose, heard by ear, seen by ear and tasted by tongue. The scientific and technological inventions and discoveries in the seventeenth century had profound impact on the supporters of physical realism and they professed that the origin of truth or knowledge was nature, and natural means should be adopted to impart knowledge, and that the artificial means were not suitable for it.

Physical realism claimed that education system should be such which imparted education by nature and natural process in which the knowledge of the natural things and processes is imparted. Physical realism had impact on the educational thoughts and it could be seen in the change of system in education which now started education in the mother tongue, study of natural and physical sciences in place of literature and languages, education of the useful and practical secondary schools, preference to inductive method in place of deductive method, and this culminated in assistance to the development of psychology.

Physical realism, or realism by sense organs got support from the following scholars

**Mulcaster (1530-1611)** : Mulcaster was a British educationist, who worked as the head of several schools in England for 37 years. He has written several books; his thoughts on education can be found in his two books - *Elementarie* and *Positions.* He brought about a change in the thinking about imparting education to the students. He said that the child was the centre of education and that education should be imparted using the mother tongue. He said : The end of education and training is to help nature to her perfection." He said that primary education should include the study of mother tongue, reading-writing, music, art, etc. and science subjects should be included at intermediate level. He opposed any kind of pressure on the child and said that efforts should be made to impart education in a natural way by developing intellect, prudence and memory of the child. He was also a supporter of the psychological methods and was of the view that the teacher is like an artist who has complete knowledge of the colours and designs. He said that a teacher without suitable teaching methods was not effective.

**Francis Bacon (1562-1623) :** Bacon was a great writer, writer and philosopher of England. He has enlightened the world of education with his practical thoughts, which can be chiefly found in his two books-The *New Atlantis* and *Advancement of Learning.* He was of the view that education should transform the child as useful for society. He believed that then prevalent education could not meet this target, so he changed the teaching methods into a scientific or inductive form. He wrote : "The object of all knowledge is to give man power over nature." His method presupposes the opportunities of observation and experimentation by sense organs. It was due to his efforts that the deductive method of **Aristotle** receded in significance. The curriculum of

Bacon accorded chief significance to subjects like science and natural education, and receded literature, philosophy and religion to the secondary place.

**Ratke (1571-1625) :** This German educationist considered education as the process of development and that its aim should be to develop the child according to his nature. He said that the sense organs were the entry points of knowledge and formulated certain educational formulae. He said that the interest, ability and capacity of the child must be kept in view, so one thing should be taught at one time using the sense organs. He said that repetition was the key to learning. He favoured using mother tongue for education and was against learning by rote. He did not favour repressionistic discipline. He advocated that things should precede words. He said that knowledge is gained by experience.

**Comenius (1592-1671) :** Comenius occupies the highest place in the physical or sensual realism; according to him, the sole aim of education is to make the child wise, moral and spiritual. He says "Ultimate end of man is eternal happiness." He believed in universal education and said that the right to education should not be restricted to the high and elite, and said that the poor people will not be able to succeed in life without education. He favoured natural methods and considered that the inductive method as professed by Bacon was not sufficient. He said that knowledge can be gained by sense organs, intellect and spiritual viewpoint, and no errors could be committed with a balance in these three factors. He propounded nine principles about teaching methods which included that the teaching methods should be simple and the purpose of the things taught should be made clear. He said that the thing being taught should have practical value and be useful for life. He preferred analysis of the principles taught and the parts of education ;should come in a due sequence. He said that file child should continue to study unless the topic is clear to him fully. He said that the study of the mother tongue should come first and the study of other languages should come later. He was against physical punishment and was in favour of psychological education. He laid stress on educational-psychology, educational organisation, teaching methods and coordination in education. His thoughts were later assimilated by other scholars the chief ones of whom are Rousseau, Pestalozzi and Herbart Spencer. His thoughts have found manifestation in the modem education, and here lies his significance in the field of education.

**4. Neo-realism**

Neo-realism is considered to be more important in the fields of philosophy and science than in the field of education. Rusk has written in this regard : "The positive contribution of neo-realism is its acceptance of the methods and results of modern developments in physics." This ideology believes that the rules of science are also changeable which prove themselves in conditioned, limited and controlled circumstances only. A change in circumstances needs a change in the law too. The scholars following this ideology have supported the education of both art and science.

The chief scholars who have contributed to this ideology are as follows

**Whitehead :** Whitehead opined that besides scientific values, other values too must be given a place and understood. He considered that conscious and unconscious beings were an organism and their attributes should be properly analysed and assimilated. He has written in this regard : "When you understand all about sun, all about the atmosphere, all about the rotations of earth, you may still miss the radiance of the sunset." Thus, we can see that the opinion expressed by him was fine in essence.

**Bertrand Russel :** He also believed in acquiring knowledge by sense organs and he emphasised on the sensual development of the child. He writes : "First and foremost, there must be as little emotional strain as possible in connection with the acquisition of knowledge. Emotional strain is the chief cause of harmful fatigue." He professes analytical method in education. He accepted liberal education and did not accord a place to religion in education. He has also opposed arousal of emotional sentiments.

Logical Empiricism(positives)

In its present form logical empiricism is a combination of two separate schools of though. One, known originally as the Vienna

Circle and later *as logical Positivism,* emphasized linguistic *and'* mathematical problems. It was led by Schlick, Hahn, Feigl, Frank, Neurath, and Carnap. The other school, concentrating on scientific methodology and mathematics, became known as *scientific empiricism.* It was headed by Reichenbach, Kohler and Lewin.

One of the most distinctive features of logical empiricism is its "theory of verification," which states that empirical propositions may be verified either directly or indirectly. The direct method is simple-we test the proposition by sense perception. Thus, the proposition "I see a book" can be proved or disproved with ease. I either see a book or I do not-that is all there is to it. Logical empiricists are interested mainly in the indirect method of verification. Rudolf Camap defines the criterion *of* indirect verification as follows: "A proposition P which *is* not directly verifiable can only be verified by direct verification of propositions deduced from P together with other already verified propositions." To illustrate:

Proposition $P_1$: This book is made of paper. Such a proposition is not *directly* verifiable, but we may set up the following premises in order to test it:

$P_2$: "If fire is placed under paper, it burns." This is a physical law, already directly verified.

$P_3$: "This flame is fire." This proposition is also directly verified: that is, wwe can see flame or feel it.

$P_4$: "`I lie fire is placed under the book." The proposition is, now directly verified by observation.

We may now deduce the conclusion from our premises:

$P_5$,: The book will now burn.

Our final proposition is a prediction or hypothesis that may be tested by observation." If observation and further tests support this hypothesis, we become more certain that the book is actuall.made of paper. But we can never become ***absolutely*** certain. Indeed, statements about the material world can only carry a "very high degree of probability." By the same token an hypothesis may be discredited, but never completely so.

The point is that if we cannot directly verify what we read or hear, we must verify it deductively from a series of statements that can be directly verified. If, in the example cited, we had been unable to arrive logically at $P_4$ from $P_{1i}$ the statement, "This book is made of paper," would not have made empirical sense.

The principle of verification is based in part on the distinction between what are called *analytic* and *synthetic* statements. Analytic statements are true by virtue of the terms that they contain. They are true *a priori* or by definition. The analytic statement, "Old maids are females," is true because of the meaning of the terms is "old maid" and "female." Mathematical statements are likewise analytic. Their truth springs solely from the meanings of the terms they contain. Thus, "2 X 5 = 10" is true by virtue of the previously defined natures of 2, 5, and 10. Analytic statements are also known as *tautologies,* because they tell us nothing beyond what already is implicit in the meaning of their terms.

Synthetic propositions, on the other hand, are true or false because they assert a matter of fact or fancy. Their truth is not internal to themselves. It is not implicit at the outset-a *priori* but is discovered afterwards-a *posteriori.* The statement, "The air is calm today," is not true by virtue of the meaning of the terms "air," "calm," and "today"; it is true only if it asserts what happens to be the case. Were a wind to arise, the statement at once would become false: Thus, synthetic statements assert more than their terms imply. They tell us things about the external world that we did not know before. Their truth is never *necessary* but always *contingent.* The analytic statement, "This Ford is a vehicle," is *necessarily* true, because the meaning of Ford has already been defined to include the property of being a vehicle. But the synthetic statement, "This vehicle is a Ford," is only *contingently* true, depending on whether or not the vehicle is *verifiably a* Ford.

According to logical empiricism, every empirically meaningful statement automatically must be synthetic. Most statements in metaphysics, ethics, religion, and poetry are not empirically meaningful because they cannot be empirically verified. In Camap's words,

The suppositious sentences of metaphysics, of the *philosophy* of values, of ethics (insofar as it is treated as a normative discipline and not as a psycho-sociological investigation of facts) are pseudo-sentences; they have no logical content, but are only expressions of feeling which *in* their turn stimulate feelings and volitional tendencies on the part of the hearer.

Thus, the expression, "Thou shalt not murder," is not a meaningful statement, because it is neither analytic nor empirically verifiable. It is an expression of a belief or preference, not a statement of fact. We *may believe* that it is wrong to commit murder, but can we verify that it is *in fact* wrong? We can discover, certainly, whether or not a majority of the earth's inhabitants believe that it is wrong. But this would only verify the factual statement "Most people believe that murder is wrong." We cannot, says the logical empiricist, verify ethical sentences, because there are no *objective* criteria of right and wrong on which we can draw.

Recently, however, logical empiricists have come to distinguish between purely emotive statements and statements that, although primarily emotive, also have cognitive content. Thus, when a teacher discovers that a student has cheated, he may tell the student: "That is the wrong thing to do." His purpose is not to impart cognitive knowledge but to direct the student's future behavior. If, on the other hand, a teacher tells a student to check a certain reference book because it explains a certain topic *very well,* the statement has cognitive content. To a considerable extent the statement can be checked by examining the book in question. Thus, in all ethical or value judgments we must .separate the emotive from the cognitive content."

Logical empiricism is an extremely complex philosophy, but it can be reduced to four basic theses.

*1. The function of philosophy is logical analysis. A* true philosophy is exclusively critical and analytic, not speculative. It does not create new knowledge but clarifies old knowledge by examining the meanings of terms and the logical relations between them. It refuses to raise or answer such questions as "What is the meaning of life?" or "Are men immortal?," because they admit of no empirically verifiable reply.

*2. Most normative assertions, whether moral, religious, or esthetic, are empirically unverifiable, and therefore meaningless.* If we say, "Most Americans are opposed to totalitarian government," or "Modern art has many critics," we are speaking meaningfully, for we are making statements of fact, which can he verified empirically. If, on the other hand, we say, "Totalitarian government is evil" or "Modern art should not be criticized," we cease to speak sense, because neither of these statements is empirically verifiable but rather an expression of personal feelings.

*3. All meaningful discourse consists of analytic or synthetic propositions.* These include the formal sentences of logic and mathematics, scientific statements, and all other propositions that are verifiable empirically.

*4. All synthetic propositions can be reduced to statements of elementary experiences which can be expressed in terms of a logicosymbolic language.* At the outset, logical empiricists hoped to develop a single, logical language for all the sciences, similar in form to the language of physics, thus providing a basis for unifying all the different sciences. Logical empiricists today realize that there is no *one* language for all the sciences. They believe, however, that many scientific statements can be translated into a language of logical forms without losing too much of their meaning. The important considerations are that the logical language be firm and precise, that there be specific rules for the manipulation of terms, and that the system be self-consistent. Thus, any symbolic language, including simple arithmetic, is counted as a language of science.

The preceding summary has, of necessity, interpreted logical empiricism somewhat narrowly. Few, if any, of its present adherents would wield the verification principle with the same vigor as did their predecessors. They are more likely to grant that different kinds of statements should be tested in different ways. Ethical statements cannot be dismissed as meaningless, for morality is an indispensable factor in life. There must be something wrong with a philosophy that says it is senseless to judge how men ought and ought not to behave. As a consequence, logical empiricism seems to be becoming rather less stringent; it now recognizes that ethical statements have a definite linguistic function to perform-that of directing conduct. Morality and beauty play a vital part in people's lives. Religious and esthetic propositions cannot be dismissed as merely nonsensical.

Since it rejects system building for analysis, logical empiricism has produced no formal theory of education like perennialism, progressivism, or essentialism (see Chapter 4). Yet, in recent years it has exerted a growing influence on educational thought not so much through formal philosophy as through the behavioral sciences, which increasingly affect education.[20] The search for theoretical models to explain and predict educational behavior seems more and more to be usurping traditional methods of educational thought. In fact, much of the theory behind automated instruction is based on experimentally verifiable models of learning behavior. The programming of specific subject matter assumes that the objectives implicit in the subject matter-the importance of learning arithmetic, for example-are firm; what cannot be programmed for automatic instruction is rejected. Although advocates of this approach do not deny the value of subject matter that is incapable of being programmed, the inevitable tendency is to depreciate what is overlooked, a fact which so far has tended to obstruct the growth of empirical educational theory.

Nevertheless, automated instruction would transform the classroom into a laboratory. Every step of the teaching program the order, kind of material, testing procedure-would be checked constantly within an experimental framework. Such a program has been justified by a learning theory that emphasizes immediate rewards or, more technically, *positive reinforcement.* A distinctive feature of automated instruction, this learning theory itself depends on experiments whose hypotheses are tested through largely statistical procedures-that is, statistical language. For that matter, almost all theories of learning, as well as such factors as criteria for teacher selection, curriculum studies, and counseling techniques, have been framed into hypotheses that are capable of verification and evaluation through statistical techniques. As mentioned earlier, professional educators who consider education primarily as a scientific discipline insist on the use of statistical language and experimental procedures for validating *any* educational theory or practice.

## EXISTENTIALISM

Existentialism is the youngest philosophy. It is very difficult to find its ,loots in any of the ancient philosophies. It may be described as a modern twentieth century philosophy. However, it has not vet received a wide general recognition in the educational field.

Its chief exponents are: 1. Soren Kiergeard, the Danish philosopher (1813-1835 A.D.), 2. Jean Paul Sartre, a French writer of the twentieth century, 3. Karl Jaspers, a German philosopher, 4. Paul T'llich, and 5. Reinhold Niebuhr, the two leading protestant theologians.

Existentialism may be described as a modern philosophy, which is primarily built upon the work of the contemporary scholars of the twentieth century.

Soren Kierkegaard (1813-1855) is considered the originator of existentialism, a philosophy that emphasizes the subjectivity of human experience and the importance of individual creativity and choice in a nonrational world. Friedrich Wilhelm Nietzsche (1844-1900), Martin Heidegger (18891976), Jean-Paul Sartre (1905-1980), Albert Camus (1913-1960), Paul Tillich (1886-1965), Martin Buber

(1878-1965), and others have developed existentialist thought by attempting to describe reality not as separate from or beyond the comprehension of humans, but as the result of individual passion and life experience.

Existentialists believe that the physical universe has no inherent meaning apart from human experience. The world and forces of nature exist, but they are not ordered in some grand scheme in which humans play their appropriate part. Human life, too, exists; we are here, but we are only what we make of ourselves. Sartre's (1947, p. 28) often-quoted phrase states that "Existence precedes essence." We owe our existence to nature, but we define ourselves through our actions.

Nietzsche (1924, 1961) revealed the dark side of this view. He characterized life as a grim battle in which one requires strength, pride, and intelligence just to survive. Sensitivity, kindness, and consideration were signs of weakness. There was no God of mercy who ruled benevolently and rewarded the worthy with eternal life in heaven. Indeed, there was no God at all. And if there ever had been, He was surely dead. Nietzsche believed that we should strive not to better the majority of people, who were mostly worthless,but to promote genius and to develop superior personalities. From an aristocracy of talent and power-one cultivated by those who choose to restrain and discipline themselves-would arise the superman.

For existentialists, choice is a critical concept. People choose who they will be. Some allow others to decide for them, but exercising this default option is also a choice. Although existentialists do not reject morals or norms of behavior, they repudiate habitual adherence to them. Existentialists encourage people faced with a difficult conflict of values to concentrate seriously on their own situations and to choose what is right for them. When we are cut loose from restrictions, we assume responsibility for our own actions. We cannot simply rely on what we are told to do or on what some scripture directs us to do. And when we are free to choose our directions, we prize that freedom for others.

Martin Buber, existentialist and Hasidic Jew, assailed theologians' talk of God and their pretensions about knowing God. In *I and Thou (1970),* Buber did not try to prop up religion or to argue that God was present in all things. Instead, he raised the possibility that life without religion lacked an important dimension. Buber proclaimed that the secular was sacred and that God is present when people encounter one another in honest dialogue. Human relationships are central in creating meaning, in lives. Buber and existentialists the development of humanistic psychology, in which relationships free thinking, and action lead to self-actualization ,or personal fulfillment.

*1. Man's Existence.* For the existentialist, the starting point for all existence is the recognition of the individual existence. For the existentialist then, man makes himself through choices among many alter natives in the environment

*2. Self-knowledge.* The existentialist considers 'self-know thyself' is the basic premise of this philosophy.

*3. ,Freedom and Responsibility.* The existentialist considers that each man has the responsibility of or creating his own values and in doing so he is choosing freedom and responsibility.

*4. Man is not complete.* For the existentialists, man is not complete; he is in the process of 'becoming'. Man has to meet the challenge. He marches on the process of becoming a complete man to reach his completeness.

*5. No acceptance of readymade concepts.* Existentialism believes that man cannot accept the ready-made concepts of existence forced upon him. He is a free agent capable of shaping his own life and choosing his own destiny.

## Existentialism and Education

Existentialism has very little to offer as a philosophy of education, There seems to be only one major book which deals with the philosophy of existentialism as applied to education. This is George Kneller's `Existentialism and Education'.

A chapter by Ralp Harper, in *`Modern Philosophies of Education* the Fifty-fourth Year Book of the National Society for the Study of Education is another source.

## Educational Implications of Existentialism

1. According to existentialism, the primary aim of education is the making of a human person as. one who lives and makes decisions about what he will do and be.

2. The school should provide an environment where the individuals find security, encouragement and acceptance by teachers.

3. All school subjects and activities should present situations for the development of human beings.

4. The teacher should facilitate development or originality and creativity by providing necessary material and equipment.

5. The teacher is very active and welcomes challenges to his ideas from the students.

6. Democratic ideas must pervade the school environment in which the students grow.

7. Concern and respect for the individual student should be the main concern of the school. Mechanization and impersonality are to be counteacted in schools.

## Limitations in Existentialism

1. The educational methods in existentialism appear to be impractical and inapplicable in an industrial society.

2. It requires a good deal of time and effort on the part of teacher to develop individual relationship with the students for having a closer understanding of their personalities.

3. Terminology used in existentialism is not very clear. Concepts like `Being', `Meaning', `Person', `Existence' are ambiguous.

## On the Exkstentialist Teacher

George F Kneller, philosopher of education formerly at the University of California at Los Angeles, argued that if teachers were to adopt an existentialist view, their choices would be important and difficult and their pedagogical strategies would be clear.

If we accept [existentialism as a world view] ... as free men and free teachers we must seek to expose and combat all those forces in culture and society that tend to dehumanize men by denying their freedom. We must repudiate the subordination of the person to economic "laws," the tyranny of the majority over the dissenting minority, and the stifling of individuality by social conformism. We must urge our students to recognize and fulfill the freedom that is theirs as persons. What we urge we must also practice by respecting their freedom as we value our own..

Most choices we make are admittedly trivial and inconsequential-choice of a necktie, choice of a restaurant, choice of a movie. A serious choice is a choice between actions involving fundamental values. It calls for deep concentration, a looking into oneself. However% I must not be content merely to apply an abstract moral principle. This is a weak choice, reliance on a rule rather than on myself. I should choose the course of action that seems uniquely right in this particular situation. I should seek not the way but my way. The hardest choices to make are often those between alternative goods. Two courses of action seem to have an equally good claim on us-which course do we take?

If I am an existentialist teacher, I urge the student to take responsibility for, and to deal with, the results of his actions. To act is to produce consequences. He must accept that these consequences are the issue of his choice, but at the same time he must not submit to them as unalterable, for this is to assume that freedom is exhausted in a single act. Freedom is never exhausted, and each consequence poses the need for further choice. I would teach him that his life is his own to lead and that no one else can lead it for him. It is pointless to blame his failures on environment, family, temperament, or the influence of others. These conditions are for choice to challenge. Whatever may have happened to the student in the past, the future is his to make.

Does this attitude lead to a ruthless disregard for others, to my fulfillment at the expense of yours? Not at all. True freedom implies not egoism but communion. The egoist is driven by a narrow self-interest. With him choice is not self-fulfillment but self-limitation. Freedom, open and dynamic, longs for other centers of freedom, other persons. It does not calculate but gives. The fulfillment of freedom is communion with others.
If as a teacher I assume the style and gestures for which convention calls, I may touch only surfaces of my students' lives. I must go beyond familiarity and open myself to them. I must come to them unreservedly, creating the trust from which springs communion and true self-fulfillment.

## Marxism

Marxism is a philosophy based on the belief that the human condition is determined by forces in history that prevent people from achieving economic freedom and social and political equality. Karl Marx (1818-1883) was a historian, philosopher, and social theorist born to Jewish parents in Germany. In the main, his work was not taken seriously until after his death.

As a university student Marx was influenced greatly by the idealist Georg Wilhelm Friedrich Hegel (1770-1831), who at the time was the grand master of German philosophy. Although Marx grew to reject Hegel's political philosophy, he was influenced greatly by Hegel's thought, particularly his development of the concept of the dialectic, or the process by which human thought and human history progress.

The dialectic is a constant intellectual movement from thesis, to antithesis, and finally to synthesis. Movement in thought occurs, for example, when one plays a thesis or idea against its opposite, which for Hegel was the reality of nature. Thought moves along a continuum by *way* of the dialectic process to richer, more complex syntheses. Hegel argued that ultimately this process would reach the Absolute Idea, or an idea that bore close resemblance to idealists' conceptions of truth. He rejected the realist view that truth is independent of our minds. People become and remain alienated, according to Hegel, until they understand that they are thinking beings and that truth is a function of this self-realization.

The process, Hegel maintained, works also for history. Civilization progresses along a continuum toward richer, more complex syntheses. Culture moves forward, building on what has come before. To Marx, progress meant revolution. Marx thought of the dialectical process as a clash of economic forces in which the capitalist system exploited the worker. The ruling class seized workers' productive capacities and offered money in return, making workers subservient to the system.

Within this context, Marx saw progress as a mixed blessing. In capitalist society, the forces of production continually increase. Simultaneously, People create a more oppressive social organization as they characterize society by unequal classes. Capitalists, Mark contended, accumulate great wealth, but they create imequalities and tehumanize people.Marx thought that in time exploited Would rise up and overthrow the ruling class.

Marx recognized the value of science as a way to acquire knowledge. For Marx, human perception is based on sense experience of the material world, and this perceptual experience shapes one's knowledge. The social order, therefore, is not fixed. Human nature is malleable-people and social institutions can be shaped and formed. A person's social class is a matter of education and circumstance. The aim of Marxism, then, is to change the material conditions of society. When these conditions change, consciousness changes; when consciousness changes, ideology changes, and the perfect, classless, communistic society will result.

In the 20th century, Marxism has been articulated and developed intellectually most notably by people referred to as the Frankfurt School-a school of thought based on Marxist assumptions about the social world, including Max Horkheimer, (1895-1973), Theodor Adorno (1903-1969), Herbert Marcuse (1898-1979), and Jurgen Habermas (born 1929). Habermas in particular has exerted considerable influence on educational theory (Ewert, 1991). Critical theorists such as Habermas attempt to reveal the covert values in schooling and society, claiming that schools alienate students and "de-skill" them by establishing the goals of education instead of encouraging students to set their own goals. The process of schooling thus breeds dependency on authority, promotes top-down communication, and advances a distorted view of history (Apple, 1995).

## MARXISM IN EDUCATION

### Main Characteristics of Marxism

Karl Marx (1818-1883), a revolutionary thinker, philosopher and author, is regarded as the originator of Marxism. He along with his colleague and friend Friedrich Engles propounded a body of socio-economic doctrine which came to be called Marxism. Marxism is a theory of revolutionary change. Capture of political power by the working class is the beginning and after it the dictatorship of proletariat should be established and massive task of social and economic transformation should start so that the way for a classless society may be paved. In practice Marxism has divided the world into two main blocks - the Capitalist or liberal block and the Communist/Socialist block. With the disintegration of the U.S.S.R., Marxism has received a great setback. Some of the most important characteristics of marxism are mentioned below:

1. Marxism believes in the materialistic philosophy of life.

2. Man's essence is defined in terms of productivity - i.e. man is a productive animal.

3. Man possesses no personal or individual freedom but fords his freedom in following the collective will of the people.

4. The working class must seize the power and abolish all private ownership. Then there will be a classless society. All the people will own all the natural resources.

5. Religion is considered as the `opium' of the people.

**Implications of Marxism in Education**

**Central Aim of Education.** Under Marxism, the ultimate purpose of education is to strengthen the State and the building up of a classless society. Knowledge is not to be imparted or acquired for its own sake. It has a social purpose --namely the service of the state.

**Production-oriented Education.** According to Marx, education should be combined with productive work. He appreciated the work of a British factory owner, Robert Owen, for initiating this idea. Marx observed, "From the factory system budded, as Robert Owen has shown us in detail, the genii of education of the future, an education that will, in the case of every child over a given age, combine productive labour with instruction and gymnastics, not only as one of the methods of adding to the efficiency of production, but as the only method of producing fully developed human beings"

**Curriculum.** As stated above, the teaching of productive work and the teaching of practical activities of life must be made essential and these activities should be social as well as useful. Marx stressed the importance of studying history scientifically. The significance of "class struggle" could be fully understood through the study of social sciences: competence in vocational fields should be encouraged.

**Stress on Group Work.** Marxian education mitigates competition and substitutes it by group work of different kinds. The child is made to feel from the very beginning that he is a unit in society and has a duty to society.

**Educational Agencies.** The state is the sole agency of education. It has absolute power and control of all educational institutions. There is no decentralization of educational administration or educational planning or curriculum. The methods of instruction, textbooks and evaluation systems are all centrally controlled and administered by the state. Discipline is very- rigid. Nursery education is given due importance.

**Free and Compulsory Education.** Education is compulsory at the school stage. It is free at all levels.

## Limitations

1. There is very little scope for creative expression as education is state controlled.

2. There is an absence of academic freedom for teachers. Individual initiative is not encouraged.

3. Discipline is very rigid and students are treated like machines.

4. There is an overemphasis on scientific technology.

# UNIT-3

**LEARNING OBJECTIVE**

**Contributions of following Indians Philosophers to Education Thought:-**

- **Vivekananda**
- **Tagore**
- **Gandhi**
- **Aurobindo, and**
- **J.Krishanamurthy**

## PROGRESSIVE EDUCATION

**Meaning of Progressive Education.** The progressive education may be regarded both as a protest as well as a vision. In the beginning it started as a protest against the standardization of education. and regimentation of mind. As a vision, it is child-centred and quite alive ro the social implications of education. William Kilpatrick (1871-1965) has been one of its most influential advocates. He has helped greatly in developing its practices.

The term 'Progressive Education' was first used in 1919 while founding the Progressive Education Association in Washington, D.C. The Progressive Association embraced the following principles:

1. Recognition of the child as a complete, dynamic and living organism
2. Freedom to the child to develop naturally.

# Swami Vivekananda

## (1863-1902)

## BRIEF LIFE SKETCH

Swami Vivekananda whose original name was Narendranath Datta, was born in Calcutta which at that time was the centre of an intellectual upsurge. As a child he developed great taste for music and was adept in sports. He began mastering the Hindu classics under the tutelage of his mother. He proved a voracious reader with a prodigious memory. Later he could often display a verbatim familiarity with the *Ency-copaedia Britannica.* Rev. W.W. Hastie, his principal, was once moved to remark, "Narendranath is really a genius. I have travelled far and wide but I have never yet come across a lad of his talents and possibilities, even in German Universities, among philosophical students." And it was from Hastie that he first came to hear about th; famed spiritual leader Sri Ramakrishna. At the age of 18, urged by his burning thirst for divine enlightenment, lie first met Sri Ramakrishna. During the ensuing six years of association with the master he had a spiritual transformation and emerged as Swami Vivekananda.

After the death of Sri Ramakrishna in 1886, Swami Vivekananda organized the master's disciples into the illustrious Ramakrishna Mission. He devoted most of the last fifteen years of his strenuous life to communicating his universal message of unity and tolerance. The impact of his dynamic personality and brilliant oratory was often overwhelming by his utter sincerity and informality. He travelled to all corners of India and he, who had known personal adversity, experienced the anguish of the country's impoverished multitudes. He visited much of Eastern Asia, Europe and the United States. It was it Chicago at the Parliament of Religions in 1893 that he first gained international attention.

## PHILOSOPHY OF SWAMI VIVEKANANDA

### Harmony and Peace

In his famous address at the Parliament of Religions in 1893 at Chicago he summed up his message and philosophy by saving that upon the- banner of every religion will soon be written, in spite of resistance; `Help and not Fight', `Assimilation and not Destruction', `Harmony and Peace and not Dissension'. The fundamental elements of all religions, divested of all special forms and names were conceived to be the Universal Religion. Religions of the world are not contradictory but they are various phases of one eternal religion. I accept all religions that were in the past and workship them all. `Not only shall I do all these but I shall keep my heart open for all that may come in the future ... salutations to all the prophets of the past, to all the greatness of the. present and to all that are to come in the future.' Swamiji has further observed, "My ideal indeed can be put into a few words and that is: to preach unto mankind their divinity and how to make it manifest in every moment of life."

Swami Vivekananda to his last days strove for the reconciliation of human contrast and conflicts and the establishment of the brotherhood of man. To the world he held out the vision of the universal religion which would recognise divinity in every man and woman and which would help humanity to realize its own true. divine nature. Swami Vivekananda declared, "It is man-making religion that we want; it is man-making theories that we want; it is man-making education all round that we want." He saw the divine in the form of the poor whom he called *Daridra Narayan.*

**God as the Universal Reality-Vedantic Philosophy and Its Implications**

Vivekanadd's philosophy and his views on religion can be summed up in the words of Dr. V. K R. V. Rao, an eminent economist and educationist as under:

"God is the one reality that exists in the world and He is the Universal Reality. All phenomena, animate and inanimate, man and animal, body, mind and soul, are all His manifestations,. Therefore, there is no difference between man and man in his basic essence anti this should lead to all men feeling about and treating each other as they would do with their own individual selves. This understanding of the real nature of man, the universe, and God is however hidden from man because of the veil cast by Maya; and it is the objective of `Vedanta' to tear this veil and let man see himself in reality. And this can be done through learning .and practising 'Jnana Yoga' or `Raja Yoga.' The Vedanta however does not only propound the Advaita doctrine. It also puts forward the dualistic understanding of God through the worship of the Personal God or one's `Ishta Yoga' because it proceeds on man's natural feeling for loving one's nearest and dearest. And for doing this, he has to find a guru who has the power to transmit spirituality, while he himself should be fit to receive and get stimulated by this transmission. When a man reaches this stage he gets filled with overwhelming love for God and the universe which he finds enveloped with God and for all men whom he finds are but manifestations of his Personal God. His religion thus leads him to love all men and find in their service his means for worshipping God. There is yet a third method of obtaining liberation from the shackles of one's ego and reaching God-consciousness. And this is Karma Yoga, the gospel of work without attachment, without selfishness, and for the service of one's fellowmen. Even if one does not believe in God, one can follow the path of Karma Yoga and obtain liberation, harmony, and the peace that passes all understanding as was shown by Buddha. To these he added the teachings of Buddha, Christ and Mohammed with their special stress on compassion, service and equality. And he concluded by talking of One, who he felt, was the perfect example in actual life of all that he taught, Sri Ramakrishna Paramahansa.

**Religion means Realisation**

To Vivekananda, religion was not just a question of belief. "Religion", he said "was realisation, nor talk, nor doctrine, nor theories however beautiful they may be. It is being and becoming; not hearing and acknowledging. It is the whole soul becoming changed into what it believes. That is Religion. Religion has to be practised if it was to have meaning, and the practice had to take account of the call of social reality. In a letter written from Washington on 27 October 1894, he made his position very clear. I quote: "I do not believe in a God or religion which cannot wipe the widow's tears or bring' a piece of bread to the orphan's mouth. However sublime the theories, however well-spun may be the philosophy, I do not call it religion as long as it is confined to books and dogmas. The eye is in the forehead and not in the back. Move onward and carry into practice that which you are very proud to call your religion, and may God bless you."

The essence of Vivekananda's teachings on religion was the universality of God and his accessibility both in form and without form, the divinity of man, respect and understanding of all religions, the equality and brotherhood of men, the supreme virtue of compassion, work without attachment, devotion without renunciation of the personal ego, and service of all men and especially of those who were poor or maimed or illiterate or disinherited, the 'daridra-narayanas' of this world.

## Ethics and Morality-the Real Basis of Life

The basis of all system, social or political, rests upon the goodness of men. No nation is great or good because Parliament enacts this or that, but because its men are great and good-People often work for the same ends but fail to recognise that fact. One must admit that law, government, politics are phases not final in any way. There is a goal beyond them where law is not needed-All great Masters teach the same thing. Christ saw that the basis is not law, that morality and purity are the only strength.

### Love and Renunciation-the Motive Power of the Universe

Vivekananda has observed, "What is the watchword of all ethical codes? `Not I, but thou', and this `I' is the outcome of the Infinite behind trying to manifest itself on the outside world. This little, 'I' is the result, and it will have to go back and join the Infinite, its own nature. Every time you say, `Not I, my brother, but thou' you are trying to go back, and every time you say `I', and not thou, you take the false step of trying to manifest the Infinite through the sense-world. That brings struggles and evils into the world, but after a time renunciation must come, eternal renunciation. The little 'I' is dead and gone. Why care so much for this little life? All these vain desires of living and enjoying this life, here or in some other place, bring death.

We have been degraded down to the animal, and are now going up, to emerge out of this bondage. But we shall never be able entirely to manifest the Infinite here. We shall struggle hard, but there will come a time when we shall find that it is impossible to be perfect here, while we are bound by the senses. And then the march back to our original state of Infinity will be sounded.

This is renunciation. We shall have to get out of the difficulty by reversing the process by which we got in, and then morality and charity will begin.

**Main Features of the Philosophy of Vivekananda**

1.Vedanta constitute the essence of the highest spiritual and ethical values of mankind.

2. The .teachings of the Upanishads have strength enough to provide solutions to our social problems.

3. Man is the incarnation of God.

4. The essential parts of all religions are the same.

5. Atma is the true reality.

6. Karmayoga as a system of ethics and religion is needed for the attainment of self-control and self-realization.

7. Service to mankind is the highest goal of religion.

8. The best image for worshipping God is man who resides in every human heart.

**Educational Philosophy of Vivekananda**

His educational philosophy may be encompassed within these ten words, "Education is the manifestation of the perfection already in man." All knowledge, secular or spiritual is in the human mind. Man manifests knowledge, discovers it within himself, which is pre-existing, through eternity. What we call powers, secrets of Nature, and force are all within. Like fire in a piece of flint, knowledge exists in the mind; suggestion is the friction which rings it out. Swami Vivekananda explains this as, "Knowledge is inherent in man, no knowledge comes from outside, it is all inside. What we say a man `knows', should exist, in strict psychological language, be what he `discovers' or `unveils'. What a man `learns' is really what he `discovers' by taking the cover off his own soul, which is a mine of infinite knowledge. We say Newton discovered gravitation. Was it sitting anywhere in a corner waiting for him? It was in his own mind; the time came and he found it out. All knowledge that the world has ever received came from mind; the infinite library of the universe is in your own mind. The external world is only the suggestion, the occasion, which sets you to study your own mind. The falling of an apple gave the suggestion to Newton, and he studied his own mind. He rearranged all the previous links of thought in his mind and discovered a new link among them, which we call the law of gravitation. It was not in the apple nor in anything in the centre of the earth."

## CHARACTER-BUILDING EDUCATION

Vivekananda was a firm believer in education as an instrument of human betterment. He was greatly distressed to see the degradation in which the masses had fallen because of the denial of literacy and education to them. He was highly critical of the educational system itself with its western bias and lack of attention to the development of the mental ability and moral character in its pupils. He wanted a thorough re-orientation, of the educational system. He declared, "We must have life-building, man-making, character-making assimilation of ideas. If education is identical with information, the libraries are the greatest sages of the world and encyclopaedias are the rishis." He quoted an old Sanskrit saying *"yatha kharaschandanabharavahi bharasya yetta na tu chandanasya"* which means "The ass carrying its load of sandle wood knows only the weight and not the value of the sandle wood." Vivekananda scoffed at the importance being given by the educational system to book-learning and memory training. "Education", he said, "is not the amount of information that is put in your brain and run-riots there, undigested all your life." Swami Vivekananda observed, "We want that education by which character is formed, strength of mind is increased, the intellect is expanded and by which one can stand on one's own feet."

**How to judge a Man of Character**

Swami Vivekananda observed, "If you really want to judge the character of man, look not at his great performances. Watch a man do his most common actions. Those are indeed the things which will tell you the real character of the great man. Great occasions rouse even the lowest of human beings to some kind of greatness, but he alone is really great whose character is great always-the same whatever be." According to him `intellectuality' is not the highest good. `Morality' and `Spirituality' are the things for which we strive. He remarks, "Our women are not so learned, but they are more pure." He does not consider a man as educated if only he car. pass some examination and deliver good lectures. The basis of all system, social or political, rests upon the goodness of man. No nation is great or good because Parliament enacts this or that,. but because its men are great and good.

**Cultivation of Heart**

"It is the heart", he said, "which takes one to the highest plane, which intellect can never reach. Always cultivate the heart." He always attached the greatest importance to the development of the compassion and fellow-feeling for the common man. In fact his Vedantic philosophy convinced him that education must play an important role in making the pupil discover his identity with the rest of humanity and especially with those who were much such worse 'off than himself in economic and social condition. What is the watchword of all ethical codes? 'Not I, but thou', and this `I' is the outcome of the infinite behind, trying to manifest itself on the outside world.

Vivekananda reminded that the nation lived in the cottage and therefore it was the duty of every educated youngman to go from village to village and make the people understand their real condition, awake them from their long slumber and advise them how to improve their own miserable lot. The sunken vitality of the helpless victims of social injustice was to be restored physically, intellectually as well as spiritually. "I call him a Mahatma who feels for the poor. Let these people he your God-think of them, work for them, pray for them incessantly-the Lord will show you the way."

**Aims of Education**

Swami Vivekananda enunciated the following goals:

1. Education for character-building.
2. Education for making people self-reliant.
3. Education for developing spiritual life.
4. Education for serving humanity.
5. Education for developing feeling of brotherhood.
6. Education for developing spirit of renunciation.
7. Education for attaining self-sufficiency.
8. Education for physical development.

**Function of the Teacher**

Vivekananda laid great emphasis on the personal contact of the pupil with the teacher-"Guru grihavasa". One should live from his very boyhood with one whose character is blazing fire and should have before him a living example of the highest teaching. The first condition necessary for the teacher is sinlessness. The question is often asked: `Why should we look into the character and personality of the teacher?' This is not right. The `sine quo non' of acquiring truth for oneself, or for imparting to others, is purity of heart and soul. He must be perfectly pure and then only comes the value of his words.

The second condition necessary for a teacher is that he must know the spirit of the scriptures. `The whole world reads Bibles, Vedas . and Korans; but they are only words, syntax, etymology, philology-the dry bones of religion. The teacher who deals too much in words and allows the mind to be carried away by the force of words loses the spirit. It is the knowledge of the spirit of the scriptures that constitutes the true teacher. The third condition is in regard to the motive. The teacher must remember that the only medium through which spiritual force can be transmitted is love.

The fourth condition is that the teacher should not think that he is making the child grow. "You cannot teach a child to grow," he said, "you can only help. A child teaches itself. The external teacher offers only the suggestion which a rouses the internal teacher to work to understand things."

## METHODS OF TEACHING-LEARNING

Swami Vivekananda stressed the following:

1. A child educates itself. We have to do only so much for the boys that they may learn to apply their own intellect to the proper use of their hands, legs, ears, eyes etc., and finally everything will become easy. "Like fire in a piece of flint, knowledge exists in the mind; suggestion is the friction which brings it out."

2. The mind works through various stages to attain its fuller development. First it lays hold of the concrete, and only gradually deals with abstractions.

3. The teaching must be modified according to the needs of the taught. The true teacher is one who can immediately come- down to the level of the student and transfer his soul to the student's soul and see through and understand through his mind.

4. Positive suggestions encourage learning. Negative thoughts only weaken them.

5. Concentration is the best method and is the key to the treasure house of knowledge. Vivekananda observed, "To me the very essence of education is the concentration of mind, not the collecting of facts." Brahmacharya is necessary for concentration.

6. The learner must have great power of endurance.

7. The learner must be able to control the internal and external senses. There must be a continuous struggle, a constant fight, an unremitting grappling with our lower nature, till the higher want is actually felt and victory is achieved.

8. The pupil's faith in himself will enable him to imbibe knowledge effectively.

9. Reverence for the guru should be inculcated in the pupil.

10. Learning and intellecual development can be fostered through frank and open discussion on all topics of study between the teacher and the taught.

11. Purity in thought, speech and act is absolutely necessary in the taught and also in the teacher.

12. Travel leads to broadening our horizon and enables us to share our knowledge with others.

## EDUCATION OF THE MASSES

Vivekananda gave prime importance to the education of the masses. He asserted, "The chief cause of India's ruin has been the monopolising of the whole education of the land, by dint of pride and royal authority, among a handful of men." He further observed, "If we are to rise again, we shall have to do it in the same way, that is, by spreading education among the masses." He considers that "the great national sin is the neglect of the masses, and that is one of the causes of our downfall. No amount of politics would be of any avail until the masses in India are once more well-educated, well-fed, and well cared for. They pay for our education, they build our temples, but in return they get kicks. They are practically our slaves. If we want to regenerate India, we must work for them."

## Social Education

Vivekananda had the most modern idea about social education. "If the poor boy cannot come to education, education must go to him. There are thousands of single-minded, self-sacrificing *sanyasis in* our country going from village to village, teaching religion. If some of them can be organised as teachers of secular things also, not only preaching but teaching also. Suppose two of them go to a village in the evening with a camera, a globe, some map etc., they can teach a great deal of astronomy and geography to the ignorant. By telling stories about different nations, they can give the poor a hundred times more information through the ear than they can get in a life time through books. But this requires an organisation."

### Physical and Health Education

Vivekananda was not satisfied with an education that merely looked to the development of the mind. He was also greatly concerned about the proper care of the body and the healthy development of one's physique. "Be strong, my young friends", he urged, "that is my advice to you. You will be nearer to heaven through football than through the `Gita'. These are bold words, but. I have to say them to you, I know where the shoe pinches. You will understand the Gita better, with your biceps, your muscles a little stronger. You will understand the mighty genius and the mighty strength of Krishna better with a little of strong blood in you. You will understand the `Upanishads' better and the glory of the 'Atman' when Your body stands firm upon your feet and you feel yourself as men." "Strength, strength is 'what the `Upanishads' speak to me from every page." "Freedom, physical freedom, mental freedom and spiritual freedom are the watchwords of the Upanishads." "Strength is goodness. Weakness is sin."

**Religious or Secular Education**

Vivekananda preached "Religion is realization. No scriptures can make us religious. We may study all the books that are in the world, yet we may not understand a word of religion or of God." His was a practical religion. He declared, "It will not do merely to listen to great principles. You must apply them in the practical field, turn them into constant practice." Service of the poor was the best religion.

Vivekananda had great regard for all religions. "Let us take in all that has been in the past, enjoy the light of the present and open every window of the heart for all that will come in the future. Salutation to all the prophets of the past, to all the great ones of the present and to all that are to come in the future."

**Education of Women**

Vivekananda was an ardent champion of education of women. He remarked, "Women have many and grave problems but none that cannot be solved by that magic word: education?" What does our Manu enjoin, "Daughters should be supported and educated with as much care and attention as the sons." His view was that `our Indian Women are as capable of doing it as any in the world. It is only in the homes of educated and pious mothers that great men are born. By raising the women, their children will by their noble actions glorify the name of the country. Then culture, knowledge, power and devotion will awaken in the country. Vivekananda, while advocating the cause of women also continued, "Any attempt to modernise our women, if it tries to take our women away from the ideal of Sita, is immediately a failure as we see every day." He suggested the following programme for educating the women:

1. Female education should be spread with religions as the centre. Religious training. the formation of character and observance of the views of celibacy these should be attended to.

2. Brahmacharins of education and character should take up the task of teaching. Through such devout preachers of character, there will be die real spread of female education in the country.

3. History and 'Puranas.' house-keeping and the arts, the duties of home life and principles that make for the development of character have to be taught.

4. Sewing, culinary art, rules of domestic work and upbringing of children will also he taught.

5. Japa, worship and meditation shall form an indispensable part of the teaching.

6. Along with other things, they should acquire the spirit of valour and heroism.

## Learning from Others but Keeping our Own

While Vivekananda welcomed the impact of Western thought, science and technology, he cautioued his countrymen against being dazzled by its materialist success and going in for a slavish imitation of its customs and way of life. He advocated, "What we want are Western sciences coupled with Vedanta, Brahmacharya as the guiding motto and also *Shraddha* in one's self. Another thing that we want is the abolition of the system which aims at educating our boys in the same manner, as that of the man who battered his ass, being advised that it should thereby be turned into a horse." `When we take anything from others we must mould it after our own way. We shall add to our stock what others have to teach, but we must always be careful to keep in tact what is essentially our own.

**National Integration**

In an article in *Modern India in 1899,* he wrote, "Forget not that the lower classes, the ignorant, the poor, the illiterate, the. cobbler, the sweeper, are thy flesh and blood, thy brothers. Proudly proclaim "I am 'an Indian, every Indian is my brother." Say `the soil of India is my highest heaven, the good of India is my good."

Dr. V. K. R. V. Rao has summed up the views of Vivekananda as "To sum up Vivekananda's ideas on education, its main base was his faith in the youth of the country for national regeneration. Hence his anxiety that they should get the right type of education and also go about the right way for getting the best out of education. Asked to define his idea of right education, he answered: `I never define anything. Still it may be described as a development of faculty, not an accumulation of words, but a training of individuals to will rightly and efficiently'. He wanted man-making education for the young and he wanted such educated young men to use their. education to Make men out of others. And when he talked of men, he included women also. it Tagore was introduced to the people of the West. The publication of the English version of Gitanjali was a turning point in his life. In 1913, Tagore was awarded the Nobel Prize for Literature. Tagore became a world figure in his own right. Besides visiting England thrice, he visited Europe, Japan, Russia and the United States. The Government made him the `Knight' in 1915 but in 1919, he renounced it as a protest against the massacre of Jallianwala Bagh, Amritsar. While giving up the title, Tagore addressed a letter to the Viceory on *29* May 1919 in which he expressed his sentiments in these words, "... Time has come when badges of honour make our shame glaring in the incongruous context of humiliation and 1, for my part, wish to stand, shorn of all special distinctions by the side of those of my contrymen who for their so-called insignificance, are liable to suffer degradation not fit for human beings." From *1921* to 1941, the poet devoted his life to develop various institutions such as Kala Bhavan, Cheena Bhavan and others at his Visvabharati. Tagore, the great apostle of peace and universal brotherhood passed away on August 7 1941.

**Tagore - A Traditionalist, Modernist, Nationalist and Internationalist**

Gurudeva represented a multitude of things. The most dominant impression which one gets about him is that he was one in the long line of the ancient sages and rishis whom India has produced from time to time. Yet this tradition did not prevent him in the slightest from being a modern of moderns and making the whole world his field of thought and action. He was a great Bengali, but being a Bengali did not come in the way of his being a very great Indian. He was an intense nationalist, yet his nationalism did not come in the way of his widest internationalism. He broke down barriers which might limit his ' personality and his message was to break down barriers wherever they were-in our customs, in our thinking, in our lives, in our general functioning and in our traditions.

**Philosophy of Humanism**

Tagore observed, "I have great faith in humanity. Like the sun it can be clouded, but never extinguished. I admit that at this time when the human races have met together as never before, the basic elements appear predominant. The powerful are exulting at the number of their victims. They take the name of science to cultivate in the school boy superstitions that they have certain physical signs indicating their eternal right to rule, as the explosive force of the earthquake once might have claimed, with enough of evidence, its never-ending sway over the destiny of this earth. But they in their turn will be disappointed."

## Universal Culture

The best and noblest gifts of humanity, cannot be the monopoly of a particular race of country, its scope may not be limited nor may it be regarded as the miser's hoard buried underground. We should remember that the doctrine of special creation is out of date and the idea of a specially favoured race belongs to a barbaric age. We have come to understand in modern times that any special culture which is wholly dissociated from the universal is not true at all. Only a prisoner condemned .to a solitary cell is separate from the world. It will not do to keep our culture so reverently shackled with chains of gold. The age has come when all artificial fences are breaking down. Only that will serve which is basically consistent with the universal.

**Synthesis of Culture**

But before we are in a position to stand a comparison with the other cultures of the world, or truly to co-operate with them, we must base our own culture on a synthesis of all the different cultures we have.

**Religious View of Tagore**

Tagore observed, "My religion is a poet's religion; all that I feel about it is from vision and not from knowledge. I frankly say that I cannot satisfactorily answer your questions about evil, or about what happens after death. And yet I am sure that there have come moments when my soul has touched the infinite and has become intensely conscious of it-through the illumination of joy. It has been said in our Upanishads that our mind and our words come away baffled from the Supreme Truth, but he who .knows that, through the, immediate joy of his own soul, is saved from all doubts and fears."

**Spiritual Unity**

" In the night we stumble over things and become actually conscious of their individual separateness, but the day reveals the great unity which embraces them. And, the man, whose inner vision is bathed in an illumination of his consciousness, at once realizes the spiritual unity reigning supreme over all differences of race, and his mind no longer awkwardly stumbles over individual facts of sepaia

# Rabindranath Tagore
# (1861 to 1941)

## BRIEF LIFE SKETCH

Tagore was born in 1861 in Tagore family which was famous for its. progressive and enlightened views. He was the fourteenth and the youngest son of Maharshi Devendranath and grandson of Dwarkanath Tagore. He received his early education at home from a private tutor. He also studied the Upanishads, Astronomy and Sanskrit from his father. By nature he loved beauty, music and poetry. He attended the seminary and the Bengal Academy for his other studies. When he had grown a little older he was sent to St. Xavier's School, Calcutta. Tagore was unable to adjust himself to the `dead routine and lifless teaching' of the educational institutions. His teachers pronounced that he was `unfit' for studies. Tagore considered himself `fortunate to escape' from these `book-learning factories'. He observed later on, "The Masters and Pandits who were charged with my education soon abandoned the thankless task ... and realised that this boy could never be driven along the beaten track of learning."

At the age of 16 in 1877, Tagore was sent to England to study Law but this subject did not appeal to him and he returned to India after a year. While in England he developed a taste in English literature and joined the London University for three months only. While, still young, he commenced writing for Bengali Periodicals. His first collection of poems was published when he was only twenty.

In 1901, Tagore established a school at Bolpur; 93 miles from Calcutta which became in 1921, the famous Visvabharati, an international university seeking to -bring about an understanding between eastern and western cultures.

In 1909, his world famous work *`Gitanjali' was* published. He visited England in 1912. An English edition of Gitanjali was published in 1912 and an introduction to it was written by the renowned Irish poet W.B. Yeats who regarded this `work of supreme culture.' Through teness in the human world, accepting them as final, he realizes that peace is in the inner harmony which dwells in truth, and not in any outer adjustments, that beauty carries an eternal assurance of our spiritual relationship to reality, which waits for its perfection in the response of our love."

## EDUCATION AS THE FULLEST GROWTH AND FREEDOM OF SOUL

Education is nothing short of the highest purpose of man-the fullest growth and freedom of soul. To the child, the environment will provide an ever-ready background for its spontaneous activity; to the adolescent, it will be an object of scientific or artistic curiosity; the adult will see in her the soil on which his country and his people grow, the cultural and economic background of human existence.

### All-round Education

There is a close and inseparable connection between the faculties of mind and the body. Each gains strength by cooperating with the other. If the education of the body does not proceed along with the education of the mind, the latter cannot gather strength. We should know that the great task of our educational effort in our institution is to provide for the education of the mind and all the senses through various activities. I believe that in our Ashram every pupil should be taught to master some form of handwork or other. To learn the particular type of handwork is not the main objective. The fact is that through the exercise of the limbs the mind is also strengthened.

### Realism in Education

The last point is that our education should be in full touch with our complete life, economic, intellectual, aesthetic, social and spiritual; and our educational institutions should be in the very heart of society, connected with it by the living bonds of varied coopera-ation. For true education is to realise at every step how training and knowledge have organic connection with our surroundings.

### Education and Freedom of Mind

I believe that the object of education is the freedom of mind which can only be achieved through the path of freedom-though freedom has its risk and responsibility as !ife itself has. I know it for certain, though most people seem to have forgotten it, that children are living beings-more living than grown-up people, who' have built their shells of habit around them. Therefore, it is absolutely necessary for their mental health and development that they should not have mere schools for their lessons, but a world whose guiding spirit is personal love. It must be an Ashram where men have gathered for the highest end of life. In the peace of nature, where life is not merely meditatiye, but fully awake in its activities, where boys' minds are not being perpetually drilled into believing that the ideal of the self idolatry of the nation is the truest ideal for them to accept; where they are bidden to realize man's world as God's Kingdom to whose citizenship they have to aspire; where the sunrise and sunset and the silent glory of stars are not daily ignored; where nature's festivities of flowers and fruit have their joyous recognition from man; and where the young and the old, the teacher and the student, sit at the same table to partake of their daily food and the food of their eternal life."

## Discipline and Freedom

"I never said to them: Don't do this, or don't do that. I never prevented them from climbing trees or going about where they liked. From the very first I trusted them and .hey always responded to my trust. Parents used to send me their most difficult children, who were supposed to be incorrigible. When the children found themselves in an atmosphere of freedom and trust, they never gave me any trouble. The boys were encouraged to manage their own affairs, and to elect their own judge, if any punishment was to be given. I never punished them myself."

**Discipline through Self-Government**

"No coercion is employed to enfore discipline among the boys, they must come to realize, of their own accord, what is anti-social and what is desirable. Cooperation here again is encouraged and any disputes that arise are dealt with first in the Vichara Sabha, or court of justice, where they are settled or punishments meted out to the offenders. A record is kept of these cases, the offences and punishments. Should, however, the Vichara Sabha find itself incompetent to settle a dispute, the matter is taken to the teacher who is addressed as dada (elder brother) and who takes this as an opportunity of demonstrating how useless, wasteful and disturbing to fruitful work are dissensions and quarrels."

**An Ideal School**

"An *ashram* must be an ideal school where men have gathered for the highest end of life, in the peace of nature; where life is not merely meditative, but fully awake in its activities, where boys' minds are not being perpetually drilled into believing that the ideal of the self-idolatry of the nation is the truest ideal for them to accept; where they are bidden to realize man's world as God's kingdom to whose citizenship they have to aspire; where the sunrise and sunset and the silent glory of stars are not daily ignored; where nature's festivities of flowers and fruit have their joyous recognition from man; and where the young and the old, the teacher and the student, sit at the same table to partake of their daily food and the food of their eternal life."

**Learning through Mother Tongue**

It was because we were taught in our own language that our mind quickened; learning should as far as possible follow the process of eating. When the taste begins from the first bite the stomach is awakened to its function before it is loaded, so that its digestive juices get full play. Nothing like this happens, however, when the Bengali boy is taught in English.

The first bite bids fair to wrench loose both rows of teeth-like a veritable earthquake in the mouth! And by the time he discovers that the morsel is not of the genus stone, but a digestible' bonbon, half his allotted span of life is over. While one is choking and spluttering over the spilling and grammar, the inside remains starved, and when at length the taste is felt, the appetite: has vanished.

**English Language**

"We must admit that the English language cannot lose its seat of honour in our universities. It is not because it is indispensable to the present needs of our daily life, but because the science and learning of Europe have today won the respect of all mankind. To deny this fact out of sheer national vanity will forebode evil. English education is as necessary for our economic . and political security as for its powerful influence towards emancipating our mind and conduct from stupidity.

## Religious Education

What is really necessary is neither temples nor external rites and rituals. We want the ashram, where the clear beauty of nature combined with the pure pursuits of the human mind has created a sacred site for worthy end eavours. Nature and the human spirit wedded together shall constitute our temple, and selfless good deed our worship ... Such a spot, if found, shall provide the true atmosphere for religious education. For, as I have said before, according to the mysteries of human nature, religious education is possible only in the natural atmosphere of piety; all artificial means only pervert or obstruct it.

## Teaching of Religion

Teaching of religion can never be imparted in the form of lessons, it is there where there is religion in living. Therefore, the ideal of the forest colony of the seekers of God as the true schooı of spiritual life holds good even in this age. Religion is not a fractional thing that can be doled out in fixed weekly or daily measures as one among various subjects in the school syllabus. It is the truth of our complete being, the consciousness of our personal relationship, with the infinite; it is the true centre of gravity of our life. This we can attain during our childhood by daily living in a place where the truth of the spiritual world is not obscured by a crowd of necessities assuming artificial importance; where life is simple, surrounded by fullness of leisured by ample space and pure air and profound peace of nature; and where men live with a perfect faith in the eternal life before, them.

## True Culture

Culture brings fulfilment from the depths of the self to the faculties and aptitudes of a man as a whole. Under its influence man spontaneously attains an all-around filfilment, and the pursuit of knowledge for its own sake and the enthusiasm for unselfish actions become natural. True culture sets greater store by natural courtesy than mechanical observance of custom and convention. It does not encourage artificial politeness calculated to serve practical ends in human dealings. A cultured man will rather injure than humiliate himself. He is ashamed of purposely parading himself or selfishly forcing himself to the forefront. Whatever is mean or false pains him. He takes delight in respecting excellence in all spheres, because of his intimate acquaintance with all that is best in art, literature and history. He can judge and forgive and can appreciate the good point in others in spite of divergence of views. To be envious of others' success is to humiliate himself.

## Tagore's Naturalism in Education

Tagore pleads in his essay `Abaran' to let fresh air and free light into our mind and our life, and to uphold and honour the supremacy of the simple and the natural. Another essay titled 'Tapovan' (Forest Colony) may be considered a valuable supplement to `Shiksa Samasya'. 'It interprets the spirit of the forest, the birthplace of ancient civilization. The unity or the universal consciousness runs through all existenceand forest is its grand manifestation. The forests hold a message to us of peace and purity, of sublime feeling and pure joy-of austerity and renunciation. Nature in the forest `Provides a grand perspective against which all objects, all feelings, lose their exaggerated shape and assume due proportions'. In 'Tapo-van' a new idea is introduced. The message of the forest can be received and felt only through the expansion of sympathy or enlarging the `feeling' aspect within us. It is not the eye nor the ear, nor all the senses, not even the intellect that could read this grand message. It is only the feeling. One has to learn to feel, to enlarge the depth of feeling and the scope of sympathy. 'Bodher Sadhana', or what we may call `Education of the Feeling'-that is really wanted. `We must constantly remember that neither the education of the senses, nor the education of the intellect, but the education of the feeling should receive the place of honour in our schools.' That is why he pleads that `our true education is possible only in the forest, through intimate contact with Nature and purifying austere pursuits'.

A Poet's School' is an important writing showing the place of Nature in life and education. Children have the gift of freshness of senses. They can become natural with Nature and human with the human society. `For our perfection we have to be vitally savage and mentally civilized.' But the misery is that a child is offered crowded solitude in a city where man is everywhere, with never a gap for the immense non-human, the Nature. The inexpensive power to be happy that the children bring to this world is `Constantly worn away by friction with the brick-and-mortar arrangement of life'. The., city-built education does take no heed of the non-civilized in us, which thirst for colour, for music, for the movement of life. This is why Tagore tried his best to develop in the children of his school `the freshness of their feeling for Nature, a sensitiveness of soul in their relationship with their human surrounding'.

He pointed out the great significance of the school atmosphere in the life of children whose mind, like the tree, has the power to gather food and nourishment from its surroundings. The cultural atmosphere keeps the mind sensitive to rich racial inheritance, glorious traditions and concentrated wisdom of ages. The school atmosphere must also develop- sensitiveness of soul and allow freedom to the mind from bondage of ignorance and apathy.

**Tagore's Message of Freedom of Mind, Peace and Universal Love**

At the doorsteps of the atom and hydrogen bomb, the world has much to learn from Tagore's message of freedom of mind, of peace and universal love, of fullness of life and human loyalty, so' that a better world could be created out of the ashes of the old, a world:

"Where the mind is without fear and the need is held high, Where knowledge is free,

Where the world has not been broken into fragments by narrow domestic walls, where words come out from the depths of truth,

Where tireless striving stretches its arms towards perfection,

Where the clear stream of reason has lost its way into the dreary desert-sand of dead habit,

Where the mind is led forward by Thee into ever widening thought and action,

Into that heaven of Freedom, my Father, let my country awake".

## SHANTINIKETAN ASHRAM (ABODE OF PEACE)

**Background**

Rabindranath was a great educational practitioner, He was not a dreamer only to leave behind a legacy of his principles and philosophy of life. He worked them out in the most constructive way. He had always in his mind to create an atmosphere which he felt was more important than the teaching of life. From his own experience at school, he was convinced that the four walls of the classroom restricted the freedom of young children. The traditional school to him was like a prison house. He has observed, "the house was more like a pigeon-holed box than a human habitation. .. Naturally our whole being was depressed." "The time spent had been thoroughly wasted." About his teachers he writes, "Of the teachers, I remember only one, whose language was so foul that, out of sheer contempt for him, I steadily refused to answer any one of his questions." Again he had to remark, "I learnt about all the - injustice, impatience, anger and partiality underlying the process of instruction, more easily than my lessons." The school according to him was "completely isolated from the surrounding life and beauty." It was a "relentless nightmare like 'a jail". The atmosphere was suffocating where no attempt was made "to attract the boyish heart". "The whole being was depressed."

**Bases of Shantiniketan**

It was in this background that the school was established in 1901 at Bolpur which is located at a distance of about one hundred miles from Calcutta. Tagore established this school for giving practical shape to his ideals. Following were the main objectives of the school

1. To give spiritual training to the students.

2. To help the children for the cultivation of love of Nature and sympathy with all living creatures.

3. To impart knowledge to children through mother tongue.

4. To educate children by providing an atmosphere of freedom.

5. To educate children by making them alive to their natural surroundings.

6. To educate children by providing an environment of living aspiration, based upon living contact between the teacher and the taught.

7. To provide an enviornment after the fashion of ancient 'Topavanas'- forest schools about which he had read so much in the Upanishads.

**Main Characteristics of the School**

1. It is based on the concept of freedom of-the mind.

2. It is a co-educational and residential institution

3. It is a community school where there is no distinction of caste and creed.

4. Mother-tongue is the medium of instruction.

5. Teaching of crafts like sewing, book-binding, weaving, carpentry is provided in the school.

6. Drawing, art and music form an integral part of the curriculum.

7. Students are provided adequate opportunities for choosing their hobbies and occupations.

8. It is a self-governing institution-has a dairy farm, post office, hospital and workshop. Students hold their own courts.

9. It provides for close personal contact with the teacher. The number of students in classes is very small.

10. There is an atmosphere of freedom; free from do's and don'ts.

11. There is a well-equipped library.

12. It provides for manual labour.

13. It is situated in natural surroundings. There prevails the atmosphere of Nature's own beauty with her varied gifts of colours and dance, flowers and fruit, with the joy of her mornings and the peace of her starry nights.

## VISVA BHARATI

### Main Features

Tagore describes them as:

1. At first, I had founded the school in Santiniketan and invited children here with the purpose of liberating them in the wide field of Nature. But gradually it occurred to me that the formidable gulf that existed between man and man had to be removed and all of men had to be released in the vast Universe of Man. This inner aspiration found expression in the history of the evolution of my institution. For, the institution that bore the name of Visva Bharati was founded with this call that man had to be set free not only in the field of Nature but also among mankind.

2. The greatest distinction of our school is the direct and immediate emotional contact of our pupils with their teachers and with external nature.

3. A speciality of our institution is that we want to bring up our pupils in inseparable association with Nature. We do not aim at the acute development of some particular faculties. Our aim is to bring about an all-round development of individual personality through harmonious union of the spirit with the environment.

4. The power of man has reached its limit. The limit has come for striving for union. Shall we not succeed in initiating at our institution this supreme mission of our age? Shall we not succeed in holding before the world the ideal of the University of Man?

5. Our centre of culture should not only be centre of the intellectual life of India, but the centre of her economic life also.

6. Being strongly impressed with the need and the responsibility which every individual today must realize according to his power. i have formed the nucleus of an International University, as one of the best means of promoting mutual understanding between the East and the West.

7. Before Asia is in a position to co-operate with the culture of Europe she must base her own structure on a synthesis of all different cultures which she has.'

In this belief, it is my desire to extend by degree the scope of this University on simple lines, until it comprehends the whole range of eastern cultures-the Aryan, Semitic, Mongolian and others. Its object will be to reveal the eastern mind to the world.'

## SRINIKETAN-CENTRE OF RURAL RECONSTURCTION

The object of Sriniketan is to bring back life in its completeness into the villages snaking them self-reliant and self-respectful acquainted with the cultural traditions of their own country, and competent to make an efficient use of the modern resources for the improvement of their physical, intellectual and economic condition.

The aims and objects of the institute, as originally set forth in detail, are as follows:

1. To' win the friendship and affection of villagers and cultivators by taking a real interest in all that concern their life and welfare, and by making a lively effort to assist them in solving their most pressing problems

2. To take the problems of the village and the field to the class room for study and discussion and to the experimental farm for solution.

3. To carry the knowledge and experience gained in the class-room and the experimental farm to the villagers in the endeavour to improve their sanitation and

health; to develop their resources and credit; to help them to sell their produce and buy their requirements to the best advantage; to reach them better method of growing crops and vegetables and of keeping live-stock; to encourage them to learn and practice arts and crafts; and to bring home to them the benefits of associated life, mutual aid and common endeavour.

4. To work out practically an all-round system of elementary education irr the villages based on the boy scout ideal and training, with the object of developing ideas of citizenship and public duty such as may appeal to the villagers and be within their means and capacity.

5. To encourage in the staff and the students of the Department itself a spirit of sincere service and willing sacrifice in the interest of and on terms of comradeship with their poorer, 'less educated and greatly harassed neighbours in the village.

6. To train the students to a due sense of their own intrinsic worth, physical. and moral, and in particular to teach them to do with their own hands everything which a village householder or cultivator does or should do for a living, possibly, more efficiently.

7. To put the students in the way of acquiring practical experience in cultivation, dairying, animal husbandry, poultry-keeping, carpentry, smithing, weaving, tanning, practical sanitation work and in the art and spirit of co-operation.

8. To give the students elementary instruction in the science connected with their practical work to train them to think and record the knowledge acquired by them for their own benefit and for that of their fellowmen.

Following are the various institutions which have developed there and form an integral part of this university:

1. Sisu Bhavan (Nursery School)
2. Path Bhavan (School Section-Matriculation Examination)
3. Siksha Bhavan (Higher Secondary)
4. Vidya Bhavan (College of Under-Graduate and Post-Graduate Studies and Research)
5. Vinaya Bhavan (Teachers' College)
6. Kala Bhavan (College of Fine Arts and Crafts)
7. Sangit Bhavan (College of Music and Dance)

8. Sriniketan (Department of Rural Reconstruction)
9. Siksa Satra (Rural High School)
10. Silpa Sadana (College of Industrial Training)
11. Cheena Bhavan (School of Languages *e.g.* Chinese, Tibetan etc.)

## CONTRIBUTION AND INFLUENCE OF TAGORE

Tagore was a great practitioner. He worked out his ideas and ideals in a very constructive way. The fulfilment of all his theories and concepts found expression in various directions. He 'struggled to implement his social ideals and strove to build up a social structure through education'. He created Shantiniketan to realise his educational ideals. In the words of Calcutta University Syndicate, "Through him (Tagore) India has given her message to mankind and his unique achievements in the field of literature, philosophy, education and art have when imperishable fame for himself and have raised the status of India in the estimation of the world.

Tagore, the ,versatile genius and the giver of our National Anthem *Jana gana mana* called upon the Indians to nourish the unity of the country and to be devoted to it.

As a naturalist philosopher, Tagore surpasses Rousseau, Pestalozzi and Froebel. Foster Watson observes in *Encyclopaedia and Dictionary of Education,* "Tagore substantially adopts Rousseau's ideal of return to nature, but included human nature, as well as external nature, basing both upon a primal sympathy." In place of 'Negative Education' of Rousseau, Tagore wanted richer environment of experience and ideas. Rousseau's ideology remained theoretical. On the other hand, Tagore gave a practical shape to his ideology. Tagore was a realist. He also deserves credit for having attempted for the revival of ancient Indian ideals of education in the modern times and combining what is best in western arts and sciences with the manners, customs and arts of Indian .His stature stands out at the cross road of two ages – traditional and modern, of two worlds- The East and the west.

# Mahatma Gandhi

# (1869-1948)

## BRIEF LIFE SKETCH

M. K. Gandhi (Mohandas Karam Chand Gandhi)" was born on 2 October 1869 at Porbander in Kathiawad. His father was a Dewan of a petty state. As a student at school, he was slow, shy and hesitant. However, his observance of truth was real and continuous. After matriculating at the age of 18, he was sent to England for qualifying himself for the bar. On return to India after four years he practised law in Bombay but was not very successful. In April 1893, he sailed for Durban in South Africa in connection with professional work on behalf of a firm. His stay in South Africa for about 20 years was the formative period of his political life. It was in South Africa that he put into practice his weapon of Satyagraha, when he saw a series of insulting events of disgracing Indians. He founded the Natal Indian Congress in 1894.

Gandhiji's educational philosophy took shape through his educational experience at the Tolstoy Farm at Transval in South Africa. On the Farm he undertook the responsibility of educating his own sons and other children. The children had to devote 8 hours a day for vocational training and only 2 hours to book learning. The children aged from 6 to 16 were very happy in `learning by doing' and `learning by cooperation.'

Having won his laurels in South Africa, Gandhiji came to India in 1914. Gandhiji continued his educational experiments for a short time at Shantiniketan and then at Sabarmati and Sewagram, where Gandhiji established his own Ashrams. Sewagram Ashram is located 11 miles from Wardha. It was here that Gandhiji not only conceived the ideas of his new system of education but also fought his battle for freedom.

## GANDHIJI'S PHILOSOPHY OF LIFE-SENSE OF HUMAN UNITY

The purpose of human life is the realization of the benevolent law; and the duty of every individual is to order his own life in accordance with it. Thus he has to help in the historical task of promoting human freedom and unity. If we wish to break down the narrowness which circumscribes the human life, our method of change also should be guided by a high sense of human brotherhood and of the dignity of man. While not co-operating with certain institutions, people should bear no ill-will against their adversaries. They should patiently try to convert their adversaries into willing partners in the establishment of anew order based upon a more comprehensive sense of human unity.

He believed that the mind of the modern man, who has inherited a vast accumulation of cultural and cognate achievements would be far superior to the mind of one who lived in the prehistoric times. Therefore, progress is the result of education, rather than of heredity. There has been an unbroken succession of thinkers and of prophets who have led mankind from higher to still higher aims and objectives. This phenomenon is by itself the proof of the operation of a higher law, which rules the destiny of mankind. In many of Gandhiji's writings such a faith is clearly implied.

**Self-Discipline and Self-Purification .**

Gandhiji personified in himself the high ideals of charity, purity, sacrifice and service. He had an ardent desire that India should establish a socialist society where the peasant and the worker will be provided with the means for full development and freedom of expression. As a staunch believer in Ahimsa and Truth, Gandhiji strove hard to make the people realize the futility of resort to violence. Moreover his advice to the statesmen of various countries was to the effect that reliance on violence for solving international controversies ought to be avoided. He made the fear-ridden people, fear-less and they became bold enough to demand freedom for India. The prison houses and the gallows which used to frighten the people were transformed into holy shrines. He taught the virtue of self-discipline and self-purification to the people. He inculcated in them the importance of organized action for overcoming social, economic and political maladies. He introduced religious principles into, politics and set about the task of spiritualizing politics with some success. Not only did he uplift a down-trodden people into a self-respecting nation. Handling of public funds, he emphasized, was a trust which should never be betrayed. He himself would spend hours, if need be, accounting for the last pie. Gandhiji's personal example and disciplined life tended to wean even the wicked away from graft and corruption. And he imparted to his followers a concern for the well-being of the down trodden. The present Government of India has been striving hard to promote the well-being of the oppressed sections of the Indian society.

## Factors which Inspired Gandhiji's Views

Gandhiji was influenced by the teachings of Lord Buddha, Lord Mahavir and also by several ancient Hindu philosophical monographs. The Upanishads, Patanjali's Yogasutra, Mahabharta of Ved Vyas, and last but not least the Bhagwad Gita. From the Upanishads, Buddhism and Jainism, he learnt the concept of Ahimsa. The Bhagwad Gita inspired him to become a Karmayogi. Self-realisation and disinterested performance of one's duty were the principles which he learnt from the Gita. Gandhiji was influenced by the teachings of the Christianity and Islam as well. He was very much impressed by the noble and simple life of Christ. He particularly liked one impressive sentence in the Bible that is "Hate the sin, don't hate the sinner". Jesus Christ's adherence to non-violence also deeply influenced him. Moreover, Gandhiji learnt the value of Satyagraha from the Christian teachings. The points out that "It was the New Testament, especially the Sermon on the Mount, which really awaken me to the rightness and value of Satyagraha." Tolstoy's "The Kingdom of God is within You" was another source of inspiration to Gandhiji. He admits that Tolstoy is one of the three modern writers who have exerted, the greatest spiritual influence on his life. From Ruskin, Gandhiji learnt three basic principles: (i) the good of man is to be found in the good of all; *(ii)* the work of a barber is as good as that of a lawyer, both being the means to earn one's livelihood; *(iii)* the farmer, the labourer or any other individual who is doing physical labour must be given due importance. He learnt from Ruskin the principle of dignity of labour. From

Henry David Thoreau, an American philosopher anarchist Gandhiji learnt the "concept of Civil Disobedience". In a word, from several sources-religious and philosophical-Gandhiji learnt many concepts, which were developed and accepted to Indian conditions.

**Service for Humanity as the Core of his Philosophy**

Service for humanity from whatever premises, he reaches to the same conclusion. He believes in the absolute oneness of God no matter with whatever name we call Him and thus there is the essential unity among His living creation. Man's ultimate aim is the realization of God and all his endeavour-social, political and religious-must be guided to this end. "The immediate service of all human beings becomes a necessary part of the endeavour, simply because the only way to find God is to see Him in His creation and be one with it-I am a part and parcel of the whole and I cannot find Him apart from the rest of humanity." For Gandhiji, God lives in the temple of humanity and man becomes )great exactly in the degree in which he works for the welfare of his fellow men.

**True and Righteousness as the Highest Religion**

Life without religion, I hold, is life without principle, and life without principle is like a ship without a rudder'. Just as a ship without a rudder will never reach its destination so will a man without religion never reach his destined goal. By religion Gandhiji does not mean dogmas or rituals. There is no religion as something that transcends, `which changes one's very nature, which binds one indissolubly to the truth within and which ever purifies'. Gandhiji emphasizes the moral basis of religion, `True religion and true morality are inseparably bound up with each other.' He believes in the Universal Religion, propounded by Swami Vivekananda in the Parliament of Religions. In the same strain Gandhiji says, `Even as a tree has a single trunk, but many branches and leaves, so there is one true and perfect religion, but it becomes many, as it passes through the human medium.' He advocates the study of other religions besides, one's own, because it `will give one a grasp of the rock bottom unity of all religions and afford a glimpse also of the universal and absolute truth which lies beyond the dust of creeds and faiths'. We should have an attitude of respect and reverence towards all religions. `Study and appreciation. of other religions need not cause a weakening of regard for one's own religion; it should mean extension of that regard to other religions'.

**Social Order Visualised by Gandhiji**

What was the social order that Gandhiji visualized? A society that would help each man to realize the highest aim of his life in a cooperative endeavour to search after Truth-is the answer. A co-operative approach implies love and fellow feeling and excludes all thought of -hatred and exploitation. Thus the social order has to be based on truth and non-violence, the other name of love. Exploitation in any form-social, political, economic or religious-must have to disappear, for it devastates the divine dignity of man. The economic and social structure of the society must depend on decentralised industry and agriculture. Everyone has to be independent for one's vital needs; for dependence brings helplessness, and helplessness engenders exploitation. And yet one has to be inter-dependent since a co-operative living demands it. To materialize this vision of a society Gandhiji evolved a scheme of education after many trials and experiments over a period of 40 years. His ideas revolutionised the current thinking about education. In 1937 the All India National Education Conference was held in Wardha which unanimously approved of his idea and appointed a committee of the leading educationalists with Dr. Zakir Husain as its Chairman to give shape to Gandhiji's plan. The report of the committee embodies what is known as the Wardlia Scheme of Basic National Education.

**Meaning of Education**

"By education I mean an all-round drawing out of the best in child and man-body, mind and spirit." This is how Gandhiji summed up his idea of true education.

`All-round implies a harmonious development.' `Drawing out of best' recognizes a great potentiality coiled up in the child which can be realised and developed to its perfection through education. `Body, mind and spirit' is a vision of the whole man.' The first emphasis is ı the body and the culmination point is the spirit: It is through practical work that one attains intellectual development. But intellectual attainment is neither the beginning nor the end of education. It is a mid-point. The individual has yet to blossom out to perfection to bring forth all that is best in him. All development, all personal advancement is in the search of Truth, the realization of the spiritual essence that is in man. Thus education cannot be confined to childhood and youth-it has to take into account the whole life of a man; and that is the significance of the phrase `best in child and man.' So education will not be complete till one realizes the Self, the perfection. Education is through life and for life. Education must take care of the whole child, the human personality, in all its aspects-physical, intellectual and spiritual. But what is the purpose of education? It should be the function of education to bring about a harmonious development of all the aspects of human personality so that it can grow to its highest stature and serve the society at its best.

## GANDHIJI'S VIEWS ON EDUCATION

Gandhiji propounded his views on education in the following words:

*1. Education for a just social order.* "The ultimate objective of the new education is not only a balanced and harmonious individual but also a balanced and harmonious society-a just social order in which there is no unnatural dividing line between the haves and have-nots and everybody is assured of a living wage and right to freedom."

*2. Meaning of education.* "By education, I mean an all-round drawing out of the best in child and man-body, mind and spirit."

*3. Education through craft.* "The uniqueness of this scheme is that education is to be given `through' village crafts. The end in view is not to be accomplished by merely adding a village craft to the current syllabus."

***4. Self-supporting aspect.*** "Self-sufficiency is not a `prior' condition, but to me it is the acid test. This does not mean that Basic Education will be self-supporting from the very start. But taking the entire period of seven years, income and expenditure must balance each other. Otherwise it would mean that even at the end of this training the basic education student will not be fit for life. This is the negation of basic education. 'Nai Talim' without the self-support basic would be like a lifeless body."

***5. Dignity of labour.*** "It is a crime to make education merely literary, and to unfit boys and girls for manual work in later life. Indeed I hold that as the large part of our time is devoted to labour for earning our bread our children must from their infancy be taught dignity of such labour. Our children should not be so taught as to desist labour."

***6. Methods of teaching.*** "Children take in much more and with less labour through ears than through their eyes."

***7. Religious education.*** *"To* me religion means Truth and Ahimsa or rather Truth alone, because Truth includes Ahimsa, Ahimsa being the necessary and indispensable means for its discovery: Therefore anything that promotes the practice of these virtues is a means for imparting religious education and the best way to. do this, in my opinion, is for the teachers rigorously to practise these virtues in their own person. This very association with the boys, whether on the playground or in the class room, will then give the pupils a fine training in these fundamental virtues."

***8. Spiritual training.*** *"I* made the children memorize and recite hymns, and read to them from books on moral training. But that was far from satisfying me. As I came into closer contact with them I saw that it was through books that one could impart training of the spirit. Just as physical training was to be imparted through physical exercise, and intellectual through intellectual exercise, even so the training of the spirit was possible only through the exercise of the spirit. And the exercise of the spirit entirely depended on the life and character of the teacher. The teacher had always to be mindful of his Ps and Qs whether he was in the midst of his boys or not."

***9. Education and character.*** "The end of all knowledge must be building up character. What is education without character and what is character without elementary personal purity."

***10. The teacher.*** "Woe to the teacher who teaches one thing with the lips and carries another in the heart."

***11. Medium of instruction.*** "Our language is the reflection of ourselves and if you tell me that our languages_ are too poor to express the best thought, then I say that the sooner we are wiped out of existence the better for us."

***12. The foreign medium.*** "The foreign medium has caused a brain fag, put an undue strain .upon the nerves of our children, made them crammers and imitators, unfitted them for original work and thought and disabled them for filtrating' their training to their family or the masses. The foreign medium has made our children practically foreigners in their own land."

***13. Curriculum and spinning.*** "In any curriculum of the future, spinning must be a compulsory subject. Just as we cannot live without` eating, so it is impossible for us to attain economic independence and banish pauperism from the ancient land without reviving home spinning."

***14. Freedom but under discipline.*** "The pupil must have initiative. They must cease to be mere imitators. They must learn to think and act for themselves and yet be thoroughly obedient and disciplined. The highest form of freedom carries with it the 'greatest measures of discipline and humility. Freedom that comes from discipline and humility cannot be denied, unbridled licence is a sign of vulgarity injurious alike to self and one's neighbours."

***15. Co-education.*** "Before launching on such experiments, a teacher has to be both father and mother to his pupils and be prepared for all eventualities, and only the hardest penance can fit him to conduct them."

***16. Textbooks.*** *"I* have, therefore, come to the conclusion, that books are required more for the teachers than for the taught. And every teacher, if he is to do full justice to his pupils, will have to repair the daily lesson from the material available to him. This too, -he will have to suit to the 'special requirement of his class."

***17. Women's education.*** "*As* for women's education, I am not sure whether it should be different from men's and when it should begin. But I am strongly of opinion that women should have the same facilities as men and even special facilities where necessary."

***18. Handwriting.*** "Handwriting is an art. Every letter must be correctly drawn, as an artist would draw his figures. This can only be done if the boys and girls are first taught elementary drawing."

## GANDHIJI AND NATURALISM

To quote M.S. Patel "Gandhiji has a strong claim to be ranked among .the leading naturalistic educators of the world. He cannot .however be called an extreme naturalist. Like Rousseau, he believes that natural and rural environments are important educative agencies but he does not hold with him that the child should be segregated from the baneful influence of man and society. His attempt at rescuing education from the four walls of the school room cannot be passed over in silence."

Following are the important points of naturalism in the educational philosophy of new education:

(i) Gandhiji agrees with Rousseau that the child is good by nature and this fact must be kept in view by us while planning his education.

*(ii)* Like the naturalists he advocates freedom for the child. "If children are to find themselves, they must be allowed a sufficient degree of freedom, if they are to develop their powers to the fullest, they must be prepared to accept the appropriate discipline and training.

(iii) He. greatly stresses the importance of educating the child in -natural surroundings. He expects "the teachers to educate village children in their villages so as to draw out all their faculties through some handicraft.

(iv) Like all naturalists .he minimizes the importance of text-book. I do not even remember, having made much use of the books that were available. I do not find it at all necessary to load the boys with quantities of books. I have always felt that the true text-books for the pupil is the teacher. I remember very little that my teachers taught me from books, but I have even now a clear recollection of the things they taught me independently of books. Children take in much more and with less labour through their ears than through their" eyes. I do not remember having read any books from cover to cover with my boys "

(v) The Basic system is based on activity of the child. According to Zakir Husain Committee Report, "We fail to understand how this scheme based on the activity and study of the child's physical and social environment can be less child-centred."

## GANDHIJI AND IDEALISM

In the words of Shri M.S. Patel, "A study of his writings will lead to the conclusion that Gandhiji is an idealist to the core. Idealism is ingrained deeply in his nature as can be seen from his upbringing and early education."

The goal of life is self-realisation which was to be achjeved not by withdrawing from the worldly life but by serving his creatures. His . Dharma consists in training the spirit which takes place through purity in our daily lives.

The' idealism of Gandhiji is reflected in the following words: "Long before I undertook the education of the youngsters at the Tolstoy Farm I had realised that the training of spirit was a thing by itself. To develop the spirit is to build character and to enable one to work toward a knowledge of God and self realization and I held that this was an essential part of the training of the young, and that all training without culture of the spirit was of no use and might be even harmful."

Like all other idealists, Gandhiji believes in the harmonious development of personality and advocates that different types of social culture and physical activities may be undertaken to achieve this end.

## GANDHIJI AND PRAGMATISM

According to Shri M.S. Patel, Gandhiji's contribution to the pragmatic philosophy of education is unique. The introduction of a basic craft as the centre of education, the co-ordination and correlation of the content of the close relationship of education with actual life, the method of learning by doing, the individual initiative, the sense of total responsibility and emphasis on experiment as the means of discovering truth are some of the outstanding features of Gandhiji's pragmatic philosophy of education:

Gandhiji's educational philosophy is pragmatic due to following reasons:

1.He has an experimental approach towards life. Gandhiji believed that reality is that which can be verified. He himself calls his autobiography "My Experiments with Truth"

2. Gandhiji advocates like a pragmatist that a child should learn from the real experiments of life.

3. The project method of the pragmatist and the Basic scheme of Gandhiji have many common points. Like a project, a Basic craft is to be a socialised activity involving participation in social relationships.

"The greatest achievement of Gandhiji", according to Shri M. S. Patel, "is that he, in his educational philosophy, gives due place to the dominant tendencies of naturalism, idealism and pragmatism which fuse into a unity, give rise to a theory of education which would suit the needs of the day and satisfy the loftiest aspirations of the human soul."

## PRINCIPLES OF BASIC EDUCATION

**1. Free and Compulsory Education for Seven Years**

Education should be free and compulsory from the age of seven to fourteen years. Seven years' course will not only impart elementary education but also secondary education. At the age of fourteen the school should be able to produce intelligent citizens. They should acquire effective literacy and should develop proper control over their senses and should be mature for social appreciation and attitudes. The education should be both manual and intellectual.

**2. Education to Centre Round some Craft**

It should be productive, manual and should centre round some craft. It must have educative possibilities. Different subjects should be grouped around it, craft as such is not to be taught. The whole education is to be imparted through it. Craft is not added to the number of literary subjects in Basic education. A craft has got educational possibilities.

### 3.. Self-Supporting Basis of the Plan

Gandhiji was fully aware of the financial condition of our people. They could not spend a single penny on education of their children. It was the duty of the State to provide free and compulsory education to all the children of the State. He was fully aware chat the government would never spend any amount to educate the teeming millions of India. He, therefore, wanted to make education self-sufficient. He could not wait till sufficient funds were made available by the State. He, therefore, suggested. that education should be self-supporting. He, therefore, introduced a manual productive craft, the sale of which would make education self-supporting.

### 4. The Medium of Instruction

Mother tongue, according to Gandhiji, is not only to become the medium of instruction but to occupy the first place in languages. All expression in natural way is possible through mother tongue. To force a. foreign language means waste of energy, time and money. It is also un psychological for those who are not of linguistic taste. Even graduates cannot express themselves fully in English. The result is that they can neither express themselves in English nor in their mother tongue. If they express themselves in their mother tongue, they will use many English words but they won't be able to use complete sentences in English or mother tongue. In Basic system, national education is to be imparted through the mother tongue.

### 5. The Cult of Non-Violence

Gandhiji had firm conviction in non-violence. So how could this scheme of education remain uninfluenced from non-violence? Gandhiji says, "We have to make this training school as a school for winning freedom and for the solution of all our ills of which the chief one is our communal troubles. For this purpose we shall have to concentrate on non-violence. Hitlers and Mussolinis accept as a fundamental principle violence. Ours is note-violence, according to the Congress All our problems have, therefore, to be solved non-violently. Our arithmetic, our science, our history, will have a non-violent approach and the problems in these subjects will be coloured by non-violence."

According to Gandhiji, our Mathematics will always keep humanity as the centre of calculation in the evolution of power factors. History will not remain the record of kings and wars but a survey of humanity striving for the better living. Our Political Science and Economics will shift from competition and militarism to co-existence and protection. Our Engineering and Science will create things for human comforts. we will, thus. concentrate on village industries and not on city industries. We will have to review our village handicrafts if we want to keep all 700,C)0 of our villages alive and not only a fraction of them. The social order of Gandhi ji's contemplation was to be free from economic power in the hands of a few for the exploitation of many. For this accomplishment, society's politics: economic and education must stand on non-violence. truth and justice.

**6. The Ideal of Citizenship**

The ideal of citizenship is an important feature of Basic education. The, spirit of citizenship should be filled in the child..

**7. Relationship with Life**

Education should be closely related to life. Wardha Scheme unifies knowledge and does not allow division of knowledge into watertight compartments. Everything is to be taught through the principle of correlation. There are three centres of correlation-craft, physical environment and social environment of the child. These three centres of correlation ill achieve perfect integration of curriculum.

## Self-Supporting Aspect

Gandhiji observed, "Self-sufficiency is not a prior condition but to me is the acid test. This does not mean that Basic education will be self-supporting from the very start. But taking the entire period of seven years, income and expenditure must balance each other, otherwise it would mean that even at the end of this training the Basic Education student will not be fitted for life. This is the negation of Basic Education. 'Nai Talim' without the self-supporting basis 'would be like a lifeless body."

"When I used the. word `self-supporting' I did not mean that all the capital expenditure would be defrayed from it, but at least the. salary of the teacher would be found out of the proceeds of the articles made by our pupils. The economic aspect of the basic system of education is thus self-evident."

"I would, therefore, begin the child's education by teaching it a useful handicraft and by enabling it to produce from the moment it begins its ' training. Thus, every school can be made self-supporting, the condition being that the State ,takes over the manufactures of these schools."

"I am very keen on finding the expenses of a teacher through the product of the manual labour of his pupils because I am convinced that there is no other way to carry education to crores of our children."

"Primary Education thus conceived as a whole is bound to be self-supporting even though for the first or even the second years course' it may not be wholly so."

"My 'Nai Talim' is not dependent on money. The running expenses of this education should come from the educational process, itself. Whatever the criticism may be I know that the only education is that which is self-supporting.

"If such an education is given, the direct result will be that it will be self-supporting. But the test of success is not its self-supporting character, but the whole man has been drawn out through the teaching of the handicraft in a scientific manner .... The self-supporting part should be the logical corollary of the fact that the pupil. has learnt the use of everyone pf his faculties."'

"I can imagine a school entirely self-supporting. If it became, say,. a spinning and weaving institution with perhaps a cotton field attached to it."

"If every school introduced spinning, it would revolutionize our ideas of financing education. You can work a school for six hours per day and give education to the pupils."

"It is easy to see that every school can be made self-supporting without 'much effort and the nation can engage experienced teachers for its school."

"Education under Swaraj will aim at making boys self-supporting from their youth. Any other profession may be taught them, but spinning will be compulsory.""

"Surely if the State takes charge of the children between seven and fourteen, and trains their bodies and minds through productive labour, the public schools must be fraud and Teachers idiots, if- they cannot become self-supporting. "

"But as a nation we are so backward in education. that we cannot hope to fulfil our obligations to the nation in this respect in the given time during this generation, if the programme is to depend on money. I have, therefore, been bold, even at the risk of losing all reputation for constructive ability to suggest that education should be self-supporting."

"Land, building and equipment are not intended to be covered by the proceeds of the pupil's labour."

"We (Teachers) should be intellectual bankrupts, if we cannot direct the energy of our children so as to get from them after a year's training one anna worth of marketable labour per hour."

**Evaluation of the Scheme**

The Wardha Scheme is imbued with Gandhiji's cardinal creed of non-violence and idea of a co-operative community. Shri Mahadev Desai explained, "The idea of self-supporting education cannot be divorced from the ideological background of non-violence, and unless we bear in mind that the new scheme is intended to bring into being a new age from which class and communal hatred is eliminated and exploitation is eschewed, we cannot make a success of it." The self-supporting society has to eschew hatred and exploitation for its very existence and must sustain itself through love, non-violence and the spirit of co-operative living.

It was only giving to this great man of our country the courage and conviction .to launch such a revolutionary experiment. To quote the words of Dr. It was only given to this great man of our country the courage and Zakir Husain's Committee: "Thus the new scheme which we are advocating will aim at giving the citizens of the future a keen sense of personal worth, dignity and efficiency and will strengthen in them the desire for self improvement and social service in a co-operative community."

The fact is that the underlying spirit of Basic Education has not been fully understood by many. Prof. Saiyidain in the foreword of the report of the Assessment Committee on Basic Education (1956) expressed the need of a careful reorientation of ideas, attitudes and techniques: "It is therefore a matter of great surprise though it is certainly one of disappointment that the full implications of basic approach have not yet been realized by many teachers and educational administrators:" Professor Mujeeb has rightly pointed out, that "The opinions of great men do not in 'the least absolve us from the duty `of thinking for,, ourselves. They are flashes of inspiration which reveal to us aspects of truth and reality that may have remained invisible without them. 'But this is all. We cannot live for them or even by them. We can' only live for ourselves, and we should look only within ourselves for the light that guides, and the will that creates." Gandhiji would never brook the idea of the dogmatic acceptance of his own scheme by the people. He himself was 'the relentless critic of his own philosophy: "You should not accept ,anything' out of your regard for me .:.. The scheme . should be accepted after full and mature consideration so that it may not have to be given up after a little while." Though Gandhiji had a desire to teach all the subjects through hand-work, he was nevertheless aware that everyone of these subjects could not be so taught and therefore, "we will teach as much of these subjects through the takli (or any other basic craft) as possible." He would not dogmatically interpret Basic Education as education through craft. This is true to a certain extent, but that is not the whole truth. The roots of 'Nai Talim' go deeper. It is based on truth and non-violence in individual and collective life. Untruth and violence lead to bondage and can have no place in education. "Craft is taught not for craft's sake but for opening up avenues of creative self-expression, practical work and learning by doing. Neither does it stand in the way of industrial progress, for the training in practical skill, observation and creative work will certainly be a better preparation for industrial training or engineering colleges."

We must remember that Gandhiji combined in himself the visionary and practical man. He was a man experimenting with truth. His thoughts evolved and grew with time. He realized with experience: It has become clear that the scope of Basic Education has to be extended. It should include the education of everybody at every stage of life. Education has to be as broad as life itself. It has to be adjusted and reoriented with the needs of time and the temper of a new society.

## ORIGINALITY OF GANDHIJI

M. S. Patel, in the book *True Educational Philosophy of Mahatma Gandhi* rightly says that his (Gandhiji's) educational philosophy is original in the sense that he arrived at it through personal experience without drawing on the accumulated experience of others. It may not be original in the sense that the like of it was never preached by anybody in the past; but should be noted that its presentation and adaptation on a nation-wide scale are undoubedly novel and original." In the words-of Acharya Vinoba,Bhave, "It may not be a new thing but it has been presented in a new light." Gandhiji himself says: "I do know that the aim in the Middle ages or any age was never to develop the whole man through crafts. The idea is original."

### Gandhiji and other Educators

The precursors to Gandhiji's philosophy of education may belong to one of the two types viz., (i) those who exercised direct formative influences on his philosophy, and (ii) a host of others who had reached similar or identical conclusions before, though Gandhiji may have reached his conclusions independently of what they had taught.

Among those who had. exercised direct formative influence on his philosophy are Raichandbhai of Gujarat, Ruskin and Tolstoy. Those who had reached similar conclusions are Rousseau, Pestalozzi, Froebet, Dewey and Karl Marx. Rousseau had advocated manual work just, to eliminate prejudice against it.. Pestalozzi recommended it for sense training and tried to show that industrial and intellectual training could go side by side. But Gandhiji was bold enough to make craft as nucleus of the whole instruction and not an extra or additional subject. There is close resemblance between the theories of Gandhiji and Froebel in so far as both lay particular emphasis on activity and constructive work in school life. Gandhiji gave the constructive work of Froebel a concrete shape and a local habitation, though quite independently of him. Gandhiji differs from Dewey in the way that he does not mean to supplement literary with manual. Training, but makes manual training the means of literacy and intellectual training. Karl Marx maintained that education should be related. with productive process. But Gandhiji does not attach a school to a factory or workshop, to him the school itself is the workshop where work is an essential instrument of learning.

Basic Education is the result of Gandhiji's experiments and experience spread over a long time. It will have far-reaching consequences and will have its way into distant lands. In short, his new scheme of "education is `new' `epoch=making,' `original' and `revolutionary.'

Use of the intellect rather than accumulation of information, concentration rather than memorising, integrated development of the human personality in the ascending scale of body, mind and heart, cultivation of fearlessness in pursuit of truth and compassion and fraternity in dealing with fellow-men, science instead of superstition, rationality in place of obscurantism, and absorption of the spirited message of the Vedanta that all men are divine and it only needs will, strength and effort to realise their divinity, and in the process recognise the common bond that makes all humanity kin-this is the message that Vivekananda gives to those who give or seek education.

## CONTRIBUTION OF SWAMI VIVEKANANDA

1. Revived the spirit of humanism in education.
2. Advocated character-building and man-making education.
3. Recommended free and compulsory education regardless of taste, creed, wealth or poverty.

4. Placed emphasis on the inclusion of subjects on the cultural heritage of India in the school curriculum.

5. Insisted on the learning of western technology.

6. Preached for providing equal opportunities to the poor for raising and bettering their lot.

7. Established the Ramakrishna Mission in 1899 for doing social service work, The Ramakrishna Mission has centres all over India.

8. Founded the Vedanta Society at San Francisco for spreading the message

# Sri Aurobindo
# (1872-1950)

**BRIEF LIFE SKETCH**

He was born in Calcutta on 15 August 1872. At the age of 7, he went to England and lived there for 14 years. Besides English he mastered Latin and Greek and also learnt French, German, Italian and Spanish. He was a very brilliant student and passed the open competition for I.C.S. He, however, did not try to qualify in the riding test, perhaps intentionally, as he nourished a feeling of resentment against a foreign rule in India. He returned to India in 1893 and joined Baroda College. He devoted himself to self culture and literary activity, learnt Sanskrit, Marathi, Gujrati and Bengali and drank deep in the philosophy and culture of India. He began yoga by himself in 1904. Even before this he had some spiritual experiences.

In 1905, at the time of Anti-partition Agitaflon he gave up the Baroda service and openly joined in the political movement. There were slides to his political activities-a secret revolutionary propaganda with which he started, then a public propaganda intending to convert the whole nation to the ideas of Independence and lastly, nonco-operation and passive resistance. He started the journal *Bandemataram* to propagate revolutionary ideas. In 1908, he .was arrested and put into jail where he remained for a year. Shri C.R. Das, the famous lawyer, put, aside long practice and devoted himself to the defence of Sri Aurobindo in the famous trial known as 'Manicktalla Bomb case'. Being acquitted he came out of the jail after a year. . During this period his view of life was radically changed, as in the jail he had spent almost- all his time in reading the Gita, and Upanishads and in intensive meditations and practice of yoga.

In 1910, he left his political activities and went to Pondicherry in search of a more complete experience harmonising the two ends of existence, spirit and matter. It is possible for the mind to rise to a greater divine consciousness and then to redescend with its spiritual gains of light, power and bliss to transform this life. At Pondicherry more and yet more people began to come to follow his spiritual path; and so, there grew up Sri Aurobindo Ashram, its ideal being the attainment of life divine on this earth and in the earthly existence.

## AUROBINDO'S PHILOSOPHY

The basis of his entire thought is his stress on the 'Life Divine' which can be realized through Integral Yoga. Aurobindo considered that while philosophy is a quest for the truth of things by the human intellect, the endeavour to realize the truth in the inner self and in outer life is 'Dharma.' Sri Aurobindo immersed himself in Vedanta and Yoga. Instead of seeing conflict or finding inconsistencies between the East and the West, he evolved a synthesis of both. He also evolved a synthesis of spirit and matter, of science and Vedanta. According to Sri Aurobindo, everyone has in him something divine, something his own, a chance of perfection and strength in however small a measure. The task is to find it, develop it and use it. His life is based on spiritual discipline and the one end ardently sought after everything done is the attainment of the 'Life Divine' while living in the world.

Sri Aurobindo considers all forms in the universe as multiple cells of One Consciousness and Yoga as the means *through* which one can come in contact with the true self and unite the separate parts of oneself and can also see the same divine in others. In his Yoga work is as important as meditation. His Yoga is not that of a `Sanyasi' who, turns away from life in order to turn towards God. On the other hand his Yoga is of the ordinary man, who has put God on the shelf, while he carries on his worldly pursuits. The seeker must experience the 'Ananda,' love, consciousness and energy of the `Supreme.' Trust must be lived. Work done in full concentration and in the spirit of surrender takes one's consciousness nearer to the Divine. Knowledge, work, devotion and meditation are all integrated in his Yoga. The most important thing is to have an inner urge for the Divine. As Sri Aurobindo says, "one who chooses the Divine is chosen by the Divine. As the call for the Divine grows more intense, so does His help come more readily.".

Aurobindo says that we must aim not only at an inner realization but an outer realization also-the establishment of the kingdom of "within the heart but also in the world of human affairs -in economics and politics. And he assures us that this is possible.

Yoga can be practised in ordinary life. If a merchant wishes to follow this yoga, his business itself is regarded as work divine and he cannot practise corruption or do black-marketing. *In* the same way a student would look for higher values and will be saved from many useless and harmful activities. *Brahmacharya* (self-control) is the most important thing in a student's life. Sri Aurobindo says, "The practice *of brahmacharya* is the first and most necessary condition of increasing the force within and turning it to such uses as may benefit the possessor or mankind. All human energy has a physical basis. The source of life and energy is not material but spiritual, but the basis, the foundation on which the life and energy stand and work, is physical. The ancient Hindus clearly recognized this distinction between *Karan* and *pratishtha,* the north pole and the south pole of being. Earth or gross matter is the 'pratishtha', the Brahman or the spirit is the *Karan. To* raise up the physical to the spiritual *is brahmacharya,* for by the meeting of the two the energy which starts from one and produces the other is enhanced and fulfils itself. The more we can, by *Brahrnacnarya,* inc.ease the store of *tapas* (heat), *tejas* (light), *vidyut* (electricity) and *ojas* (life-force), the more we shall fill ourselves with utter energy for the works of the body, heart, mind and spirit."

## MEANING OF TRUE EDUCATION

What does a true education really signify? Sri Aurobindo said that there are three things that education must take into account: (I) the man, (2) the nation or people, and (3) universal humanity. To appreciate Sri Aurobindo's educational thesis we should understand the inter-relationship among these three, and realize that the purpose of life-individual, national, universal-is spiritual development

He said that a true and living education `helps to bring out to full advantage, makes ready for the full purpose and scope of human life all that is in the individual man, which at the same time helps him to enter- into his right relation with the life, mind and soul of the people to which he belongs and with the great total life, mind and soul of humanity of which he himself is a unit and his people or nation a living, a separate and yet inseparable member'.

### Education is the Discovery of Soul

The importance in education of the discovery of the soul is shown by Sri Aurobindo when, speaking of new educational trends evidenced by the experiments carried out in various countries, he says, "The discovery that education must be a bringing out of the child's. own intellectual and moral capacities to their highest possible value and must be based on the psychology of the child-nature was a step for-ward towards a more healthy system; but it still fell short because it still regarded him as an object to be handled and moulded by the teacher. But at least there was a glimmering of the realization that each human being is a self-developing soul and that the business of both parent and teacher is to enable and to help the child to educate himself, to develop his own intellectual, moral, aesthetic and practical capacities and to grow freely as an organic being, not to be kneaded and pressured into form like an inert plastic material. It is not yet realised what this soul is or that the true secret, whether with child or an adult help him to find his deeper self, the real psychic entity within."

The closer touch attempted with the psychical entity behind the vital and physical mentality and an increasing reliance on its possibilities must lead to the ultimate discovery that man is inwardly a soul and conscious power of the Divine and that the evocation of this real man within is the right object of education and indeed of all human life if it would find and live according to the hidden truth and deepest law of its own being.

**Integral Education**

Education to be complete must have five principal' aspects relating 'to the five principal activities of the human being: the physical, the vital, the Mental, the psychic and the spiritual. Usually, these phases of education succeed each other in a chronological order following the growth of the individual. This, however,does not mean that one should replace another but that all must continue, completing each other, till. the end of life.

**Principles of Teaching**

Sri Aurobindo enumerated three principles of teaching. The first principle of true teaching is that nothing can be taught. The teacher is not an instructor or task master, he is 'a helper and guide.

The teacher's work is to suggest and not to impose on the mind of the students. He does not actually train the mind of his student but helps him to perfect his mind, the instrument of knowledge and encourages him-every way in this process. Thus he does not impart knowledge, but shows the- way how knowledge can be acquired. Knowledge is within the pupil and the pupil has to help himself to bring it out, but ha needs help. Somebody must tell him where it is and how it can be 'habituated to rise to the surface'. Teacher alone can do this work.

The second principle is that the mind has to be consulted in its growth. The idea of hammering the child into the shape desired by the parent or teacher is a barbarous and ignorant superstition.

The third principle of teaching is to work from the near to the far, from the known to the unknown. Man's nature is moulded by his soul's past, his heredity and his environment. The past is the foundation, the present is the material and future is the aim -and each must find its due and natural place in any national system of education.

**Moral Education through Personal Example**

The best method .of suggestion is by personal example, daily conversation and the books read from day-today. These books should contain for the younger student, the lofty examples of the past given not as moral lessons, but as things of supreme human interest, and, for the elder student, the great thoughts of great souls, the passages of literature which set fire to the highest emotions and prompt the highest ideals and aspirations, the records of history and biography which exemplify the living of those great thoughts, noble emotions and aspiring ideals. This is a kind of good company, 'satsanga', which. can seldom fail to have effect so long as sentintious sermonising is avoided and becomes of the highest effect if the personal life of the teacher is itself moulded by the great things he places before his pupils. It cannot, however, have full force unless the young life is given an opportunity, within the limited sphere, of embodying in action the moral impulses which rise within it.

**Teacher-A Guide and Helper**

The teacher is not an instructor or task-master; he is a helper and guide. His business is to suggest and not to impose. He does not actually train the pupil's mind, he only shows him how to perfect his instruments of knowledge and helps and encourages him in the process. He does not impart knowledge to him; he shows him how to acquire knowledge for himself. He does not call forth the knowledge for himself. He does not call forth the knowledge that is within. He only shows him where it lies and how it can be habituated to rise to the surface.

**Discipline and Liberty**

Sri Aurobindo suggests perfect liberty for the child. He says, "I would not like any hard things to be brought into the child's experience. He advises teachers not to be arbitrary, despotic, impatient and ill tempered.'

"If education is to bring out to full advantage all that is in the individual child we should first guarantee a safe custody of all that is in the individual. Nothing is to be lost or damaged, twisted or crushed. Everyone has in him something divine, something his own, a chance of perfection and strength in however small a sphere which God offers him to take or refuse. That Divinity in man is not to be insulted, that chance of perfection is not to be lost, that spark of strength is not to be extinguished. The task of a teacher is to help the child to feel that touch of Divinity, to find that `something', to develop it, and use it. Education should help the growing soul to draw out the best that is within and make it perfect for a noble cause."

**Physical Education**

Perfection is the true aim of all culture .... If our seeking is for a total perfection of being, the physical of it cannot be left aside, for the body is the material basis, the body is the instrument which we have to use. 'Sariram Khalu dharmasadhanam', says the old Sanskrit adage-the body is the means of fulfilment of dharma, and dharma means every ideal which we can propose to ourselves and the laws of its working out and its action.

It is true that in the past the body has been regarded by spiritual seekers rather as an obstacle, as something to be overcome and discarded than as an instrument of spiritual perfection and a field of the spiritual change.

## THE AUROBINDO ASHRAM AT PONDICHERRY

The Ashram located near the seashore has a number of fine buildings scattered over a vast area. Over 800 inmates of the Ashram are drawn not only from different parts of India but also from the world. There are poets, musicians, artists, physicians, surgeons, people from all walks of life. There is no high or low in the Ashram. The Ashram is intended to provide an environment of peace and harmony. All the inmates engage themselves in one or the other fruitful activity. Efforts are made to put into practice the `Ideal of Human Unity'. A strict code of discipline has to be maintained by the 'Sadhaks', the persons who stay in the Ashram and also the visitors. All activities in the Ashram are taken in the spirit of service and dedication to the Devine. The Library and the Reading Room are well-equipped.

## The Ashram School

The school was originally started in 1943 for the children of S: Aurobindo's disciples. It expanded gradually from a Primary School to a full-fledged High School. There are resident as well as day students.

### The International Centre of Education

The objectives underlying the centre are:

1. To evolve a system of education for making it dynamic, ideal for society.

2. To organise an environment which may provide inspiration and facilities for the exercise and development of the five aspects *of* personality-the physical, the vital, the mental, the psychic and the spiritual.

3. To emphasise the unity of all knowledge.

4. To develop the sense *of* oneness *of* mankind.

5. To discover and prepare for the role India has to play in the for mation of the new international harmony.

**The Curriculum**

It includes:

(1) Psychic and spiritual studies.

(2)' Academic subjects.

(3) Physical and health education.

(4) Cultural activities like art, music, drama.

(5) Vocational training.

(6) Education for international understanding.

**Auroville**

Auroville. `the city of dawn' near Pondicherry was inaugurated by the Mother on 28 February 1968, with representatives from 121 nations pouring soil from their respective lands into a lotus shaped urn symbolising the unity of the human race. It was intended to give practical expression to Sri Aurobindo's vision of a modern, selfsupporting community, -whose members would take full advantage of scientific developments while laying greater emphasis on spirituai awareness.

According to its own charter, Auroville belongs to nobody in particular. It belongs to humanity as a whole. Conceived as "the city of human unity," its objective was that there should be somewhere upon the earth a place that no nation could claim as its sole property, a place where all could live freely as the citizens of the world.

Alas, the objective is far from reality. To-day, Auroville is a house divided against itself. Apart from the two major societies, any number of small groups within groups have taken shape to protect their own self-interest.

The most disturbing factor is that a large number of residents of this 'city of dawn' are either drug addicts or people who are simply running away from life. They feel that sex is consistent with Sri Aurobindo's philosophy of evolutionary spiral, of man evolving into a higher consciousness.

## J. Krishnamurthy

## (1895 1986)

J. Krishnamurthy was a great revolutionary thinker. He said : "As long as you have concepts, you cannot see what is true." Besides other realms, he has presented his valuable thoughts in educational philosophy which can beget us serious spiritual and moral results. He has disapproved of all kinds of external authority whether it pertains to man, book or tradition. He said that we cannot know the truth by any man, book ortradition. For this, we have to make effort by ourselves. He was against the concept of religious groups and organisations, because they do not help us in coming face to face with the truth.

### Krishnamurthy and Education

J. Krishnamurthy was not orthodox in his principles of education. He has paid special attention to the problems of the new generation. He felt sorry that the most children in the modern times do not respect and listen to their parents, teachers and elders; and spare no time to think for them. He opines that this condition has arisen due to heir faulty breeding. The children should be given proper breeding from the earliest times coupled with training in proper conduct and education. He advocated the formation of such society and generation which is fearless, pragmatic, intelligent and prudent, and which can use better methods to improve upon the present situations. He said : "The function of education is to help you to face the world in a totally different intelligent way."

Criticising the prevalent educational system, Krishnamurthy said that our education is faulty because it stresses more on acquiring knowledge, but it does not develop sensibility, sensitivity and intelligence to solve the problem of the whole life. The real education of the world has to be moulded to meet the purpose of acquiring knowledge as well as enabling the child to look at the world objectively. Commenting on truth, he said : "Truth is a pathless land. Man cannot come to it through any creed, through any dogma, priest or ritual, not through any philosophic knowledge or psychological technique."

**Krishnamurthy and Educational Aims**

As we have discussed that Krishnamurthy was not orthodox. He wanted, education to work for preparing the new generation for a fruitful human life. Education is neither acquiring knowledge, nor passing examinations, nor taking degrees or earning abilities. He said : "To be really educated means not to conform, not to imitate, not to do what millions and millions are doing. If you feel like doing that, do it. But be awake to what you are doing." He further said : "Education must help in facing the world in a totally different, intelligent way, knowing you have to earn a livelihood, knowing all the responsibilities, the miseries of it all." When he saw that the present world lived more in violence of speech, thoughts, action, obedience, competition and all other spheres of life, he was pained greatly. He says when a man becomes aware of the violences present around him, he becomes free. It is the real education. According to him, education implies 'to live a life of tremendous order in which obedience is understood, in which it is seen where conformity is necessary and where it is totally unnecessary, as to see when you are imitating'. He further said education generally used to mean learning out of books, storing up information and using it either selfishly or for a particular cause, or a particular sect, and making oneself important in that sect or organisation." He says that violences among peoples, nations can be eradicated only by true form of education. He said : "We have this problem of existence with all its complexities - there is war, there is violence in our daily life, there are the religious divisions, there are the divisions caused by priests, by their idea of what is good and so on." About freedom, he has said : "Freedom is not a reaction; freedom is not a choice. It is man's pretense that because he has choice he is free. Freedom is pure observation without direction, without fear of punishment and reward."

**Krishnamurthy and Teacher**

Krishnamurthy is of the view that the teacher should assist the students in acquiring knowledge of the book and themselves. We can see that he defines education as self-realization. The process of education should produce development of intelligence and instincts, besides inner vision. By disciple he meant : "Disciple means one who learns. But the generally accepted meaning is that a disciple is one who follows someone, some guru, some silly person. But both the follower and the one who follows are not learning." He considers the present revolution of the new generation against meaningless standardised life of the present times as necessary His views on the teacher-pupil relationship are not in conformance to the ancient Indian thought.

**Krishnamurthy and Discipline**

According to Krishnamurthy, education should make available suitable opportunities to the child to express himself, so that he becomes able to lead an intelligent and prudent life. He favours freedom in the process of education which can help in the evelopment of intelligence. According to him : "Education is to help us to be sane, non-mechanical and intelligent." Education makes us practical and intelligent which is useful in this material world. Education helps us to acquire knowledge free from the past prejudices. Education should enable man to look at things independently, apply his own perception and logic, and contemplate about them. Following a teacher, book or tradition blindly can do him no good. He must live a life according to his own beliefs and intelligence. Depending on others' intelligence and advice can only misguide him.

**Krishnamurti's Message:** For the perturbed and wayward humanity ,his message was ,"First understanding the purpose of your life –the purpose of this individual existence .Understand what it is towards which you are thriving .Then utilise every emotion, every thought to strengthen you ." He observed that the man who can spilt the nation, but has no love in his heart , become a monster . The exclusive creation of technique has product scientists, mathematicians and engineers ,who have no understanding of the process of life Emphasis on efficiency without understanding what life means, brings about misery and chaos in the world.

**Shortcomings in the Present** System of Education. Krishnamurti noticed the following deficiencies in the present system of education:

1. Education at present is simply accumulating knowledge and collecting information from books.

2. To-day's education, riot only kills the spirit of the child but also debars him from becoming an integrated individual.

3. Education has come to mean acquiring skills, learning techniques which help in earning a living only.

4. Education does not encourage creativity.

5. To-day's education creates more or less 'yes men'.

6. Large impersonal schools with crowded classes and mass instruction fail to bring about the accomplishment of true education.

7. The present system of education depends upon authority and domination at all levels - the government, the head of the school and the teacher.

All exercise their powers and the pupil who is at the lowest end, suffers. He becomes fearful and his creativity is killed.

## Main Features of the Educational Philosophy of Krishnamurti

Integral Education. According to him, "The highest function of education is to bring about an integrated individual who is capable of dealing with life as a whole." Education according to him was a transformation of human mind and creation of new culture. Education must free the mind and spirit of children. He remarked, "Without a change of heart, without goodwill, without the inward transformation which is born of awareness, there can be no peace, no happiness for mankind." "Education should encourage self-observation and the experiencing of life as a whole, not to `me' and `mine' but to go above and beyond to discover the real." That was whv education should be concerned with the totality of life and not with the immediate responses to immediate challenges. Making a scathing attack on modem technical. and vocational education, he remarked, "Modern education is just like having a right arm highly developed, strong and vital while the rest of the body withers and becomes weak." This is against the concept of integral education. The task of education was showing the way to wisdom, to truth. Truth was within oneself.. To find the truth, man must be free from all bondages. The function of education is to help each pupil to discover inner psychological resources and develop his own individual strengths, as well as to realize his weakness , without imposing upon him the teachers' notion what he should be.

**The Educator's Role.** The teacher himself should be a properly integrated human being. The teacher has to be careful, thoughtful and affectionate in the creation of the right environment for the development of understanding to enable the child to deal intelligently with human problems. In order to achieve all this, the educator needs to understand himself. In order to deal with children a great deal of patience and understanding are needed . for a true teacher ,teaching was not a technique but a way of life .

**Responsibility of the Parents.**

Krishnanurti held the view that education was a dual responsibility of the parents and the teacher .he said, “The problem is not the child but parents and the teacher, the problem is to educate the educator”

# UNIT-4

**LEARNING OBJECTIVE**

**Education, national values and the constitution of India**
**Nature of knowledge and the knowledge getting process**
**Social Philosophy of Education- Freedom, equality, Democracy and Responsibility**

# National values and Constitution

The history of education in India took a significant turn from the fateful night of August 15, 1947. Slaves had finally won independence and in the free air of independence, attention turned towards changes in education, formulation of an educational policy, and the needs of the country. In the early days of independence, India's educationists felt that it was not possible to find the right path without altering the structure of education.

In order to educate itself, society, has to resort to modernisation. It must make an effort to create a class of educated individuals, drawn from every part of society, whose beliefs and ambitions bear the deep imprint of Indianism. Such persons are needed to raise the educational level of the average citizen. In a democracy, the end is the individual himself. (The major purpose of education is to grant the individual the maximum possible opportunities for the fullest development of his capabilities Today, it can be said that India's destiny is being shaped in its classroom.' In this world of ours, founded upon science 'and technology, it is education alone which determines the level of prosperity, well-being and security of individuals. The success we achieve in the task of national reconstruction depends directly upon the qualities of our students emerging from our colleges and universities. Awakening a national consciousness should be an important objective of our school education. We must endeavour to achieve these objectives by bringing about a growth in knowledge based upon over cultural heritage, by indulging in its constant re-valuation and by instilling the depest faith in its future progress. Today, education has undergone multifaceted growth and progress. In consequence, literacy has increased, but at the same time, the rapidly increasing population has also increased the problems of education. In the various sphere of education, many problems have assumed gigantic and frightening proportions Although over Five-Year plans have made some progress in this direction, education has, on the whole., to satisfy the individual's needs.

## 1. EDUCATION AND THE CONSTITUTION

From one viewpoint, it is appropriate to treat the declaration of the Constitution as the starting point of education in free India. The Constitution states explicitly that education is a State. This has been made clear in entries 63, 64, 65 and 66 of Schedule I, and the 25th entry of the Third Schedule.

The ideas expressed in the Constitution concerning education in free India are the following:

**(1) Free and Compulsory Education**-Articles 45 of the Constitution states, "The state shall endeavour to provide with in a period in ten years from the commencement of this constitution for the free and compulsory education of all the children until they complete the age of 14 years."

In this statement, the term `State' refers to the States subordinate to the Union government.

**(2) Education of Women**-According to Articles 15(3) of the Constitution the State cannot be absolved of the responsibility of framing special scheme for the education of women and children. This section does not restrain the State on any way in making special provisions for women and children.

**(3) Religious Education**-Article 28(1) of the Constitution lays down that religious education of any kind will not be imparted in any educational institution financed from the national treasury. However, according to Article 28(2), any institution established by a trust or a religious body can impart religious education, even though such an institution may be aided by the government.

It has also been made clear that, in such educational institutions, children cannot be forced to imbibe a religious education which runs counter to their own religion, without the permission of the parents. In this context, the Kothari Commission h, also pointed out that in the new generation, social and moral conflicts are coming to the force. Western thinkers have come round to the view that there should be a balance between knowledge and skill, science and technology should be linked with morality and religion, research into knowledge of oneself should be understood, the meaning of life should be understood, the real truth shout stand revealed and there should be an understanding of human relations. (Education Commission, p. 19, para 14·7).

**(4) Union and State Lists**-In the Constitution, educational activities have been divided in the following manner-(1) According to the 62nd entry of the Schedule-national libraries, national museums, the Imperial War Museum, Victoria Memorial, and historical places of national importance will be under the charge of the Union. (2) According to entry 63, Benaras, Aligarh and Delhi universities will be under the control of the Union government. (3) The 64th entry of the Schedule points out that scientific and technical institutions of national importance, so declared by Parliament, will remain under the charge of the Union. (4) According to entries 65 and 66, the union government will have the responsibility for professional and technological institutions, research institutions, institutions for research into crime eradication, etc., as well as determining the standards of higher education and research. In the same way, Article 239 gives the Union the responsibility for education in all Union Territories.

66 subjects relating to education have been placed within the jurisdiction of the States. The 12th entry in this regard classifies that the States will be responsible for libraries, museums, archeological institutions and memorials of national importance.

In addition to the above, the Constitutions also contains a Concurrent list, which lists the following subjects-(1) economic and social planning, (2) professional and technological training, (3) scientific research, (4) technological education, (5) the development and propagation of Hindi, (6) preservation of national art and culture,

(7) preservation of Sanskrit literature, (8) education of disabled persons, (9) development of educational research, (10) protection of the cultural interests of minorities, (11) educational development of the scheduled castes, regions and classes, (12) national and emotional integration, (13) provision of scholarships to brilliant students, (14) continuous professional training, (15) establishment of central institutions and agencies, (16) free and compulsory education for children upto the age of 14 years.

## 2. EDUCATION COMMISSIONS IN INDEPENDENT INDIA

### 1. Central Advisory Board of Education

In 1948, the Central Advisory Board held its 14th meeting, in which it reflected upon secondary education. It put forth the suggestion for the appointment of a commission, whose main function would be to (1) evaluate the existing secondary education in the country, and (2) give suggestions for the problems relating to it.

This suggestion was implemented when a committee was appointed under the chairmanship of the then Advisor on educational matters, Dr. Tara Chand. Its report was considered in 15th meeting of the Advisory Board, and in consequence, th government of India was requested to appoint a commission for determining the objectives and purposes, and suggesting solution for the problems of basic, secondary and university education. This requirement was then reiterated in 1951.

### 2. University Education Commission 1948

A University Education Commission was appointed in 194 under the Chairmanship of Dr. Radhakrishnan. This Commission came forward with numerous significant suggestions for the improvement of education at the university level, and in consequence the following changes occurred- (1) emphasis was placed upon teacher education and training, (2) the curriculum was made comprehensive and diverse to accommodate the interests, abilities and talent of students,(3) research began to hourlsh, (4) religious and morn education came to he imparted, (5) importance was given to the three-language formula for solving the language problem, (6) many reforms in the system of examination were carried out. In addition, many steps for student welfare, education *of* women and relate issues were taken.

**Jurisdiction**-The jurisdiction of the Commission was stated in the following words, "To report on Indian University Education,. and suggest improvements and extensions that may be desirable suit present and future requirements of the country. (Rep the U. E. C. Page 1.) This Commission stated the objective of university education in the following terms-it should seek to harmonise life and the various branches of knowledge. Hence essential that the subjects taught in the universities should bear a relationship to life. They should comprehend all elements.

The Education Commission has laid stress upon formation of character. It clarifies that the objective of education is the achievement of justice, liberty, equality and brotherhood upon the foundations of a national discipline. Highlighting the importance teachers, the Commission has declared that the success of the educational process depends upon the ability and character of the teacher. The most important aspect of any scheme for improvement of university education is the obtaining of able teachers. The Radhakrishnan Commission has reflected upon every possible way for improving the conditions of teachers. It has attached importance to raising the standards of teachers and the expansion of laboratories and libraries, etc.

The Commission has defined three objectives of the curriculum : (1) to provide general education, (2) to provide a liberal education, (3) to provide professional education.

To ensure the greater importance is given to law and medicine, the Commission has made some significant recommendations. It has also stressed the need to develop objective testing techniques. In connection with the welfare of students, the Commission has expressed the view that the prime functions of the university are imparting education to youth and searching for new truths. Students are not created for universities; instead universities are established for formation of the students' character. Hence, it is essential that the university should seek, by every conceivable means and ways, to bring about the integral physical, mental and spiritual development of the student's powers.

Throwing light on the importance of education of women, the Commission opines that without educated women, there can be no educated men. General education should not be confined to either men or women. Women, too, should get the opportunity to receive education because, it is only in this condition that knowledge can, with certainty, be transmitted to future generations.

Emphasizing the need for the setting up of rural universities. the Commission has stated that for the general progress of rural India, it is necessary to bring about a constant extension in skills, limits of training and its quality. In order to provide these, and to satisfy the need for educated citizens, it is necessary to adopt the technique of rural colleges and universities. Hence, work in this direction is very desirable.

Dr. Rajendra Prasad's opinion of this Commission was that the Commission had presented a very valuable document on the achievements of education in our universities, and that it had provided useful suggestions for the attainment of varied specialised skills.

**2. Mudaliar Commission 1952-53**

A Secondary Education Commission was appointed in 1952-53 for the reorganisation of secondary education. Dr. Lakshmanswami Mudaliar was appointed its chairman. The recommendations of this commission brought forth the following changes in education

(1) The Higher secondary programme was extended to 11 years.

(2) Stress was laid on the establishment of multipurpos schools.

(3) The curriculum was made comprehensive and vared.

(4) Objective testing was given importance.

(5) Schemes for welfare of teachers were proposed.

**Jurisdiction**-The sphere of operation of this commission and the issues it was to examine were stated thus-1. Evaluation of every aspect of secondary education in India and throwing light upon it. 2. Giving suggestions for the improvement and reorgainisation of secondary education.

This Commission considered the defects of secondary education and determined its objectives in the light of the following needs-(1) development of qualities of character through education, propagation of nationalism and secularism, , (2) increase in productive capacity so as to bring about an increase in national wealth. (3) Improvements in education.

**Objectives of Education**-(1) Development of democratio citizenship. (2) Training in the art of living. (3) Development of personality. (4) Supply of professional skills. (5)Training for leadership. (6) Propagation of love of country.

The Secondary Education Commission determined the period of education at 7 years, intended for children between 11 and 17 years of age. It was divided into two parts-(1) 3 years for middle education, and (2) 4 years of higher secondary education vision was also made for a three-years degree course.

The Commission considered it important that technical schools and other kinds of schools should be developed. It also provided for co-education. It views on the study language were as follows -(1) Hindi has been given the rank of the national language by the Constitution. (2) After some time, Hindi was expected to become the language of exchange between the center and the Slates. (3) Hindi would become the practical language of the majority. (4) As the language of the government, Hindi would bring about a growth of national unity.

Similarly, the Commission put forth the following views on the subject of English- (1) English is popular in the country. (2) English will bring about political unity. (3) English has international importance. (4) English is necessary.

The commission views on Sanskrit were -(1) Sanskrit is the mother of Indian languages. (2) It has been responsible for the growth of the cultural and religious attitude. (3) Indian knowledge can be obtained only through knowledge of Sanskrit.

The Commission also gave many valuable suggestions concerning the curriculum. It divided this into two parts-the Core and the Optional part. The Commission also advocated the nationalization of the text books. These should be cheap, and of good quality. The Commission has accepted formation of character as the basis of education. It has suggested that schools should have arrangements for consultancy and vocational guidance. It has also recommended physical or health education. In addition to improvementsin examinations, it has suggested the proper maintenance of school records. It has also given importance to improving the conditions of teachers. The Commission has also reflected upon the economics of education, and pointed towards many important sources.

**3. Kothari Commission 1964-66**

Under the Chairmanship of Dr. Daulat S. Kothari, a National Education Commission was set up in 1964. It put forward a national education scheme for the next 20 years. This Commission has given Indian education a new direction. The Commission has reflected upon the entire spectrum of education, from its objectives to its economic aspects, and in consequence, it has raised many illuminating questions for the country's educationists to reflect upon. -

In the context of the establishment of this commission, the Central government stated on July 14, 1964, that the commission had been appointed to reflect upon the advise the government on educational policies, national standards of education, and the potential for development in every sphere of education. The prefatory statement throws light on-(1) Education and national ideals, (2) method of education, its structure and level, (3) the standard of the teacher, (4) teacher training, (5) enrolment and manpower, (6) equality in the opportunities for obtaining education, (7) the parameters of educational problems of schools, (8)method of education, direction or guidance, and evaluation, (9) school education, administration and inspection, (10) environment for higher education and programmes, (11) sovereignty of universities, (12) agricultural education, (13) professional, technical and engineering education, (14) scientific education and research,(15) adult education, (16) educational planning and administration me (17) the economics of education.

With reference to the prospectus of this Commission, the contemporary minister for education, Sh.Muhammed Karem Chagla, said that the prospectus was a kind of Magna Carta, for teachers. In it, thought bad been given to national and social service, salaries of teachers, the three language formula, etc. This preface led to many important turning points in the sphere of education Of these, the three language formula became a of considerable discussion.

**4. Other Achievements**

Since independence, there has been a remarkable quantitative increase in the educational sphere. The number of school has increased, and so have the students, but the obiectives of education could not be achieved. Many new professional institution, came into existence, as did many new universities. There were many and varied experiments in education. The scales of pay of teachers underwent numerous revisions. There was progress in the s here of women's education.

The new achievements in education can he enumerated thus-

1. The Center has adopted democracy as a form of administration and way of life for the people.
2. It has reduced poverty through the means of education and thus brought about a general improvement the level of the people.
3. Modernisation has been adopted in industry and agriculture.
4. Obedience to ancient Indian traditions has gone hand in hand with the acceptance of knowledge and science.'
5. It has accepted a socialistic pattern of society.
6. Equality has been granted to the opportunities for education.
7. The rate of literacy has increased from 19 to 28 percent.

In the context of this new age, we must accept that education is that basis of our consciousness, awareness of our society and our nation According to **Acharya** Vinobha Bhave, revolution should be introduced into education, so as to bring about a synthesis between knowledge and action. It is the combination of knowledge and action which can be called education. In view of this, both physical and mental activity are essential for the individual. Every individual should possess the capacity for the complete and balanced development of both aspects. In spite of all these, achievements, our educationists continued to feel that our educational structure suffered from some shortcomings.

## THE NATURE OF KNOWLEDGE

### Epistemology

Epistemology is the theory of knowledge. It deals with knowledge as a universal matter and aims to discover what is involved in the process of knowing. It asks such questions as: Is there something common to all the different activities to which we apply the term "knowing"? Is knowing a special sort of mental act? If so, what is the difference between knowledge and belief? Can we know anything beyond the objects with which our senses acquaint us? Does knowing make any difference to the object known?

Unlike the psychologist, the epistemologist is not interested in amassing d classifying facts and subjecting them to statistical analysis. ( e epistemologist has ideas about how people think and feel, but he does not claim to be able to explain them scientifically. He examines relevant psychological concepts such as perception, memory, and reinforcement in order to determine whether they are consistent not necessarily with facts but with themselves. Knowing the psychological use of these expressions, he seeks to analyze their meaning. In general, the main epistemological problem is to state and assess the very grounds on which knowledge rests and on which claims to knowledge are made. There are, of course, different types of knowledge, the most important of which yell now be reviewed.

## TYPES OF KNOWLEDGE

### (1) Revealed Knowledge

Revealed knowledge is in part the kind of knowledge that God discloses to man.. In His omniscience God inspires certain men to record f: is revelation in permanent form, whereby it may become accessible to all mankind. For Christian and Jew it is contained in the Bible; for the Mohammedan, in the Koran; for the Hindu, in the Bhagavad-Gita and the Upanishads. Divinely authenticated, it promises that those who accept it can never, according to their own lights, be mistaken. Human interpretation may distort parts of it, but in itself it is Divine truth. Revealed knowledge is confined to whatever a religion or sect accepts as the Word of God. It-is-not-simply an individual, personal pronouncement. It is also based on supernatural phenomena, although it can apply to natural phenomena, as in Genesis. There can be *very* little argument about the credibility of its source. It can neither be proved nor disproved empirically. One accepts it on faith, buttressed whenever possible by reason and critical experience.

### (2) Authoritative Knowledge

This is knowledge accepted as true because it comes from experts. Knowledge found in encyclopedias usually is regarded as authoritative, as is that of our best textbooks. Other sources are monographs and specialized publications by recognized profession people. In school practice we accept without question formula for solving certain mathematical problems and memorize table for decimalizing English measurements. We could check the truth of these formulas and tables personally, but we prefer to accept them in order to save time and effort. After all, they have been-vouched for by authorities in mathematics for a long time Most of our factual knowledge is based on authority; much of is a record of the achievements, experiences, and facts that a cu ture considers of sufficient value to perpetuate.

(3) **Intuitive Knowledge**

Intuition is perhaps the most personal way of knowing. It a. curs on what psychologists call the *subliminal level,* beneath the "threshold of consciousness." It is intimately connected with feeling and contrasts with the logical processes usually associated with thinking at the conscious level. As persons, we see "in a sudden flash of insight" that something is the case. We apprehend knowledge directly. Yet, we do not know how we acquired this knowledge. Only an intense feeling seems to convince us that we have discovered what we were looking for. Intuition is often equated with an instinct that has become self-conscious and, hence, is viewed by many as the only true source of knowledge. To Nietzsche intuition is "the most intelligent of all kinds of in intelligence." Harvard's Jeome S. Bruner calls it "the intellectual technique of arriving at plausible but tentative formulations without going through the analytic steps by which such formulations would be found to be valid or invalid conclusions." This does not mean that intuition about a scientific the, for example, comes to an individual regardless of his knowledge of science. Unless one is familiar with the scope and structure of the knowledge involved, there can be no substantial intuitions about it.

Intuition is by no means the monopoly of mystics, saints, and females. Scientists, artists, philosophers, and religious leaders who have experienced moments of deep contemplation all testify to the fact that some of their most creative accomplishments have occurred following sudden insights or moments of inspiration. Alone, however, intuition probably is not a reliable source of knowledge. It must be checked by the concepts of reason and the percepts of the senses. Intuitive and analytic thinking must complement each other, and intuited scientific theories must be verified by normal scientific procedures before they can be cleared valid and reliable.

That our schools tend to emphasize analytical thinking to the neglect of intuition there is no doubt, largely because of the unpredictability and. extremely personal quality of intuition. But intuition, asserts Bruner, .. is an "essential feature of productive thinking, not only in formal academic disciplines but also in everyday life," and the intuitive power of a student should cultivated as a genuine source of creativity." A teacher shonl be able to differentiate the student's "educated hunch," which intuition, from the clever' trick he may use to conceal ignorance Teachers may have to develop greater powers of intuition them selves in order to recognize intuition in others!

**Rational Knowledge**

Reason is a source of knowledge from which we derive, universe v valid judgments that are harmony with one another. Certain mathematical and logical truths, for instance, are "self-evident" kinds of knowledge that appeal to our reason. Consider t proposition that two contradictory statements both cannot true at the same time, or the proposition that, if A is greater than B and B is greater than C, then A is greater than C. Bu are true statements independent of actual instances and not derived from the senses. They are valid regardless of our person experience with them.

Those who stress reason as the important factor in knowledge are known as *rationalists.* They acknowledge the contribution of the senses to knowledge in the form of bare facts and isolate_ impressions. But they believe that the intellect interprets a, organizes these bits and pieces of information into what we can call reliable and significant knowledge.

Knowledge through reason, however, has important limitation It tends to be abstract. It deals with a world of relations al, meanings, and gives little understanding of the physical wore Because our lives inevitably arc immersed in this physical wore we need the help of other types of knowledge. Moreover, of reasoning processes may be influenced by prejudices, interests, and inclinations, which often prevent reason from being objective.

Pure reason is used less now than in the early days of philosophy, when men believed that reason alone was paramour Yet, it still remains the arbiter and judge of knowledge, if knowledge is to be rational. Here reason finds itself in a rather difficult position, for the human mind, it seems, must actually judge itself.

Reason, Kant once declared, attempts "to undertake the most laborious of all tasks-that of self-examination.' "The understanding, like the eve," wrote Locke, "whilst it makes us see and perceive all other things, takes no notice of itself; and it requires art and pains to set itself at a distance, and make it its own object."

**Empirical Knowledge**

The view that knowledge comes from the senses is known as *empiricism.* By seeing, hearing, smelling, feeling, and tasting, we form our picture of the world around us. Knowledge,, therefore, is composed of ideas formed in accordance with observed facts. An empiricist cautions us to "look and see," whereas a rationalist tells us to "think things through."

Although we depend on our eases for our knowledge of the everyday world, at times these senses deceive us, as in the classic example of the stick that looks bent in water but turns out to be straight when we touch it. Our prejudices also may influence our way of seeing. At times we see what we are conditioned to see, not what is actually there. The accuracy of the senses may be reduced further by such elements as cold, fog, heat, noise, or smog. Nevertheless, the senses have their own role to play in the formation of knowledge.

Because modem science is empirical, its methodology is allied closely with this particular aspect of epistemology. Theories or hypotheses are tested through experiments to find which one best explains a certain phenomenon. Success depends on many factors such as elimination of extraneous and spurious elements, careful collection of data, proper research design and selection of methods, and the attitude and ability of the experimenter. Even so, the conclusion of an experiment is never expected to prove or:'dis= prove a hypothesis absolutely. It can only present the results as more or less probable. Empirical knowledge, then, is not necessarily the most dependable kind of knowledge that we have, as many suppose. It takes its place along with other types as one more avenue to understanding reality.

## THE NATURE OF VALUE

### *Types* of Value

The general study of values is known as *axiology.* There are, o course, different theories and types of value, and they arc logically a part of established schools of philosophy.' As a rule, a stud'. of values centers around three main issues: (1) whether values are, objective or subjective, that is, impersonal or personal; (2) whether they are changing or constant; and (3) whether there arc hiearchies of value.

**1.** Objective values exist regardless of man's personal feeling' and desires. They are cosmic in character and may be regarded' as realities deriving from the nature of the universe itself. Truth goodness, and beaus for example are by this concept *ontological* realities and possess intrinsic value. Objective truth has its own value; it is Rood to tell the truth whether we like it or not. Goodness is also a value; we do good simple for the sake of doing it and not because we desire to do good. In an objective theory of art we say that beauty resides in the object. The beauty of the sunset-its colors both changing and blending-is a quality apart from the beholder's judgment. Its beauty is all its own. Objective values exist for all men. They drawn an appreciative response from us regardless of our individual wishes. In this view, education or learning is an objective value, a "good" in itself, not dependent on monetary reward or personal gain.

Subjective values, on the other hand, are relative to personal desire, which confers value on the object considered. To value something means to desire it. We believe it is good simply because we desire it. Subjective values are man-made and vary according to the man and the circumstances. Sonic subjective values are referred to as *instrumental* because they are instruments or means used to obtain certain desired satisfaction y Bill Smith helps his classmates with their homework so that he can gain their favor, or he studies hard so that he can get a well-paid job or become a scholar

**2.**Values may also be considered either (a) absolute and eternal, or (b) variable and changing. Absolute values are constant. They derive from the character of the world and are a reflection of reality itself. They do not change from generation to generation or from society to society, but in their essence they remain constant for all time. What is wrong for us today was wrong also for our predecessors a thousand years ago.

Changing values, on the contrary, are likely to be responses to man's immediate needs. Unlike absolute values, they arise in the course of man's daily experiences. *They* are both relative and personal to him. Such values; therefore, are always subject to revision. They are generally more social than individual. They are arrived at empirically and tested publicly in order, to gain the approval of an informed group

**3.**Whether or not one believes in a permanent hierarchy of values depends on one's general philosophy. Some philosophies adhere to a more or less fixed value structure, which extols the things of the spirit above those of matter. They rank religious values highly because such values help man to become one with the spiritual order. Other philosophers agree that some values are more important than others, but they rank empirical values highly for helping us to adjust to material reality. They value the physical and mathematical sciences for disclosing -certain facts of the universe from which empirical values derive Still other philosophers refuse to establish a hierarchy of values. For them one activity is likely to be as good as another if it satisfies an urgent need and possesses instrumental value. These philosophers emphasize the process rather than the end of evaluation. They are sensitive to the values that society pries, but they delight as much in establishing ways for testing values as in contemplating them rationally. They feel this way largely because they believe that, in the long run, all values past and present are only instrumental to the establishment of further and better values.

The subject of values is long and intriguing, especially in our day when specialists are striving to establish them logically and scientifically. If, for example, researchers can demonstrate that Americans prize the same values as other people elsewhere, we shall have come a long way toward laying a foundation for international understanding.

Whereas popular opinion maintains that East and West are far apart in their social and moral values, experimental tests might show that Americans and Japanese actually agree on some values more than Americans and the British. Elaborate classifications have been made of what men *in fact* prize highly as contrasted with what they say they value. The results are startling and should be studied by every educator. In this way the statistical findings of the social scientist provide both educator and philosopher with facts for deep reflection.

## Ethics

Ethics is the philosophic study of moral values and conduct. It deals with such questions as "What is the good life for all men?" and "How ought we to behave?" It is concerned with providing right values as the basis for right actions. These values, or principles, justify or condemn one's personal conduct.[12]

An ethical system may be related closely to a religion. If so, it tends to be absolutistic, consisting of fixed rules of conduct, which people are expected to obey. Today, however, ethical systems are more likely to be secular, naturalistic, and relativistic. The ethical systems of the Western world, although largely derived from and influenced by Christianity, often justify themselves on other than religious grounds. In America an established policy of separation of church and state has led to the rejection of religious teaching in public schools. This, in turn, has led people to wonder whether certain moral values should be taught in order to take the place of religious knowledge.

Two types of ethical theory are pertinent to this introduction *intuitionism* and *naturalism.* Intuitionism states that moral values arc apprehended directly. We grasp whether a thing is right or wrong by means of an inborn moral sense. Moral values, then, cannot be assessed in terms of their consequences; *they* are right in themselves and do not need to be verified by scientific xperimentation. Furthermore, they are "nonnaturalistic"; in, deed, they are, in anything, "supranaturalistic."

Naturalism is the view that moral values derive from and are determined by man's needs, interests, and desires. Man is the originator and measure of his own values. The rightness or wrongness of his acts depends upon their consequence for him. Therefore, since consequences can be verified empirically, so can values. For example, if one believes that premarital sexual relations are morally wrong, one should believe so, not because of ethical statements already made on the subject, but rather because of the findings of scientific experimentation and observation about the actual effects of such relations. A person who accepts the naturalistic interpretation of ethics founds his principles on what he believes scientists have shown to be the proper way for human beings to conduct themselves. In other words, he insists that moral values must meet the real needs of' men living together here and now, and that they must be based on an earthly humanism rather than a heavenly one.

## Esthetics

Esthetics is the study of values in the realm of beauty and art. Esthetics deals with the theoretical aspects of art in its widest sense, not to be confused with actual works of art or specialized criticisms of them. Esthetic values are harder to assess than moral values, because they tend to be more personal and subjective and because' they relate to imagination and creativity. A particular work of art evokes varying responses among different people. De *gustibus non est disputandum.* Who is to say that this or that response should be the appropriate one?

At any rate, one basic question has occupied estheticians throughout the centuries. Should art be imitative and representative, or should it be the product of the private creative imagination? In the first view, art should faithfully reproduce life and human experience. We should clearly recognize the autumnal scene or fading sunset depicted in a landscape painting. Indeed, how many of us treasure a still life of a bowl of flowers, each flower etched so well, its petals so lifelike, that we are impelled to reach out and touch them!

The second view may be considered a reaction against- the first. Here the artist may express himself spontaneously about any aspect of life that interests him. He does not need to copy objects that he sees or experiences in actual life. "A picture," said Degas, "must never be a copy. . . . The air we see in the paintings of the old masters is never the air we breathe." [13] The artist is on his own. He enjoys limitless freedom to use his medium in a way that genuinely satisfies his creative urge. He creates out of his personal experiences; he expresses his feelings about the beauty or ugliness of the world and, perhaps, shows what he thinks the world should be. He may teach us as effectively as the representational artist how to see and experience life.

In both views, questions arise as to the proper subject matter and scope of art. If art is an expression of life, it should deal with *all* of it-the ugly, the beautiful, the grotesque, the unique. However, there are many, especially among supporters of the first view, who believe that art has *a social* function. For them art must speak to the hearts of all men. Art that fails to communicate its mood and message cannot be genuine. Art whose meaning remains forever private to the creator is, says Jung, a "neurosis."

On the other hand, if the artist is compelled constantly to bear in mind the need to communicate his message to a society that cannot possibly know and appreciate his inner feelings, his creativity will be stunted, if not completely destroyed. For many, particularly among those who hold the second view, the social function of art is not its highest function. Society itself is ephemeral; it changes, progresses, sees things differently. Anartist born in one generation may he creating for the next. Shall he be condemned for failing to please his contemporaries? An artist who has pleased his critics is probably at the end of his inventive powers, for critics tend to judge in accordance with accepted standards. The rejected creator may be the real innovator.

# THE NATURE OF ORDERLY THINKING

## Types of Logic

Logic is the study of correct thinking. It examines the rules *of valid inference,* which enable us to pass successfully from one argument to another. It establishes criteria, such as the *principle o f self-contradiction* or the *law o f the excluded middle,* that enable us to assess the internal consistency of statements. From what is given and accepted as either self-evident or already demonstrated, we pass to something that follows necessarily or most probably. Schoolchildren, for example, engage in inference when they tell their teacher that they knew it rained because the ground was wet. However, their conclusion is not decisive enough for their inference to be valid. The ground may have been wet because the gardner turned his hose on it.

Because one of the teacher's greatest responsibilities is to cultivate in students the ability to think clearly and correctly, it is imperative that he receive some training in logic. There are many types of logic, but for present purposes it will suffice to outline two of them. Later we shall consider their importance to processes of education.

## Deductive Logic

*Deduction is* a form of reasoning that moves from a general statement particular instance. It draws implications, from one or a number of basic axioms or assumptions. The syllogism is an exam le of deductivc reasoning. The major premise of a syllogism takes the form of a general statement, such as "All men are mortal." This is a universal statement, which nobody can deny. It is followed by a minor premise, usually more specific, such as "John is a man." This is a particular fact, and no one doubts it. The conclusion is inevitable: "John is mortal." In deductive reasoning, once certain premises are accepted, the conclusion is indisputable, provided it is drawn validly from the premises.

The value of deduction lies not so much in deriving particular conclusions from universal propositions as in the logical necessity with which the consequences follow from the premises. In everyday conversation people think that they are using the syllogism correctly; they say that their point of view is "logical. Take, for example, the ardent young man who sought refuge in logic to inform his sweetheart of his true sentiments: "All the world loves a lover," he said. This was his major premise. Was it correct? Minor premise: "You are all the world to me" Co0rrect? Conclusion: "Therefore you love me." Do you age· And what about the logic of the fourth grader who "deduced that the reason the pig was a "pig" was that lie was a very dirt animal? Or consider a more sophisticated example. One often hears this sort of argument: "All communists are totalitarian all fascists are totalitarian; therefore, all communists are fascists. The error lies in the assumption that if two groups share a sing! quality, they must therefore be identical.

## Inductive Logic

Inductive logic is usually defined as reasoning that moves from particular instances to a general conclusion. Certain particular with similar characteristics are put in the same category. Then generalizations are made on the basis of these particulars. Clearly, the teacher must guard against the tendency of students to jump to generalizations from insufficient particulars. A premature in duction might run like this: A man gets drunk on Monday on rye and soda, on Tuesday on scotch and soda, and on Wednes day on gin and soda. What caused his drunkenness? Obviously, the soda!

## Logic and Psychology

If logic is the study of correct thinking, does it not form par` of psychology? Not exactly, for, whereas psychology considers the actual process of thinking, logic studies the content of what is thought or, more accurately, the types of propositions into which this content is cast. Logic, then, deals with v,-hat our propositions assert; but how any individual actually thinks when he states these propositions is irrelevant to logic. Our apprehension of a syllogism, for example, may be studied as a psychological event, because it is an act of thought; however, the syllogism we apprehend is not itself a psychological event but rather a relation between the forms of three propositions.

Thus, an inference is valid or invalid depending on what is inferred, not on the actual mental operations that must occur if this inference is to be made. If I infer that because an undergraduate has taken an introductory course in the philosophy of education, he knows certain things about the philosophy of John Dewey, then my inference is true or false regardless of the neurophysiological events, mental images, and so forth that constitute the act of inferring as opposed to the content inferred.

Nevertheless, although the validity of an inference is unaffected by the psychological state of the person inferring it, a person must still be motivated to think logically; that is, he must, be psychologically conditioned so that he desires to make valid inferences and knows how to do so. Thus, at first, if a teacher rewards a student for thinking logically, the student continues to think logically in order to receive the reward. Gradually, however, the student realizes that this way of thinking is satisfying not only because it is rewarded but also because it is logical. In other words, the habit of thinking logically can be cultivated by psychological means-for example, by positive and negative reinforcement-but whether any particular inference is valid or invalid depends on the relations between the propositions in which this inference is expressed..

**5. FREEDOM IN EDUCATION**

So far an analysis has been given of the principle of liberty, an attempt has been made to justify it, and general problems of its application have been considered. Its application in the specific field of education must now be examined. The issues raised here are very different from those raised in the previous two chapters; for whereas they were concerned with the distribution and matter of education, questions to do with its manner have now to be tackled. There is, of course, an issue to do with the freedom of the parent in relation to educational provision, which is closely connected with the problem of its distribution; but the more perplexing problems relate to the freedom of the child and of the teacher. The problems are created by the differences in application necessitated by the fact that the principle has to be applied in an educational situation.

We shall begin, therefore, with the freedom of the child, pass on to the freedom of the teacher, and end up with a few brief remarks about the freedom of the parent.

***(a) The freedom of the child***

It has been maintained that the concept offreedom joins together two main components: first the notion of possible wants or decisions and secondly that of the absence of constraints upon them. In applying this concept to a situation in which adults are involved, their possible wants are tat' more or less for granted as brute facts about them. A question of freedom arises only when there is a possibility of their being constrained in respect of such wants.

In an educational situation, however, the application of the principal is not so straightforward. For, almost by definition, it is a situation n which constraints are imposed upon children's wants. To start ,with children are compelled to attend school which is not a promising start from the point of view of freedom. Some of them, of course, want to attend as well; but the combination of legal requirement and parental pressure do not readily intimate an area of free choice and action.

Secondly the conditions under which learning takes place make it imperative that something like the rule of law should be established within an educational situation. However much encouragement is given to children within a class-room to follow their own interests and to work at their own pace, there must be conditions of order sufficient to permit a large number of children to work at the same time in a small space. What such conditions are depends on the age and number of children, what is being learnt, and the amount of space available. But without minimum conditions of order a class-room would degenerate into a Tower of Babel, and the freedom of some would be exercised at the expense of others. Education could not go on.

Thirdly an educational situation involves essentially a contrived and controlled environment. Children may be encouraged to choose this and to follow their own interests in their study. Indeed emphasis may be placed on the desirability of spontaneity and autonomy. But such choice has always to be exercised within a range of what is thought desirable. Amongst the materials, with which they are encouraged u experiment, knives, and liquid paraffin are not included. Horror comics and pornography do not adorn the shelves of school libraries. Sexual, experimentation is not encouraged in the common rooms. Such controlled conditions act as general constraints on the wants of children By means of them adults exert a steady, if mild sort of pressure.

This must be the case; for no educator can take the wants of children for granted, part of his business as an educator being the transformation of wants, both in respect of their quality and in respect of their stability. To effect such a transformation a background of constraints on children wants is necessary. It may, of course, be possible ;within such a controlled environment to harness the worth-while content of education to existing wants either by developing understanding, skill, and a sense of standards in relation to existing wants as in activities like canoe building, making guitars, or dancing, or by using such existing wants as a means to developing new ones, as in the project method. But it may at times be necessary to exert pressure on children so that they master something irrespective of what they want. Many students, for instance, have been told to write an essay on something in which they were not at all interested and, as a result, have developed a new interest in something. Such possibilitics open up wider empirical questions about intrinsic and extrinsic motivation as well as moral questions about the permissibility of various methods of changing people's wants. But the basic point remains: no educator can be indifferent to what children want. He cannot, as in an ordinary social situation, say that what people want to do is their own affair, provided that they do no damage to others or interfere with their liberty. To adopt this *laissez-faire* attitude in a school would be to abdicate as an educator. Caretakers, maybe, can adopt such an attitude, but not teachers.

The justification of such a framework of order does not fall, naturally enough, in the main under the principle of liberty. It falls under the principle of the promotion of what is good, with its subordinate principle of the consideration of what is in people's interests. Nevertheless a case can be made in terms of liberty for such conditions of order in school which illustrates the paradox of freedom very well. If the rule of law imposed impartially by those in authority is absent it simply is not the case that children are actually able to do what they individually want. They are subject either to the arbitrary will of a bully or to the tyranny of peer-group pressure. Progressive schools in which the staff, as a matter of policy, withdraw from their proper function of exercising a just and levelling form of social control, are notorious for peer-group pressure and the proliferation of rules administered with severity by the children themselves. Or something like a state of nature prevails, as depicted with ghoulish exaggeration by William Golding in his *Lord of the Flies.* I once asked a colleague why his parents took him away from one of these schools. He replied that it was such hell when the headmaster was not around because of the bullying that went on. The headmaster in question prided himself on the fact that the staff laid down no rules. What he had not grasped was that there are other ways in which adults can control situations, when they are there, without having to formulate rules.

In all such situations, when human beings are gathered together, it is completely unrealistic to suppose that men or children are ever, as a *matter* of fact, free to do what they like simply because of the inherent decency and good sense of all concerned. They are in fact free because some rule or other, in addition to the moral law, is effectively enforced which prohibits interference. The practical choice is never between simply doing as one likes and being constrained; it is rather between being subject to different types of constraint. From the point of view of freedom it is a better bet for the individual to accept a system of levelling constraints which limit his freedom of action but limit also the freed of action of others to interferere with him, than to commit himself to a state of nature in which he runs the risk of being arbitrarily coerced or sub rejected to merciless group pressure. Adolescents who join in rejecting the authority of parents and teachers often make a dubious gain in terms of freedom; for they find that their opportunities for doing what they want as individuals are much more stringently curtailed by peer-group pressures.

The gist of the arguments so far has been to show that because an educational situation is one in which an environment is specifically contrived so that what is good can be promoted and passed on , there are conditions of order which must obtain in order that this overriding aim can be implicated . as ,how ever freedom is an independent principle like justice it can not be abrogated entirely for the sake of promotion of what is good .the presumptions in favors of it still holds .It has to be shown that restriction imposed on children , even in this contrived situation , are essential in terms of promotion of what is good . Rules for the sake of rules ,or as expression of a teacher's love of power, anathema to any rational man .Some type of rules , it has been argue can we justify in relation to paradox of freedom ,as will as because of there necessity for the promotion of what is good .but the fewer restriction the better , all such rules must have some point . What they are dissevered up on how they are enforced will depend up on all sorts of contingent question to do with the age of the children, the size of the school, whether or not it approximate , as does boarding school to total instruction , and so on ,Contingencies a bound when such a consort label of the implementation of general principal in reach . About such contingencies there is very little , philosophically speaking , to say 'four common since must not be passed of a philosophical analysis . philosophy is only one component in educational theory. When it comes to the formulation of particular principles for implementation in particular schools the contribution of philosophy, in terms of abstract analysis and justification of principles, must be put together with that of psychologists, sociologists, and teachers, who have practical experiences of the particularities in question. Philosophy contributes to practical wisdom but is not a substitute for it.

There is, however, another aspect of the freedom of the child which is very relevant to the ideals of progressive schools; for often such schools are not much concerned with providing conditions in which education of what they derisively call an 'academic' sort can proceed. They are much more concerned with the moral rehabilitation of misfits, or with character development, and emotional maturity.

They are particularly interested, perhaps, in the development of moral autonomy and independence. Children have to learn to make their own choices, to stand on their own feet; it is argued that this sort of permissive atmosphere encourages them to do this.

Anyone concerned seriously with answering the question 'What ought I to do?' will be equally concerned about implementing such a laudable ideal; for the search for reasons for action is the hall-mark of the autonomous person. He is not prepared to accept authoritative pronouncements and is unhappy about simply doing what others do without inquiring any further. He will thus be very concerned that people should be educated in a way which encourages independence of mind. But he will also hope that this can be done without too great a cost in terms of security and happiness-especially in view of the danger of a relapse into submission to authority or group conformity, because of the 'fear of freedom' already mentioned. He will be concerned that individuals develop who can make proper use of the areas of discretion permitted by a liberal society. Little, however, is yet known about the conditions which favour the development of such autonomy. Do children in fact learn to behave autonomously by being brought up from their earliest years in a very permissive atmosphere without a proper framework of order? This seems highly improbable both on general grounds and on the basis of the slender empirical evidence that there is about such matters. It would not be appropriate to enter into a detailed consideration of the empirical evidence, but the general grounds can be briefly mentioned as they make explicit considerations which are often forgotten in talk about children's autonomy and choice.

Autonomy implies the ability and determination to regulate one's life by rules which one has accepted for oneself-presumably because the reasons for them are both apparent and convincing. Piaget has shown that such an attitude towards rules is generally impossible before the age of about seven. Secondly there is evidence to suggest that the giving of reasons for action has little educative effect at an early stage, Yet long before this age children, for reasons both of their own survival, and for the welfare of others, must acquire in *other lays* a basic code of behaviour.[1] Thirdly they have to learn what it is to act on rules generally before the notion of determining their own code of rules for the selves can have any significance for them. If, too, such a choice is to be a real possibility for them rather than a lip-service to a shibboleth they, must have experience on the basis of which they can decide between alternatives. This is parallel to the problem of an elective curriculum What sense is there in saying that children should have 'choice' of what subjects they are to study unless they have been given some experience of such subjects on the basis of which they are in a position really choose'? There is all the difference in the world between choosing between alternatives and 'opting' for alternatives on the basis of what is immediately attractive. I was once discussing with a girl her 'choice' of a College of Education. It transpired that she was inclined towards one college rather than another because of the picture of it on the brochure! Choice should not be confused with the way of opting for things which is encouraged by advertising agencies. For children to learn to choose in this real sense they must live in a fairly predictable environment so that they can learn to make realistic assessments of consequences. human affairs the environment is mainly social, i.e. constituted by rules and standards. If predictability is not provided by something approximating to a rule of law how can the capacity for choice be developed in children? If rebellion and criticism are regarded as valuable something concrete must be provided to rebel against, so that children can learn to do this, knowing what is likely to happen. The virtue of a legal system, in relation to its encouragement of autonomy, is that it provides rules with determinate sanctions. Individuals who break the law do so with the knowledge of what is likely to happen if they are found out. They arc thus put in a position where concrete probabilities are presented to them. If children are brought up without such stable conditions it is difficult to see how they can learn to make realistic choices.

Fourthly those who are staunch advocates of autonomy, such as Existentialists, draw attention both to the necessity and virtue of the choice between rules which conflict on particular occasions. It is seldom pointed out that such conflicts are only real if the individual already accepts the rules which conflict as binding on him. But if he has not been brought up in such a way that he has internalized a set of rules, how could such conflicts ever occur out of which his independence and strength of character begin to develop?

Fifthly although there is little virtue in order for its own sake, the fact is that human beings are beset by anxiety unless minimum conditions of order are provided. If they are anxious or insecure they will be an easy prey to all sorts of irrational pressures. They will submit readily to authoritarian regulation or peer-group pressure; they will dart to and fro between alternatives that offer easy gratification. They are in the worst possible condition to learn how to direct their lives autonomously.

The development of autonomy is a slow and laborious business. Young people have to learn gradually to stand on their own feet and direct their own lives. They are not likely to do this if they are not encouraged to take responsibility and make choices about important matters within their limited experience; still less are they likely to do it if they are pitchforked into an anarchic situation in which they are told that they have to decide everything for themselves. Rationality requires a middle course between authoritarianism and permissiveness. Above all what is required is a rational attitude to and exercise of authority on the part of parents and teachers. Further consideration of this must be reserved until Chapters IX and XI.

***(b) The freedom of the teacher***

The question of the freedom of the teacher centres mainly on his right to teach what he likes and to put forward his own views about controversial matters. This is usually defended by arguments similar to those used by J. S. Mill in his essay *On Liberty.* Truth, it is argued, is only advanced if people are allowed to voice their own opinions, however heterodox. For if the orthodox opinions are true their truth will be strengthened by being challenged by conflicting opinions.' If, on the other hand, they are false, their falsity cannot be exposed unless challenge to them is permitted. To forbid freedom of thought is to presuppose in fallibility. The pursuit of truth develops only by the progressive falsification of orthodox opinions.

Such arguments are more or less unanswerable in the sphere of what Locke had previously called `speculative opinions in his *A Letter concerning Toleration.* The matter, however, is not quite so straightforward in the sphere of what he called `practical opinions'. Neither is the position of the teacher in relation to both sorts of opinions quite so simple as that of a man publishing a book for an adult public or reading a paper at a scientific congress. The qualifications required by the differences must now be explored.

Mill distinguished in his essay between freedom of thought and freedom of action. The right to the former is absolute, the right to the latter conditional upon the possible harm done to others. A difficulty, however, arises with opinions which Locke called `practical' which have a very close connection with action because of the harm that they may do to public order and to the enjoyment of rights by other individuals. Mill's failure to consider carefully the status of such opinions rather weakened his case for toleration. There are laws forbidding the expression of extreme forms of such practical opinions-laws against libel, slander, obscenity, and sedition. How far should such intervention be extended? What should the attitude be of someone who believes in toleration to opinions that are directed against a system that makes toleration possible? It is one thing to tolerate the Marxist interpretation of history, which is a matter of speculation; but what attitude should be taken to the promulgation of opinions about the tactics of revolution and to advice to party members about how to infiltrate into the main centres of control in the state? A rational course has to be steered between McCarthyism on the one hand and the feebleness of the Weimar Republic on the other. As this is a case where two fundamental moral principles conflict, that of liberty and of the consideration of people's interest, no hard and fast rule can be laid down. It is to he hoped that in a democratic society a balance in favour of toleration can he maintained, it being left to the good sense of individuals to combat such revolutionary or obnoxious opinions. There are such powerful irrational forces in man that sustain and magnify his intolerance that a bias in favour of toleration is justified. But there may come a time when sterner measures have to be taken. Race prejudice may fester and spread like a rash on a community. Insecurity and unemployment may make men disposed to listen to those who use the free speech afforded by a democratic society to suggest that the system which makes it possible is nothing but an instrument of class oppression. At what precise point the expression of such opinions has to be checked, and what form of safeguard has to be used, is a matter of Judgment.

The teacher's position in regard to the expression of opinion is complicated both by his educational role and by the fact that he is dealing with people whose minds are immature, which imposes special responsibilities on him. At university level these complications are of less importance. University teachers have in the main a firm allegiance to the pursuit of truth, in its various forms, and usually feel some obligation to initiate others into it. They are bound, of course, to some extent by syllabuses and examinations which they help to construct; but their right to interpret such syllabuses in their own way is unquestioned. Their main concern is with the pursuit of truth and what Mill says about `speculative' opinions applies pre-eminently to them. They feel little squeamishness, too, about presenting their own point of view strongly about controversial matters in their subject to students. For they know full well that there are others with different points of view to whom students can listen if they wish. They also know that many of their students have begun to acquire the manner of thinking which will enable them to sift, assess, and criticize their own views. Indeed if their students do not start producing attempted refutations of what they say they should consider that they are falling down on their job. There are, of course, too, some university teachers who have little interest in the wider educational or moral context of their activities; they are required to give lectures and accordingly conduct their private musings in public.

The situation in schools is somewhat different. To start with, though school teachers, like university teachers, should have a strong allegiance to the discipline in which they have been trained, they are concerned more specifically with education and less with developing the frontiers of knowledge than university teachers. They are subject to closer public supervision than university teachers and many of them have to prepare children for public examinations in accordance with syllabuses over which they have little control. Although headmasters in England have a very high degree of autonomy, assistant masters may often have to work very strictly in accordance with patterns prescribed by the headmaster or by the head of their department. Although their freedom to interpret such syllabuses in their own way is usually granted they often have to be much more mindful than university teachers of the rather narrow requirements of examinations, and are very conscious of their dubious role as agents of selection in a system where there is too little room at the top.

No doubt many of the restrictions set on their freedom by such facts of life are thoroughly undesirable, but even without them there are aspects of their situation which should give them cause to ponder on the extent to which they are justified in plugging their pet theories. To start with they are very often the only competent exponent of the form of thought in question. Their students will not hear another point of view about the same matter from someone else. Secondly even in a sixth form their students are still struggling to acquire the procedures as distinct from the content of the form of thought. They are not therefore properly equipped to assess and criticize what a teacher tells them. A teacher, for instance, who plugs the economic interpretation of history in a sixth form will encounter few students equipped to dispute what he says. If he presents the Reformation purely from the Protestant point of view a Catholic in the class may be thoroughly disturbed but will lack the equipment to give expression to his inarticulate uneasiness. A scrupulous and competent teacher will know that different interpretations of the evidence are possible about such matters. His concern should not be to pump opinions into his students but to see to it the his students acquire the competence to form their own. For his basic task is not to teach his students what to think but how to think.

This does not mean, of course, that a teacher must sit as inscrutable as the Buddha and never commit himself to an opinion about anything Children will usually glean where a teacher's sympathies lie, anyway, without his having to avow them. His attitude should rather be, if he is a rational man, that nothing depends on the contingent fact that hr happens to hold a particular opinion. After all he may be wrong. The important thing to get at is what grounds there might he for him anyone else to hold this opinion or a contrary one. He must be, to a certain extent, an authority on what he is teaching. If he is not, he should not have been appointed. But his claim to authority derives not from the particular opinions which he holds about any sub stantive issue but from his mastery of the form of thought by means of which such opinions are arrived at. This is what he has to impart to his students. He has to teach in such a way that his students can eventual dispense with him.

The discussion to date has only been concerned with speculative opinions that are handed on in the various school subjects. The responsibilities of a university teacher do not extend much beyond these, though there are some who think it also to be the function of a university teacher to induce some kind of moral commitment in his students. At the school level, however, the matter is again very different; for moral education is certainly a very important aspect of education at school. Here again the teacher has no right to use the special relationship in which he stands to children to parade his own idiosyncratic opinions. Maybe he is a vegetarian or a pacifist; perhaps he believes steadfastly in the virtues of nudity or of polygamy. His concern should not be to convert children to adopt such substantive positions because of their admiration for him, but to get them to see the reasons on which such positions are based; for his job is teaching, not indoctrination. He must get them to face squarely the question `What ought I to do?' and lead them on to fundamental principles on which answers to this question must be grounded. Whether they come to agree with him on matters of substance is another matter.

About some moral rules, however, on which there is a broad consensus, his attitude must be rather different. These are what have been referred to above as basic moral rules' which are those which are in anyone's interest whatever his conception of the good life may be. Rules like those prohibiting injury to the person; theft, lying, and the breaking of contracts are necessary for the life of a school as well as for that of any other community. Any teacher must insist on the observance of such rules both from the point of view of the maintenance of necessary conditions of order in the school and from the point of view of moral education. But here again he should not be just content with enunciating that it is wrong to do such things; he should try to get children to see why it is wrong. And just seeing, of course, is not enough; they have to feel it as well. Otherwise such rules will not bite on their behaviors. How this can be done is, of course, another matter about which too little is known. Is such a deepening of moral consciousness much aided by discussions in a formal situation? Is it mainly a matter of what is imparted on concrete occasions? Does it depend much more on the peer-group than on the example of adults? These are all empirical questions with which philosophy is not concerned. Answering them, however, has little bearing on the question of the teacher's freedom in relation to such opinions, though it has very great relevance practical task as a moral educator.

In the sphere of more general religious and political opinions position of the teacher is fairly straightforward. He is not employed as a missionary for any church or as a recruiting officer for any political party. It is his job, however, to initiate children into the skills, attitudes, and knowledge which are necessary for them to participate intelligently as citizens in the life of a democratic state. In so far as he deals with s matters in formal periods, e.g. in R.I. or Current Affairs, his re endeavour should be the deepening and informing of a religious political consciousness rather than the defence of particular dogmas or programmes. If, of course, a teacher is an atheist or an agnostic, an,' required to teach R.I., this is a different matter. Obviously he can teach religion as religion if he is unfamiliar with or antipathetic to form of awareness on which it is based. He has, therefore, the alt natives of teaching something else under the aegis of R.I., e.g. his: of the Hebrews, comparative religion, morals, or refusing, on conscientious grounds, to have anything to do with it. Little more can said about this topic without detailed discussion of the nature religion, of its difference from and relationship to morals, and of anomalies and complications arising from the status of R.I. under 1944. Act, which would require a chapter to itself.'

What the teacher does about his own beliefs outside school hours is, of course, his own business, provided that he does not implicate employers in his activities; his activities are subject to law and public opinion like those of any other individual. The fact that he is a teacher does not deprive him of the normal rights of a citizen. He may have unusual and perhaps mildly outrageous views on many things; political and religious affiliations may be very unorthodox; he may well indulge in bizarre `experiments in living'-to use Mill's phrase but. unless these can be shown incontrovertibly to distort or bias his condition as a teacher on the job or to influence children unduly by his public example, it is difficult to see why his employers, in a democratic society, should take active cognizance of such matters. To take a concrete case: a teacher may join some society in his spare time for the amelioration of the condition of homosexuals in society. Parents and indignant citizens might band together and start an agitation to have him dismissed' from his post, as a source of corruption. Another might drink overmuch or lead an irregular sex life, and it might be suggested that his competence was reduced as a result, or that children were corrupted by his example. What would have to be produced, however, would be concrete evidence of corruption or incompetence. General probabilities are not enough. If this demand were once abandoned the teacher's position in the community would become intolerable.

An exception, however, might be made in the case of commitment to practical opinions which must necessarily involve a particular attitude to children, if held sincerely. A man may have homosexual tendencies, but it has to be shown that these necessarily take the form of attempts to seduce small boys. Most `normal' men have strong heterosexual tendencies; but in a co-educational school the girls in the class are not necessarily in a permanent state of moral danger. Hence the necessity for evidence that such tendencies take this concrete form of expression in a school situation. It might be the case, however, that a man who sincerely holds Fascist opinions must have a certain type of attitude to Jewish or coloured children in his class. It might be argued, too, that even if there was little evidence to support the assumption that such a man would in fact discriminate against Jewish or coloured children, the children in question might live in perpetual fear of him because of his known opinions. A similar argument might be advanced in relation to the probable attitude of an active Communist towards children of the bourgeoisie, though the connection in this case is looser. Such extreme cases might be cited as exceptions to the general principle that concrete evidence must be produced before the presumption in favour of toleration is abandoned. But such cases are mercifully rare in England at the moment.

***(c) The freedom of the parent***

The ground of a parent's right to educate his children as he thinks fit is not altogether perspicuous. It presupposes all sorts of things about the parent-child relationship which would take a long time to discuss. Some regard the parent's rights in this sphere rather like rights to property; others assimilate them to those of' a trustee. But though the grounds of this right are obscure there are few in Britain who would question that the parent has such a right. Indeed in England the right of a parent to educate his child as he likes is one of the most long-standing rights of the subject. Burke, for all his attack on `abstract rights', includes the right to `the nourishment and improvement of their offspring' amongst the `real rights' of the subject. Even Hobbes, thought to be one of the precursors of modern totalitarianism, presumed that the sovereign would not interfere with matters such as the subject's choice of vocation, choice of wife, and choice of education for his children. This right is of particular importance for those whose religion requires a special sort of education.

This right was established, of course, long before compulsory education for all was ever contemplated. Such compulsion was obviously enough an infringement of liberty in so far as parents were no longer free to exercise their discretion by not having their children educated at all. The arguments for such a limitation of freedom are obvious. enough too. A highly industrialized society cannot he run effective' unless a certain level of literacy and numeracy is attained by all and high degree of specialized knowledge and skill by many. Also without certain minimum conditions being insisted on, individuals would be. deprived of the necessary conditions for attaining the quality of life in such a society which is handed on in a good educational system. Compulsion cannot force people to become educated. But without it many children would be deprived of their opportunities for entering into their cultural heritage. Such a limitation on freedom can therefore be justified both in terms of the interests of the community and the long--term interest of individuals potentially composing it. For matters as important as this cannot be left purely to the good sense of parents.

Since the development of state education the right of the parent ha, come to mean that of educating his children in a private school if he should wish to spend his money in this way. For most people such a right is `formal' rather than `actual'; for only a small minority have the money necessary to exercise it. Naturally enough the state cannot be expected to pay for such a luxury and naturally it is reasonable for the state to insist that a certain minimum standard of educational provision should be maintained. In this way the point of a compulsory system is retained without insisting on uniformity in implementation. For without this latter condition the children themselves might suffer as a result of the parent's exercise of their freedom of choice and so, derivatively, would the state.

There are few who dare challenge this watered-down prima facie right of parents in a democratic society. Arguments against the existence of private schools derive from a conviction that it is unfair that the possession of money should put some in a privileged position, especially as much of the wealth so used is inherited rather than earned by the parents in question. When so few have actual access to a formal right of this sort it is argued that there is a case for abolishing it. Fairness must take precedence over freedom-especially as the present division in the educational system tends to perpetuate class attitudes, which encourage lack of respect for persons.

At this point another principle becomes relevant-that of the promotion of what is good; for one of the main reasons why parents, who can afford it, insist on exercising their right is that the quality of education provided in the best independent schools is very good indeed. Of course there are many exceptions. Some independent schools, especially at the preparatory level, are not very good, and some parents have predominantly social motives for exercising their right of choice at such a great expense. They do not want their children to mix with children from another social class; or they see that education at an independent school may enhance their children's prospects of high social status and good employment. But the fact is that there are many very good independent schools with long traditions, which have built up by long experience and trial and error a system which successfully combines academic achievement with character-training. Historically these schools have been pioneers in many spheres of educational experiment and the state system owes an enormous amount to their example. It would be criminal folly to dismantle a system of education which contributes and has contributed so much to the quality of education in England. The real scandal is that both the major political parties and the public as a whole have cared so little about education in the past that they have never spent enough money either on schools or on salaries of teachers to cater adequately for the nation as a whole. They have, of course, paid lipservice to the importance of education; but when it has come to producing enough money to develop a really effective and fair educational system, other demands on the Exchequer have always seemed more pressing. The reply to this is obvious enough-that radical improvements will only bb effected in the state system when the wealthier and more influential minority of the population have to send their children to the same schools as everybody else.

And so the debate proceeds over the status of independent schools with arguments deriving from liberty, equality, and the quality of life. It represents *par excellence* an issue where these basic principles conflict. Obviously some compromise which does not involve abandoning altogether the right of parents to educate their children they think fit will have to be found. The point at which such a compromise can be found must depend on the ingenuity of practical men. It cannot be determined by philosophical analysis alone, though such analysis can do much to get clearer on what fundamental points decisions have to be made

## (4) EQUALITY OF EDUCATION

The simpler case of wage and of voting have been taken to illustrate some input an. general points about the application of the principle of equality. The first is that consideration of equality alone can not determine what out to be done in concrete case of distribution where there is a dispute about wether exceptions should be made or categories created .at that the principle lays down presumption. But if it is challenged relevant consideration must necessary fall under principle other than that of equality. Voting is a case of equals being treated equally, wages of unequally, being trated unequally; but in both case the point of the actively has to be picked out in terms of general principle before relevant criteria can be produced either for claiming that difference in treatment is grounded on irrelevant distinctions, or for setting uo categories on the basis of relevant distinction. This is because though boating and earning a wage are through to be desirable they are not usually thought to be desirable in themselves. There value derives from fundamental principle other than that of equality. As in each case more than one fundamental principle is involved in addition to equality, irreconcilable disagreements may arise owing to the different weight given to the different fundamental principle. Determining the relevance if criteria, e.g. of desert rather then of need rustication is required to assess their relative importance as applied to a concrete situation.

Secondly these simpler cases have been used to make the contrast between a formal analysis of a situation in terms of a what is priscribed by law custom or morality, and what actually happens. This raises the question of the extent to which formal arrangements should be extended To minimize the influence of actual difference. Again other principal are involved because objection to the pursuit of positive equality usually are based on other principal which are infringed in the process. This general point can now be made in relation to the more complex case of education.

Education is unlike voting and earning a wages in many respect, but especially in respect of its intrinsic value. It was argued in the first part of the book that education involves imitation into what a community considers to be worth while, and that it is impossible to represent it in terms of taking means to a worth while end or bringing about a worth while product by method which are morally natural. Being educated marks a group of achievement, which are internally related to a family of takes. Nevertheless it was also pointed out that an educational system or a school can be regarded from an external point of view as a method of preparing people for job in a community .it can also be a regarded, by the individual as a avenue to power and pressing in a community. Indeed it is now becoming the chef mode of social aslant. Obviously enough, there for, question of access to it and of its distribution are some of the most explosive issue in the modern world. how, then ,is the principal of equality to be applied in this sphere.

**(a) Interpretation of the principal in USA and England**

In some countries, e.g. the USA, education at any rate up to high school level is regarded almost as a kind of commodity to which all have an equal right. It is rather like the right to vote, a case where the explicit presumption is that equal should be treated equally. Selection is delayed and works rather like a free market economy on the basis of the survival of the fittest . it approximate to what turner calls a contest system in which all can have a go and see how far they can get. The wastage is high , but as there is plenty of room at the level above the high school , and as the country is very rich ,this is not disastrous .by the time the fittest struggle through to there ph.ds .some are very well educated , and a large percentage of the population pick up some sort of traning as well as a modicum of knowledge about many things

In such a system there is provision, of course, for differences in aptitude and ability. American high schools usually have at least three types of courses, college, technical, and commercial. But the students have the right to opt for whichever course they want, to try and see how they get on. Naturally enough the general provision tends accordingly to cater for the `average' child. There has recently been a widespread revulsion. against this `levelling down' of educational provision with the neglect of `excellence' that it entails. Advanced placements schemes have therefore been started, by means of which the courses of able children can be supplemented so as to accelerate their development. Another significant trend has been the mushroom-like growth of private schools which claim to provide an education of a better quality for those who can pay for it. These trends are accompanied by arguments much more familiar in English education.

In the English system, at any rate in the decades preceding and succeeding the 1944 Act, the necessity for different categories of education was generally accepted. There was not the presumption that children should all go to the same school. The situation was more like the case of the `fair wage' than of the right to vote. Differences in educational provision were accepted; the problem was to determine relevant grounds for assigning children to different schools. The system was more like what Turner calls a `sponsored' system. There was much less room at the top and far smaller resources to be spent on education. The problem was that of determining relevant grounds for recruiting people to positions of authority and prestige in the community. As is well known the old scholarship examination, by means of which children from elementary schools were sorted out as being eligible for a grammar or central school, was elevated into the II+ examination. On the basis of this examination, which included tests in English and matih; nitics, as well as an intelligence test and teachers' reports, judgment was made on basis of the age, aptitude, and ability of children, and they were dispatched to their destiny in a grammar, technical or secondary modern school.

This, it was argued, constituted a substantial move towards remedying existing injustices. Secondary education, at least up to 15, was proclaimed to be the right of all. Access to the appropriate type of education was granted on what were thought to be relevant criteria. It could no longer be argued that lack of money could deprive a person of the type of education that a grammar school or independent school (such as Eton) could provide. It was admitted that the wealth of parents vas an irrelevant consideration. No one now, with the relevant qualities, need be deprived of the most suitable type of education for him. This was part of the general new deal for the underprivileged which was characteristic of legislation generally at the end of the Second World War.

It would be very difficult to maintain that abstract considerations of justice, in the main, determined these main lines of educational pr, vision in both countries. This, in fact, depended on a great number contingent circumstances. The Americans, for instance, are so aware to children from the same community going to different schools that they are prepared to tolerate mammoth-size institutions in defence of this interpretation of the maxim that equals should be treated equally. This is not because of any deep-seated love of uniformity; for there was a time when the Americans were highly individualistic. Nor is it due purely to their fear that if their neighbor's child goes to a different school he may in fact be getting a better start in the race. It is also to be seen in terms of the school's historic role of helping to make a nation out of immigrants with a great variety of cultural backgrounds. This combination of contingent circumstances leads to the insistence that differences in provision must be made within the same school, whatever i' differences in educational aims.

The English, on the other hand, have assumed that it is reasonable that unequals should be treated unequally. But they have also been h i to assume that there are three different types of education-grammar technical, and modern-which suit different types of children, and the these should be provided in different types of schools. Again this interpretation is not to be seen as due purely to a love of diversity or to the Platonic vision of administrators who imagined that they were dealing with the three classes in *The Republic*. It is to be seen rather in terms of the historic evolution of the grammar schools, senior schools and central schools and the practical means that were available, on limited resources, of raising the school-leaving age to 15.

In neither the USA nor in England have agitations about equality in education taken the form of abstract pleas for ideal systems in which education is to be distributed in accordance with clear-cut criteria derivative from unitary aims. In both countries interpretations of the principle have to be seen in terms of these contingent circumstances, and arguments advanced in terms of it have almost always been related to particular injustices, to distinctions made on the basis of irrelevant differences. In the USA, as has been already explained, the main issue is the plight of the negroes. In England it used to be and still is, in the case of the privileged position of those attending independent schools, the injustice of a system that denies the best forms of education to those without wealth. It has now shifted to the new injustices created by the implementation of the 1944 Act which was in part designed to remedy the old injustices connected with wealth. A new problem, too, is looming rather like the American problem, which is due to the influx of immigrants.

When such agitations develop they are always complicated by disagreements not only, as would be expected, about the aims of education, but also about what education is. This dimension of disagreement makes arguments about voting and wages straightforward in comparison. For instance it can be argued that devices for distribution distort education and deprive it of its intrinsic value. On the one hand it is argued that an efficient system of selection by examinations may transform education into a matter of 'knowledge to be acquired and facts to be stored'. On the other hand it is claimed that attempts to distribute education 'equally' in a large school, on the basis of individual interest and aptitude, turns a school into a sort of supermarket with all the attendant losses in quality. Education, it is argued, can only really take root on an apprenticeship basis; a supermarket type of institution renders such a relationship very difficult to contrive.

If an educational system could be thought of in purely instrumental terms, like a wages system, discussions would be much more straightforward. Michael Young, for instance, in his satire entitled *The Rise of the Meritocracy* imagines a community devoted whole-heartedly to economic productivity, in which positions in the community and training for them are determined solely on the criterion of merit. Schools in such a community become training institutions. The problems of selection are purely technical; for the criteria determining what is `fair' are agreed and unambiguous, namely those to do with ability to contribute to the community's good, defined in terms of increasing productivity.

The flaws in such a conception, which the satire was written to expose, are obvious enough. No community has or could set itself such a limited end as increase in productivity; for what quality of life is such an increase intended to sustain? In so far as schools are concerned with education, and not simply with training, they are concerned with initiating children gradually into this quality of life. The forms of knowledge and awareness into which they are initiated are not just convenient vade-mecums for operatives, technocrats, and bureaucrats. The rights of individuals to such a quality of life can therefore be set against their duty to contribute to the state, with all that is implied in the way of training. Furthermore, even at the level of mere training, the skills necessary to run a rapidly changing industrial society change so rapidly with it that the notion of `vocational training' has only limited application at the school level under modem conditions.

But included in the general notion of `a quality of life' are different values on which different emphasis is placed in disputes about the aims of education. Some emphasize the supreme importance of individual choice; others emphasize the importance of mastery of certain forms of knowledge or skills; others emphasize the training of character; others stress the need for all-round development. All such aims must be ct alongside the state's requirement for training in essential skills and in `citizenship'. They are not necessarily incompatible; but difference emphasis will suggest differences in educational provision and, perhaps different criteria of access. Supposing, for instance, that a person is much impressed by the community's need for industrial development and the pool of technicians and statisticians that goes with it. He will ten stress the importance of training in educational institutions and the portance of mathematics, science, and technology. In a time of limited resources he may advocate criteria of selection related to these priori? His proposals may be backed by someone else who values precision and rigour of thought as a cardinal educational value, irrespective of benefit to the community. Someone else, however, may he led by stress on the importance of individual choice, to deprecate selection a to advocate a situation where individuals are given the maximum opportunity to discover for themselves what they want to explore. He may be supported by another who thinks that 'wholeness' is important and who therefore deprecates any form of selection which will lead to premature specialization.

Such possible types of disagreement could be multiplied indefinitely; but there is no point in labouring the obvious. Enough has been said to substantiate the main claim that discussions about the fairness of the distribution of education are different in at least two ways from discussions of the distribution of simpler commodities. Firstly the nature of education can be seriously influenced by its manner of distribution; secondly it is something which is of intrinsic value, although what goes on in educational institutions can also be viewed instrumentally in relation to the needs of the community or purposes of the individual. As, however, there are different intrinsic values involved in the quality of life that is passed on in educational institutions, and as these can be seriously affected both by its manner of distribution and by the determination to relate this to the extrinsic ends of the community or of the individual, the possibilities of disagreements deriving from different values are endless.

It is obvious enough, therefore, why disagreements about what is 'fair' in education depend upon other values which a person has, which provide criteria for determining relevance in matters of distribution. Most people would admit that the wealth of parents is a completely irrelevant criterion. But there is not a corresponding measure of agreement about the criteria of aptitude and ability that have in England been substituted for it. Lack of agreement about the relevance of such criteria does not derive solely from the difficulties actually encountered in the attempt to categorize children in accordance with these criteria. Rather it reflects basic differences in emphasis about what is vital in education and about the extent to which what goes on in schools should be closely related to the extrinsic requirements of the community.

There is also a further basic source of disagreement, which relates not so much to what is fair but to the importance to be attached to fairness in relation to other principles. This usually happens when the pursuit of equality comes into conflict with liberty or with the demands for a quality of life. Defenders, for instance, both of the grammar school and of the independent schools often take their stand on these two principles. They argue for the right of parents to have their children educated at schools of their own choosing, especially if this entails paying large fees. They also argue that it takes many years to build up educational institutions which actually succeed in initiating children into the forms of thought and awareness, with their built-in standards of excellence, which are constitutive of a quality of life. There is a danger; they argue, that well-meaning ideologues should be driven by their unbridled passion for equality into dismantling schools which have achieved the rare distinction of knowing how to educate people. They also point out the great service done to education by pioneers such as Arnold and Froebel who used this liberty to carry out experiments in independent schools and to the standards set by grammar schools within the star system. They ruefully note that the modern Levellers are bent on making the English educational system as much like the American system I; possible at a time when enlightened Americans are becoming profound l disturbed about the inadequacies of their own system.

***(b) The formal and the actual***

Modern agitations about `equality of opportunity' in the USA and England are also related in part to the contrast between formal arrangements and what in fact happens. Here again the important question arises, which has just been raised, about how far the claims of equality, are to be pressed. How far are formal arrangements to be extended order to minimize actual inequalities?

In the USA, for instance, realities make the plight of the Negroes on facet of a more general problem. The standard of educational provision differs considerably in the different states as well as in different neighborhoods. As there is a widespread ideological insistence on children, going to the same school as their neighbors, this means that the type educational provision in fact varies according to contingent circumstances prevailing in different states. Furthermore, as neighborhood differ widely in standards and cost of housing, and as the local community contributes considerably towards the cost of education, this means, in effect, that wealth can indirectly buy a more lavish type of education. American professors debate whether they arc to invest their money in a cheap house in a poor area and spend the income_ so saved w a private school, as the standard of public education in the neighborhood is so deplorable; or whether they are to spend more money on house in a better class area where the quality of education is suitable f their children.

Similarly in England the I I + examination is not in fact an objective test; for its standard varies according to different localities depending on the number of grammar and technical places available. It is even different from year to year in the same locality. Furthermore though, formally speaking, everyone is competing on equal terms, evidence shows that IQ score is very much affected by socio-economic class, especially by the speech habits of the family to which the child belongs.' The plight, therefore, of culturally deprived children, is unenviable; for they suffer from cumulative obstacles in attaining the level necessary for success.

Perhaps most serious of all has been the unintended plight of many children attending secondary modern schools. The intention of those who devised the 1944 Act was that the secondary modem school should provide a different, not an inferior, form of education, which was meant to be suited to the distinctive ability and aptitude of those who attended them. Headmasters were encouraged to experiment and to devise a new form of exciting `modern' education. This seldom happened. Children who went to such schools felt that they were inferior, as they had `failed' the test. They could no longer claim, as they used to be able to claim under the old system, that they lacked education because their fathers could not afford it. They now had had their chance and had been found `wanting'. The schools that they attended were often poorly equipped and housed in antiquated and lavatory-like premises. The staffs were often disgruntled because they had failed to find employment in grammar or technical schools. Few attempts were made to develop a distinctive curriculum, which was adapted to the ability and aptitude of the children. Courses of a vocational naturh were, of course, laid on but, with the growing tendency for children to stay at school longer, the curriculum became increasingly a watered-down version of that of grammar and technical schools. This tendency was strengthened by the demand of employers for some objective sign, which meant in effect an examination, by means of which the attainment of school-leavers could be assessed. In brief a variety of social pressures combined to stultify the intentions of those who framed the 1944 Act with regard to the secondary modem school. The system has turned out to be so manifestly unfair in the way in which it actually works that various schemes are in train or in mind for revising it.

### *(c) Remedying actual inequalities*

In the light of this experience most English educationists now query the basic presumption that unequal should be treated unequally, if this is interpreted as entailing attendance at a different school from the age of eleven onwards, the type of school being determined by a crucial test It is argued that, if there is to be selection, it should be delayed as long as possible and be made less irrevocable in its probable consequences Over and above this common measure of agreement there exist a splendid variety of alternative proposals. Some argue that the difference in provision should be provided within vast comprehensive schools to be attended by all from a given neighborhood from the age of eleven upwards, as in the American high school system. Others argue that all should attend the equivalent of the American junior high school from the age of nine to thirteen and then pass on to different types of school' Others argue that there should be `comprehensive' education for all up to fifteen and that there should be different types of provision after that There are disputes, too, about whether parents should be allowed to choose to which of such multifunctional schools they send their children. or whether they should be compelled to send them to a school which arbitrarily fixed for them on a neighborhood basis.'

Arguments for adjusting institutions in order to remedy such obvious sources of injustice depend upon contingent factors which are more the concern of the social scientist and psychologist than of the philosopher They only get philosophically interesting when a question of principle raised about the limits to which equalitarians are prepared to go order to remove such actual sources of inequality. Most enlightens

Americans are prepared to support Federal intervention in order to en sure that negroes are not in fact debarred from good schools and universities. But to what extent arc they prepared to support Federal intervention in order to redress actual inequalities existing between the different states in terms of educational provision? To what extent arc they prepared to agitate against housing regulations which ensure that only people with a certain level of income can live within a given district?

English equalitarians are never tired of stressing that being brought up in a working-class home in fact imposes all sorts of handicaps or children. Are they then prepared to advocate compulsory attendance at nursery schools (supposing that this were economically feasible) to make up for this? Are they prepared for the state to intervene in order to regulate other crucial factors, such as the size of families, perhaps by refusing to grant family allowances for more than three children? If they are prepared to admit the claims of liberty and of quality of life at this level why do they seem so oblivious of them at other levels?

Lieberman' suggests two meanings for `equality of educational opportunity'. One is that A and B have it when `they live under conditions which do not provide either person with any material advantage over the other in selecting or pursuing his educational goals'. He argues that such equality is almost non-existent, though many imagine that it exists. The other is that A and B have it `when the material advantages which one of them possesses over the other in selecting or pursuing his educational goals cannot be removed without endangering other important values'. Because `other important values' vary from person to person, so also does the interpretation of `equality of educational opportunity'. This second meaning, however, is a sham. For people have not got it in any actual sense and are not prepared, for reasons which have nothing to do with equality, to take the steps necessary to ensure that they have it. To call the second state of affairs one in which `equality of educational opportunity' prevails is to misrepresent the facts of life in order to retain a shibboleth. The plea for `equality of opportunity' is more properly understood as either an attack on irrelevant aids to opportunity (e.g. wealth) or as a demand for replacing unreasonable by reasonable grounds for providing access to opportunities.

The obvious fact is that, descriptively speaking, there is no equality of opportunity and never can be unless equalitarians are prepared to control early upbringing, size of families, and breeding. Without taking such steps there will always be ineradicable differences between people which will affect how any system works in practice. Were there not such differences the principle of equality would have little point. For, as has been argued, an equalitarian is not necessarily committed to any factual assertions about men, but only to the determination to treat people the same unless the differences between them can be shown to be *relevant* to how they should be treated. What makes differences relevant is, as has been shown, a very complex matter which necessarily involves recourse to other principles. To extend the meaning of `equality' of opportunity' in the way suggested by Lieberman has the effect of soft-pedalling the importance of such other principles in discussions educational provision. It is to fall in with the modern fashion assuming that the only moral issues involved in educational provision are issues of equality. This chapter has attempted to demonstrate, only that this is not so, but that it necessarily cannot be so.

Mill argued in his essay *On Liberty* that the only legitimate ground for interfering with individual liberty was that others were harmed by it. In other words he saw that one principle, that of the consideration of people's interests, sets limits to the pursuit of liberty. In a similar way. it has been argued that other principles such as liberty and the develop ment of a quality of life (which is involved in the consideration interest)' both set limits to the pursuit of equality and, in the case of education provide content for what is to be justly distributed. But it has not been claimed that philosophical analysis or argument can show at what particular points such limits are to be set. This depends upon practice judgment which has to be exercised in the light of a multitude of contingent circumstances. Philosophers can only map the contours of such arguments; they cannot pronounce upon the details of the view.

## DEMOCRACY IN EDUCATION

"Democracy", the term indicates that it is the "Government by the people, for the people and of the people". By this definition of democracy has now taken a widened meaning an it has various connotations. The above said working of the Government can said as Political Democracy. This is only one aspect of true democracy. The other aspects being, economic and social democracy. Economic Democracy means that economic power will be in the hand of the people as a whole, not in the hands of a few capitalists or of a particular class. The economic organization of the community will be co-operative rather than competitive: To economic projects will be undertaken for the benefit of the community as a whole and not for private profit. Work will be provided for every individual according to his abilities and capacities. Social Democracy connotes absence of distinctions based on class, both or possession of money. Everyone will have equality of opportunity - money or birth or class will not stand in the way of progress. In social democracy, it is recognized that each individual is of supreme to worth as an individual and that he is sovereign with power to govern.

Thus democracy in its complete sense, means a way of living and organization of community that has political, economic and social aspects. In such a democracy, every human individual will be given the freedom to develop, to the fullest extent possible. all the potentialities - freedom to express, to discuss and to work and act - freedom to create and to change, freedom to co-operate. Besides freedom for every 'individual in a true democracy will have an equal chance of living a full life, and of exercising his powers in social, economic and political spheres. The individual will he valued as a person, whatever his caste, creed or religion. In true democracy, faith in the common man to do the noble things in life will ever inspire the citizen who will serve the community realizing "that all he has and is, he owes to the community"

These democratic aims, democratic content, democratic administration, organization, principles and procedures are sure to go a long way in creating a society which has all great thinkers, philosophers and statesmen. Therefore, the whole educational process should breathe this spirit of democracy. In planning our education, this should be the prime consideration.

## Democratic Education

Dewey tells us, "A society which makes provision for participation in the good of all its members on equal terms and which secures flexible readjustment of its institutions through interaction of the different forms of associated life is in so far democratic. Such a society must have a type of education, which gives individuals a personal interest in social relationship and control, and habits of mind which secure social changes without introducing disorder.

Some ethical dimensions of the this democratic education are:

1. Dignity of the individual
2. Equalitarianism
3. Brotherhood
4. Freedom
5. Faith in the educability of man
6. Cooperation of all individuals
7. Appreciation of the contribution of individuals to group welfare
8. Character and intelligence to form judgments
9. Good Citizenship

## Dignity of the Individual

*The individual must be respected. It does not mean indulging or coddling him, but by engaging him in activities which may develop his resourcefulness and initiative* and drive. Educational programme should be such that it should nurture this intelligence *in the individual. His education should be conducted in such way., that tic may* Progressively grow in his abilities, attitudes, and skills.

## Equalitarianism

This envisages equal opportunities to every member of the society for realizing and enjoying his own capacities and aptitudes. Every individual is born with unique abilities. aptitudes, talents and capacities. It would be very unfair and undemocratic it' they were not given the opportunities to accomplish the abilities which nature gave them to do. It has to be understood this does not mean identicalism in education. Educational opportunities should be equal and not identical.

**Brotherhood**

The realisation of brotherhood of mar. and fatherhood of God is the sheet anchor of democracy. Democracy does not know the distinction of caste, creed or color If all the members of the mankind realize that they are the creations of one God, they are sure to inculcate democratic trends in them. Love, justice and fairness and equity are the fruits of prosperity

**Freedom**

One great essence of democracy is freedom –freedom for action., speech and movement. It is in the very atmosphere of freedom that one gets the stimulus to express himself and to realize his full potentialiedties. Man loves freedom his complete growth depends upon this. This full flowering of the personality takes place only when he is allowed elasticity and flexibility. It does not, how a work, mean license. The freedom maeas liberty in this context of a existing rule and regulation of the society.

**Faith in the educability of man**

*Democracy prospers only when we believe that every man is educable. He is* superior and supreme of all the living kind. The lower animals does not have this sort of greater intellectual capacity. They have direction but not self-direction, consciousness but not self-consciousness, inherited instinct but not conceptual reasoning. Man has history, literature, science and the arts of civilization. Man is therefore, a fit subject for education. Democracy succeeds if we have this faith that man is educable.

**Co-operation of all individuals**

Another essence of democracy is that all individual must cooperate. Prosperity and progress lies in co-operation rather than in cut-throat competition.

**Appreciation of contribution of individuals of the group welfare**

The contribution of individuals should be appreciated. If everyone contributes with dedicated service and happiness arid according to his own abilities, this society will remain the happiest one.

**Character and Intelligence to form Judgments**

For the working and success of democracy, character of an individual is supreme and fundamental. The real strength of democracy lies in the individual and national character. It is the character *of a person that gives him the power of judgment and discriminating the right form the wrong.

**Good citizenship**

In democracy effective participation in civic life is an asset. A person who has got a progressive outlook and understanding and the quality of recognizing leadership will always advocate democratic ideals of life. He will appreciate the rights and privileges of others, while at the same time; he will also realize his own obligation. Good citizenship means the establishment of balance between rights and duties.

## Educational Implications of the Democratic Principles

Democracy cannot be thought of in isolation from education. In fact, democracy is the result of education. Unless the principles of democracy are reflected in the aims f and ideals of education, curriculum, methods of teaching, administration, and organization, in discipline, in the atmosphere of the school and in the outlook of the teacher, democracy cannot grow. If democracy can catch roots in these, it would result as a rich and fertile filed for the growth and development of the children.

## Democracy and Aims of Education

According to Dewey, "All which the school can or need to do for children, so far as their minds are concerned is to develop their ability to think." But the condition prevalent in today's schools is that, before they can progress in thinking, they are made to learn a large mass of facts through rote memory. They just become mechanical store house of facts unable to think or reason.

But democracy in education means that children should acquire mastery over facts and skills that are meaningful as well as individually and socially useful to them. The schools should provide a wide range of activities which not only develops interest in the child but also encourages him in the acquisition of the subject matter, keeps him, happy and as a well balanced personality.

Another aim is to develop the social outlook which in turn would create traits such as social interests, concern for one's fellow beings, sense of obligation, social understanding and the ability to solve social problems.

The Educational Policies Commission of the USA has established objectives for a democratic education. The four large areas of these objectives are as follows:

1.The aim of self-realisation :is achieved through inquiring minds - speech, reading, writing, number, sight, hearing, health knowledge, health objectives, public health, recreation, intellectual, interests, aesthetic interest, character.

2. The aim of human relationship: respect for humanity friendships, co-operation, courtesy, appreciation of the home conservation, home making democracy in home

3.The aim of economic efficiency: such, as work, occupational information occupational choice, occupational efficiency. occupational adjustment etc.

4.' The objective of civil responsibility: such as' social justice,, social activity, social understanding' critical judgment, tolerance, conservation, world citizenship, law observance, political citizenship etc.

**Democracy and Curriculum**

One of the major aims of democracy is that the individuals must be allowed to develop according to his own abilities. Therefore the curriculum aims at providing a wide range of activities such that each of which stimulates the child's creative abilities. The curriculum is also characterized by flexibility. It is based upon the tastes and talents of the children. In such a curriculum, only the basic or core curriculum is prescribed for all the pupils. Addition subjects are offered only in accordance with the ability, intelligence and needs of the individual pupils.

The social element is also greatly emphasized. Besides, the curriculum lays stress on promoting the growth of the child's intelligence. The business of the teacher is not to present the pupils with ready-made ideas, concepts. Conclusions and attitudes but to help them in making use of the same to evolve their own ideas. Such a curriculum involves problem solving activities in arithmetics, telling or writing a story, organizing a tea-party or producing a play. These activities mean purposing, planning, thinking, and judging.

Bearing in mind the above aims, the subjects suggested for an Indian Democratic School are: Crafts, Agriculture, Nature study, Mother Tongue, and other languages Practical Mathematics. Science, History. Geography, Civics. Hygiene and Artwork.

**Democracy and The Methods of Teaching**

The child of today is living in an era of "space" and "speed". The education which we provide to him today must help him to meet the demands of tomorrow. The methods of teaching which cope up which changes in the development will help him meet the challenges. There should be much of planning and purposing and minimum of command compulsion. Instead of dogmatically compelling him to imbibe the information doled out by him, the pupil is encouraged to take an active part in the learning process. Initiativeness in children should be encouraged. He should be given freedom to ask question, to reason, to criticize and even to differ view points with the teacher. Group work, discussion, problem solving, learning through experiences, and group evaluation of results are some effective democratic teaching methods. Stress is on intelligence and enquiry. The inductive, deductive, analytic and synthetic methods develop the art of thinking scientifically and forming sound generalizations. Problem solving techniques teach the children to establish criteria, weigh alternatives, secure information relative to the problems and arrive at the conclusion. It is this method advocated by Dalton Plan, Montessori system, heuristic method, Socialized recitation etc.

Constant scolding and discouragement of low ability children no longer exists in a democratic educational system. Rather, the teacher takes pain to understand the child and help them to discover their abilities.

**<u>Democracy and Co-curricular Activities</u>**

In order to develop the qualities of self-reliance, leadership. initiative, co-operation, intelligent obedience and responsible behavior etc and to develop and increased mastery of the physical. environment, the learner must by able to understand himself, his needs, abilities, social needs and social responsibilities. To inculcate such abilities in a child, a democratic education decides the following activities.

1., Introduction of self government in schools - students being associated with the management of the schools.

2. Provision for manual work - this goes a long way in making students realize the dignity of labour.

3. Encouragement to group work - this provides opportunities to the students to participate in group work.

4: Promotion of self-expression - with a view to promote this activities such as debate, declamation contest etc. may be planned.

5 Opportunities for Social - Service - which will bring the students into direct contact with the community and enable them to understand its problem

6. Vocational Efficiency - Craft education is very helpful in preparing our students with a practical bias.

7. Development of hobbies – hobby are very helpful in preparing the student to make the best use of there leisure.

8. Hostel life –wherever possible hostel opportunity should provide to the student. This is an effective way of tanning the student in the art of leaving together.

9. Student parliament – students union and parliament may be formed in the school and the office borers of these elected.

10. Visits to legislatures –such visits provides the student first hand opportunity to see for themselves the working of a democracy.

## Democracy of the Teacher

The teacher is the vitalizing force behind the dome created organization for a society. Beside her usual qualification, she should be well equipped for a domestic education. She should be a believer in the fact such as the role played by the environment in the development of the individual, individual difference between the learner, and the capability of individual in making there own moral choice, to distinguish good and bad, the right of very child to think, to choice and to get an equal chance to participate. The process of teaching in democratic education is a co-operative enterprise where both the teacher and the learner participate in the teaching –learning process. The teacher should not impose anything. She should be guide, supervisor an inspire.

## Democracy Administration and organization

In the words of Herbert Spencer "Whatever be the special function of an institution. It must have a family likeness." School administration in democracy depends. Largely on increased opportunity of the teacher and of student to share in formulating to policy of the school. It envisages a life of give- and take and of balance between tights and duties. It further ensure that the teacher are given to our teachers in our school. In democratic education too the administrator criticizes the teacher. But this is just a structive criticm. The administrator has to encourage each member of the group. A democratic in a administrator seeks to avoid the extreme connection of power. The unshared responsibility, and the regimentation of authoritarianism. He should rather be friendly, helpful and advisory

In a democratic school, the student share in making the rules the shoulder responsibilities in running clubs, societies and association and in organing function in school. Activities like organizing games, running to school store are school canteen looking after the clean lines of the school bringing out a school a general magazine or new bulletin system the write person at the right job and there fore every one makes a worth while contribution.

There practical result if such a democratic administration is followed in school

The teacher makes a distinct contribution to the policy of the school. All the teacher are in a position to know more about the children, school, and administrator.

The teacher gains in professional maturity by working with the administrator in the purpose and planning

Co-operation between the administrator and teacher helps in the development of a democratic sprit between them this improve the moral and enthusiasm of the teacher.

**Democracy and discipline** –

Democratic discipline does not each about threats, punishment promises and rational good behaviour. There will be apontaneous discipline when children are provided contant work, which is a stimulating waiting and interesting." an ideal brain is a devils work shop' freedom given in a democratic education is not to flout the truth the regulate on the life in a knowledge of it.

Love, sympathy human relation ship should be the bonus between the teacher and the taught. "Sit still ","Don't shout "; "Don't move around" are trite phrase aline in democratic education. "A school, humming with activity, with din of powerful pursuit is more disciplined and then institution was there is passive listening.

In training our students for democracy, we should stimulate in them not only willing subordination the constituted, authority but also such desirable quality as intellectual honesty Fairless reasoning and respect core order based on inner conviction and willing acquiescence.

# NOTES